Risk-First Software Development Menagerie

By Rob Moffat

Copyright ©2018 Kite9 Ltd.

All rights reserved. No part of this publication may be reproduced, distributed, or transmitted in any form or by any means, including photocopying, recording, or other electronic or mechanical methods, without the prior written permission of the publisher, except in the case of brief quotations embodied in critical reviews and certain other noncommercial uses permitted by copyright law. For permission requests, write to the publisher, addressed "Attention: Permissions Coordinator," at the address below.

ISBN: 9781717491855

Credits

Ideas, issues and proof-reading:

- Gustavo Andrade
- George Bashi
- Michael Geary
- Jan Hovancik
- Bertold Kolics
- Richard Moffat
- Ilja Neumann
- Ian Obermiller
- Stephan Westen

Cover Images: Biodiversity Heritage Library; Biologia Centrali-Americana; Insecta. Rhynchota; Hemiptera-Homoptera. Volume 1 (1881-1905)

Cover Design By P. Moffat (peter@petermoffat.com)

Books In The Series

- **Risk-First Software Development Volume 1: The Menagerie.** Volume one of the Risk-First series argues the case for viewing *all* of the activities on a software project through the lens of *managing risk*. It introduces the menagerie of different risks you're likely to meet on a software project, naming and classifying them so that we can try to understand them better.
- **Risk-First Software Development Volume 2: Tools and Practices.** Volume two of the Risk-First series explores the relationship between software project risks and the tools and practices we use to mitigate them. Due for publication in 2020.

Online

Material for the books is freely available to read, drawn from `risk-first.org`.

Published By

```
Kite9 Ltd.
14 Manor Close
Colchester
CO6 4AR
```

Contents

Contents		ii
Preface		v
Quick Summary		xi
I	Introduction	1
1	A Simple Scenario	3
2	Development Process	7
3	Meeting Reality	15
4	Just Risk	21
5	Evaluating Risk	27
6	Cadence	41
7	De-Risking	45
8	A Conversation	51
9	One Size Fits No-One	55
II	The Risk Landscape	65
10	The Risk Landscape	67
11	Feature Risk	73

12	Communication Risk	83
13	Complexity Risk	103
14	Dependency Risk	119
15	Scarcity Risk	125
16	Deadline Risk	133
17	Software Dependency Risk	137
18	Process Risk	155
19	Boundary Risk	165
20	Agency Risk	179
21	Coordination Risk	189
22	Map And Territory Risk	205
23	Operational Risk	219
24	Staging and Classifying	229

III Tools & Practices — 235

25	Coming Next	237
26	Estimates	239
	Glossary	257
	Index	261

Preface

Welcome to Risk-First!

Let's cover some of the big questions up-front: the why, what, who, how and where of *The Menagerie*.

Why

> "Scrum, Waterfall, Lean, Prince2: what do they all have in common?"

I've started this because, on my career journey, I've noticed that the way I do things doesn't seem to match up with the way the books *say* it should be done. And, I found this odd and wanted to explore it further. Hopefully, you, the reader, will find something of use in this.

I started with this observation: *Development Teams* put a lot of faith in methodology. Sometimes, this faith is often so strong it borders on religion. (Which in itself is a concern.) For some, this is Prince2. For others, it might be Lean or Agile.

Developers put a lot of faith in *particular tools* too. Some developers are pro-or-anti-Java, others are pro-or-anti-XML. All of them have their views coloured by their *experiences* (or lack of) with these tools. Was this because their past projects *succeeded* or *failed* because of them?

As time went by, I came to see that the choice of methodology, process or tool was contingent on the problem being solved, and the person solving the problem. We don't face a shortage of tools in IT, or a shortage of methodologies, or a shortage of practices. Essentially, all the tools and methodologies that the industry had supplied were there to help *minimize the risk of my project failing*.

This book considers that perspective: building software is all about *managing risk*, and that these methodologies are acknowledgements of this fact, and they differ because they have *different ideas* about which are the most important *risks to manage*.

What This Is

Hopefully, after reading this, you'll come away with:

- An appreciation of how risk underpins everything we do as developers, whether we want it to or not.
- A framework for evaluating methodologies, tools and practices and choosing the right one for the task-at-hand.
- A new way to look at the software development process: it's an exercise in managing different kinds of risk.
- The tools to help you decide when a methodology or tool is *letting you down*, and the vocabulary to argue for when it's a good idea to deviate from it.

Patterns

This is not intended to be a rigorous, scientific work: I don't believe it's possible to objectively analyze a field like software development in any meaningful, statistically significant way (things just change too fast).

Does that diminish it? If you have visited the TVTropes[1] website, you'll know that it's a set of web-pages describing *common patterns* of narrative, production, character design etc. to do with fiction.

> "Sometimes, at the end of a 'Dream Sequence' or an 'All Just a Dream' episode, after the character in question has woken up and demonstrated any '[lesson]' that the dream might have been communicating, there's some small hint that it wasn't a dream after all, even though it quite obviously was... right?."
> —Or Was It a Dream?, *TVTropes*[2]

Is it scientific? No. Is it correct? Almost certainly. TVTropes is a set of *empirical patterns* for how stories on TV and other media work. It's really useful, and a lot of fun. (Warning: it's also incredibly addictive).

In the same way, "Design Patterns: Elements of Reusable Object-Oriented Software[3]", is a book detailing patterns of *structure* within Object-Oriented

---

[1] https://tvtropes.org
[2] https://tvtropes.org/pmwiki/pmwiki.php/Main/OrWasItADream
[3] http://amzn.eu/d/3cOwTkH

programming, such as:

> "[The] Adapter [pattern] allows classes with incompatible interfaces to work together by wrapping its own interface around that of an already existing class..."
> —Design Patterns, *Wikipedia*[4]

Patterns For Practitioners

Design Patterns aims to be a set of *useful* patterns which practitioners could use in their software to achieve certain goals. "I have this pattern"[5] was a phrase used to describe how they had seen a certain set of constraints before, and how they had solved it in software.

That book was a set of experts handing down their battle-tested practices for other developers to use, and, whether you like patterns or not, knowing them is an important part of being a software developer, as you will see them used everywhere you go and probably use them yourself.

In the same way, Risk-First aims to be a set of *Patterns for Software Risk*. Hopefully after reading this, you will see where risk hides in software projects, and have a name for it when you see it.

Towards a "Periodic Table"

In the latter chapters of "The Menagerie" we try to assemble these risk patterns into a cohesive whole. Projects fail because of risks, and risks arise from predictable sources.

What This is Not

Risk-First isn't an exhaustive guide to every possible software development practice and methodology. That would just be too long and tedious.

Neither is this a practitioner's guide to using any particular methodology: if you've come here to learn the best way to do Retrospectives, then you're in the wrong place. There are plenty of places you can find that information already. Where possible, this site will link to or reference concepts on Wikipedia or the wider Internet for further reading on each subject.

---

[4]https://en.wikipedia.org/wiki/Design_Patterns
[5]http://c2.com/ppr/wiki/WikiPagesAboutWhatArePatterns/HaveThisPattern.html

Who

This work is intended to be read by people who work on software projects, and those who are involved in managing software projects.

If you work collaboratively with other people in a software process, you should find Risk-First a useful lexicon of terms to help describe the risks you face.

So, if you are interested in *avoiding your project failing*, this is probably going to be useful knowledge.

For Team Members

Risk-First is a toolkit you can deploy to immediately improve your ability to plan your work and avoid pitfalls. But that's not the only goal. Frequently, we find software methodologies "done to us" from above. Risk-First is a toolkit to help *take apart* methodologies like Scrum, Lean or Prince2, and understand them.

Methodologies are *bicycles*, rather than *religions*. Rather than simply *believing*, we can take them apart and see how they work.

For Project Managers and Team Leads

All too often, Project Managers don't have a full grasp of the technical details of their projects. And this is perfectly normal, as the specialisation belongs below them. However, projects fail because risks materialize, and risks materialize because the devil is in those details.

This seems like a lost cause, but there is hope: the way in which risks materialize on technical projects follows a pattern. With Risk-First we attempt to name each of these types of risk, which allows for a dialog with developers about which risks they face, and the order in which they should be tackled.

Risk-First allows a project manager to pry open the black box of development and talk with developers about their work, and how it will affect the project. It is another tool in the (limited) arsenal of techniques a project manager can bring to bear on the task of delivering a successful project.

How

One of the original authors of the Agile Manifesto[6], Kent Beck states in his book:

---

[6] https://en.wikipedia.org/wiki/Agile_software_development#The_Agile_Manifesto

> "It's all about risk"
>
> —Kent Beck, *Extreme Programming Explained*[7]

This is a promising start. From there, he introduces his methodology, Extreme Programming[8], and explains how you can adopt it in your team, the features to observe and the characteristics of success and failure. However, while *Risk* has clearly driven the conception of Extreme Programming, there is no clear model of software risk underpinning the work.

Risk-First introduces a model of software risk. This means that we can properly analyse Extreme Programming (and Scrum, Waterfall, Lean and all the others) and *understand* what drives them. Since they are designed to deliver successful software projects, they must be about managing risks, and we will uncover *exactly which risks* and *how they do it*.

But here's a warning: this is going to be a depressing book to read. It is book one of a two-book series, but in **Book One** you only get to meet the bad guy:

- Part One argues that all the actions we take to complete a software project are actually about risk.
- Part Two introduces us to various types of software project risk, so we know them when we see them.

Conversely, **Book Two** is all about *how to succeed*: how to choose tools and techniques to use on a project in order to cope with the risks we've covered here.

Where

All of the material for both of these books is available Open Source on github.com[9], and at the risk-first.org[10] website. Please visit, your feedback is appreciated.

There is no compulsion to buy print or digital versions, but we'd really appreciate the support. So, if you've read this and enjoyed it, how about buying a copy for someone else to read?

---

[7] http://amzn.eu/d/gUQjnbF
[8] https://en.wikipedia.org/wiki/Extreme_programming
[9] https://github.com
[10] https://risk-first.org

A Note on References

Where possible, references are to the Wikipedia[11] website. Wikipedia is not perfect. There is a case for linking to the original articles and papers, but Wikipedia references are free and easy for everyone to access, and hopefully will exist for a long time into the future.

On to The Quick Summary

---

[11] https://wikipedia.org

Quick Summary

1. There are Lots of Ways to Run Software Projects

There are lots of ways to look at a project in-flight. For example, metrics such as "number of open tickets", "story points", "code coverage" or "release cadence" give us a numerical feel for how things are going and what needs to happen next. We also judge the health of projects by the practices used on them, such as Continuous Integration, Unit Testing or Pair Programming.

Software methodologies, then, are collections of tools and practices: "Agile", "Waterfall", "Lean" or "Phased Delivery" all prescribe different approaches to running a project, and are opinionated about the way they think projects should be done and the tools that should be used.

None of these is necessarily more "right" than another: they are suitable on different projects at different times.

A key question then is: **how do we select the right tools for the job?**

2. We Can Look at Projects in Terms of Risks

One way to examine the project in-flight is by looking at the risks it faces.

Commonly, tools such as RAID logs[12] and RAG status[13] reporting are used. These techniques should be familiar to project managers and developers everywhere.

However, the Risk-First view is that we can go much further: that each item of work being done on the project is to manage a particular risk. Risk isn't something that just appears in a report, it actually drives *everything we do*.

For example:

---
[12]https://www.projectmanager.com/blog/raid-log-use-one
[13]https://pmtips.net/blog-new/what-does-rag-status-mean

- A story about improving the user login screen can be seen as reducing *the risk of users not signing up*.
- A task about improving the health indicators could be seen as mitigating *the risk of the application failing and no-one reacting to it*.
- Even a task as basic as implementing a new function in the application is mitigating *the risk that users are dissatisfied and go elsewhere*.

One assertion of Risk-First is that **every action you take on a project is to manage a risk.**

3. We Can Break Down Risks on a Project Methodically

Although risk is usually complicated and messy, other industries have found value in breaking down the types of risks that affect them and addressing them individually.

For example:

- In manufacturing, *tolerances* allow for calculating the likelihood of defects in production.
- In finance, projects and teams are structured around monitoring risks like *credit risk*, *market risk* and *liquidity risk*.
- *Insurance* is founded on identifying particular risks and providing financial safety-nets for when they occur, such as death, injury, accident and so on.

Software risks are difficult to quantify, and mostly, the effort involved in doing so *exactly* would outweigh the benefit. Nevertheless, there is value in spending time building *classifications of risk for software*. That's what Risk-First does: it describes a set of *risk patterns* we see every day on software projects.

With this in place, we can:

- Talk about the types of risks we face on our projects, using an appropriate language.
- Anticipate Hidden Risks that we hadn't considered before.
- Weigh the risks against each other, and decide which order to tackle them.

4. We Can Analyse Tools and Techniques in Terms of how they Manage Risk

If we accept the assertion that *all* the actions we take on a project are about mitigating risks, then it stands to reason that the tools and techniques available to us on a project are there for mitigating different types of risks.

For example:

- If we do a Code Review, we are partly trying to minimise the risks of bugs slipping through into production, and also manage the Key Person Risk of knowledge not being widely-enough shared.
- If we write Unit Tests, we're addressing the risk of bugs going to production, but we're also mitigating against the risk of *regression*, and future changes breaking our existing functionality.
- If we enter into a contract with a supplier, we are mitigating the risk of the supplier vanishing and leaving us exposed. With the contract in place, we have legal recourse against this risk.

From the above examples, it's clear that **different tools are appropriate for managing different types of risks.**

5. Different Methodologies are for Different Risk Profiles

In the same way that our tools and techniques are appropriate for dealing with different risks, the same is true of the methodologies we use on our projects. We can use a Risk-First approach to examine the different methodologies, and see which risks they address.

For example:

- **Agile** methodologies prioritise the risk that requirements capture is complicated, error-prone and that requirements change easily.
- **Waterfall** takes the view that development effort is an expensive risk, and that we should build plans up-front to avoid re-work.
- **Lean** takes the view that risk lies in incomplete work and wasted work, and aims to minimise that.

Although many developers have a methodology-of-choice, the argument here is that there are trade-offs with all of these choices.

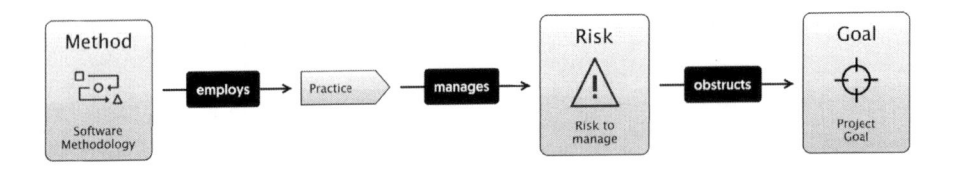

Figure 1: Methodologies, Risks, Practices

"Methodologies are like *bicycles*, rather than *religions*. Rather than simply *believing*, we can take them apart and see how they work."

6. We can Drive Development With a Risk-First Perspective

We have described a model of risk within software projects, looking something like this:

How do we take this further?

One idea explored is the *Risk Landscape*: although the software team can't remove risk from their project, they can take actions that move them to a place in the Risk Landscape where the risks on the project are more favourable than where they started.

From there, we examine basic risk archetypes you will encounter on the software project, to build up a vocabulary of Software Risk, and look at which specific tools you can use to mitigate each kind of risk.

Then, we look at software practices, and how they manage various risks. Beyond this we examine the question: *how can a Risk-First approach inform the use of this practice?*

For example:

- If we are introducing a **Sign-Off** in our process, we have to balance the risks it *mitigates* (coordination of effort, quality control, information sharing) with the risks it *introduces* (delays and process bottlenecks).
- If we build in **Redundancy**, this mitigates the risk of a *single point of failure*, but introduces risks around *synchronizing data* and *communication* between the systems.

- If we introduce **Process**, this may make it easier to *coordinate as a team* and *measure performance* but may lead to bureaucracy, focusing on the wrong goals or over-rigid interfaces to those processes.

Risk-First aims to provide a framework in which we can *analyse these actions* and weigh up *accepting* versus *mitigating* risks.

Still interested? Then dive into reading the introduction.

Part I

Introduction

CHAPTER 1

A Simple Scenario

In this chapter, I'm going to introduce some terms for thinking about risk.

For a moment forget about software completely, and think about *any endeavour at all* in life. It could be passing a test, mowing the lawn or going on holiday. Choose something now. I'll discuss from the point of view of "cooking a meal for some friends", but you can play along with your own example.

1.1 Goal In Mind

Now, in this endeavour, we want to be successful. That is to say, we have a **Goal In Mind**: we want our friends to go home satisfied after a decent meal, and not to feel hungry. As a bonus, we might also want to spend time talking with them before and during the meal. So, now to achieve our Goal In Mind we *probably* have to do some tasks.

Since our goal only exists *in our head*, we can say it is part of our **Internal Model** of the world. That is, the model we have of reality. This model extends to *predicting what will happen*.

If we do nothing, our friends will turn up and maybe there's nothing in the house for them to eat. Or maybe, the thing that you're going to cook is going to take hours and they'll have to sit around and wait for you to cook it and they'll leave before it's ready. Maybe you'll be some ingredients short, or maybe you're not confident of the steps to prepare the meal and you're worried about messing it all up.

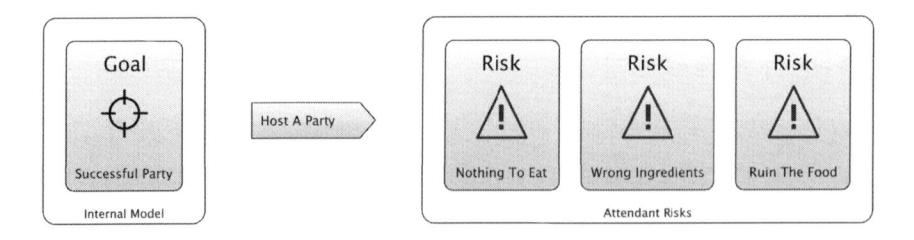

Figure 1.1: Goal In Mind, with the risks you know about

1.2 Attendant Risk

These *nagging doubts* that are going through your head are what I'll call the Attendant Risks: they're the ones that will occur to you as you start to think about what will happen.

When we go about preparing for this wonderful evening, we can choose to deal with these risks: shop for the ingredients in advance, prepare parts of the meal and maybe practice the cooking in advance. Or, we can wing it, and sometimes we'll get lucky.

How much effort we expend on these Attendant Risks depends on how big we think they are. For example, if you know there's a 24-hour shop, you'll probably not worry too much about getting the ingredients well in advance (although, the shop *could still be closed*).

1.3 Hidden Risks

Attendant Risks are risks you are aware of. You may not be able to exactly *quantify* them, but you know they exist. But there are also **Hidden Risks** that you *don't* know about: if you're poaching eggs for dinner, perhaps you didn't know that fresh eggs poach best. Donald Rumsfeld famously called these kinds of risks "Unknown Unknowns":

> "Reports that say that something hasn't happened are always interesting to me, because as we know, there are known knowns; there are things we know we know. We also know there are known unknowns; that is to say we know there are some things we do not know. But there are also unknown unknowns—the ones we don't know we don't know. And if one looks throughout

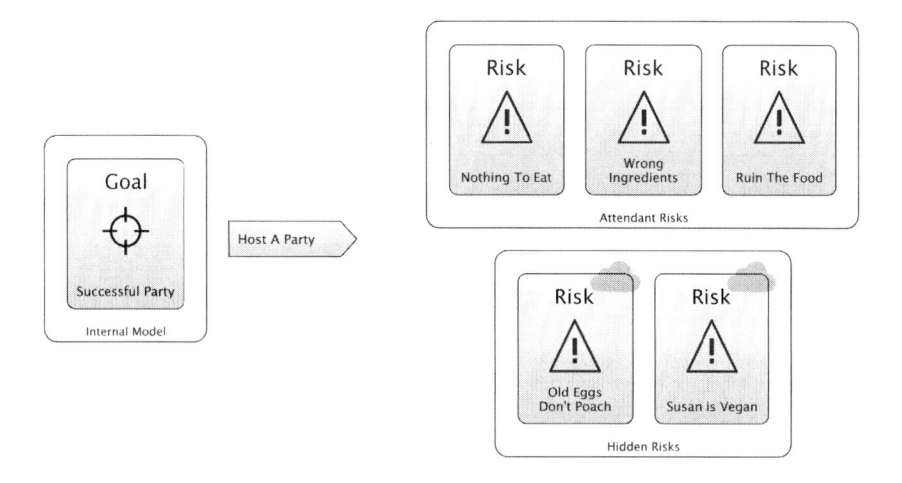

Figure 1.2: Goal In Mind, the risks you know about and the ones you don't

the history of our country and other free countries, it is the latter category that tend to be the difficult ones."
—Donald Rumsfeld, *Wikipedia*[1]

Different people evaluate risks differently, and they'll also *know* about different risks. What is an Attendant Risk for one person is a Hidden Risk for another.

Which risks we know about depends on our **knowledge** and **experience**, then. And that varies from person to person (or team to team).

1.4 Meeting Reality

As the dinner party gets closer, we make our preparations, and the inadequacies of the Internal Model become apparent. We learn what we didn't know and the Hidden Risks reveal themselves. Other things we were worried about don't materialise. Things we thought would be minor risks turn out to be greater.

Our model is forced to Meet Reality, and the model changes, forcing us to deal with these risks, as shown in Figure 1.3. Whenever we try to *do something* about a risk, it is called Taking Action. Taking Action *changes* reality, and with it your Internal Model of the risks you're facing. That's because it's only by

---
[1] https://en.wikipedia.org/wiki/There_are_known_knowns

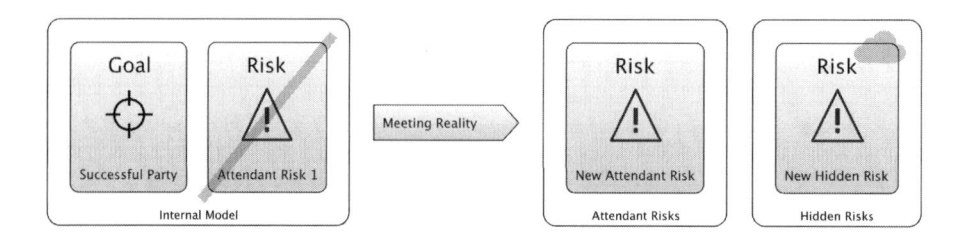

Figure 1.3: How Taking Action affects Reality, and also changes your Internal Model

interacting with the world that we add knowledge to our Internal Model about what works and what doesn't. Even something as passive as *checking the shop opening times* is an action, and it improves on our Internal Model of the world.

If we had a good Internal Model, and took the right actions, we should see positive outcomes. If we failed to manage the risks, or took inappropriate actions, we'll probably see negative outcomes.

1.5 On To Software

Here, we've introduced some new terms that we're going to use a lot: Meet Reality, Attendant Risk, Hidden Risk, Internal Model, Taking Action and Goal In Mind. And, we've applied them in a simple scenario.

But Risk-First is about understanding risk in software development, so let's examine the scenario of a new software project, and expand on the simple model being outlined above: instead of a single person, we are likely to have a team, and our model will not just exist in our heads, but in the code we write.

On to Development Process...

CHAPTER 2

Development Process

In the previous chapter we introduced some terms for talking about risk (such as Attendant Risk, Hidden Risk and Internal Model) via a simple scenario.

Now, let's look at the everyday process of developing *a new feature* on a software project, and see how our risk model informs it.

2.1 A Toy Process

Let's ignore for now the specifics of what methodology is being used - we'll come to that later. Let's say your team have settled for a process something like the following:

1. **Specification**: a new feature is requested somehow, and a business analyst works to specify it.
2. **Code And Unit Test**: a developer writes some code, and some unit tests.
3. **Integration**: they integrate their code into the code base.
4. **UAT**: they put the code into a User Acceptance Test (UAT) environment, and user(s) test it.
5. ... All being well, the code is **Released to Production**.

Can't We Improve This?

Is this a *good* process? Probably, it's not that great: you could add code review, a pilot phase, integration testing, whatever.

Also, the *methodology* being used might be Waterfall, it might be Agile. We're not going to commit to specifics at this stage.

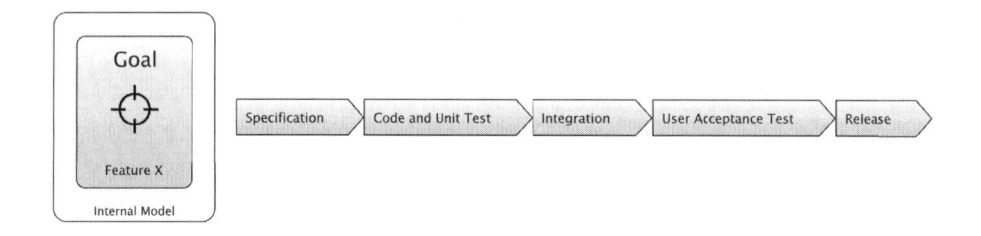

Figure 2.1: A Simple Development Process

For now though, let's just assume that *it works for this project* and everyone is reasonably happy with it.

We're just doing some analysis of *what process gives us*.

Minimising Risks - Overview

I am going to argue that this entire process is *informed by software risk*:

1. We have *a business analyst* who talks to users and fleshes out the details of the feature properly. This is to minimize the risk of **building the wrong thing**.
2. We *write unit tests* to minimize the risk that our code **isn't doing what we expected, and that it matches the specifications**.
3. We *integrate our code* to minimize the risk that it's **inconsistent with the other, existing code on the project**.
4. We have *acceptance testing* and quality gates generally to **minimize the risk of breaking production**, somehow.

A Much Simpler Process

We could skip all those steps above and just do this:

1. Developer gets wind of new idea from user, logs onto production and changes some code directly.

We can all see this might end in disaster, but why?

Two reasons:

1. You're Meeting Reality all-in-one-go: all of these risks materialize at the same time, and you have to deal with them all at once.

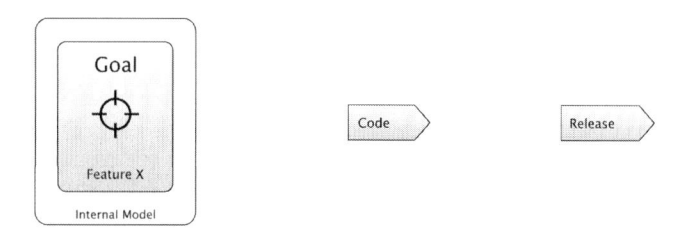

Figure 2.2: A Dangerous Development Process

2. Because of this, at the point you put code into the hands of your users, your Internal Model is at its least-developed. All the Hidden Risks now need to be dealt with at the same time, in production.

2.2 Applying the Process

Let's look at how our process should act to prevent these risks materializing by considering an unhappy path, one where at the outset, we have lots of Hidden Risks. Let's say a particularly vocal user rings up someone in the office and asks for new **Feature X** to be added to the software. It's logged as a new feature request, but:

- Unfortunately, this feature once programmed will break an existing **Feature Y**.
- Implementing the feature will use some api in a library, which contains bugs and have to be coded around.
- It's going to get misunderstood by the developer too, who is new on the project and doesn't understand how the software is used.
- Actually, this functionality is mainly served by **Feature Z**...
- which is already there but hard to find.

Figure 2.3 shows how this plays out.

This is a slightly contrived example, as you'll see. But let's follow our feature through the process and see how it meets reality slowly, and the Hidden Risks are discovered:

Specification

The first stage of the journey for the feature is that it meets the Business Analyst (BA). The *purpose* of the BA is to examine new goals for the project

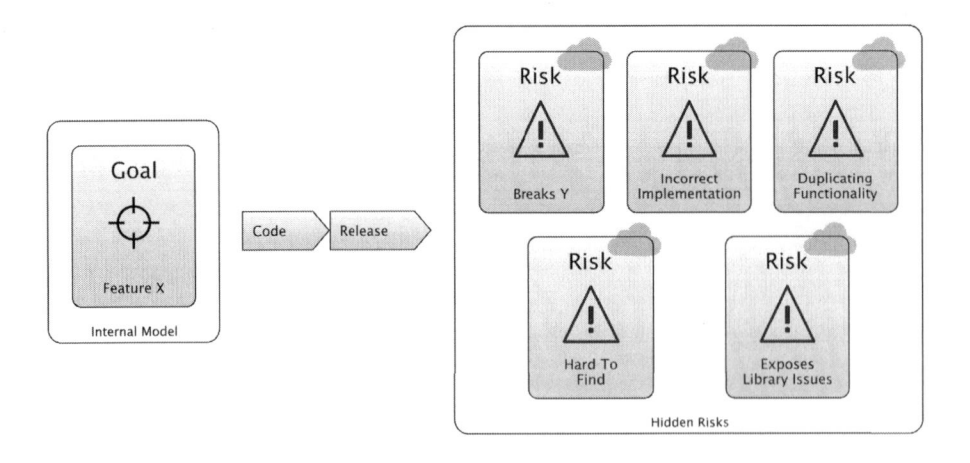

Figure 2.3: Development Process - Exposing Hidden Risks

and try to integrate them with *reality as they understand it*. A good BA might take a feature request and vet it against his Internal Model, saying something like:

- "This feature doesn't belong on the User screen, it belongs on the New Account screen"
- "90% of this functionality is already present in the Document Merge Process"
- "We need a control on the form that allows the user to select between Internal and External projects"

In the process of doing this, the BA is turning the simple feature request *idea* into a more consistent, well-explained *specification* or *requirement* which the developer can pick up. But why is this a useful step in our simple methodology? From the perspective of our Internal Model, we can say that the BA is responsible for:

- Trying to surface Hidden Risks
- Trying to evaluate Attendant Risks and make them clear to everyone on the project.

In surfacing these risks, there is another outcome: while **Feature X** might be flawed as originally presented, the BA can "evolve" it into a specification, and tie it down sufficiently to reduce the risks. The BA does all this by simply *thinking about it*, *talking to people* and *writing stuff down*.

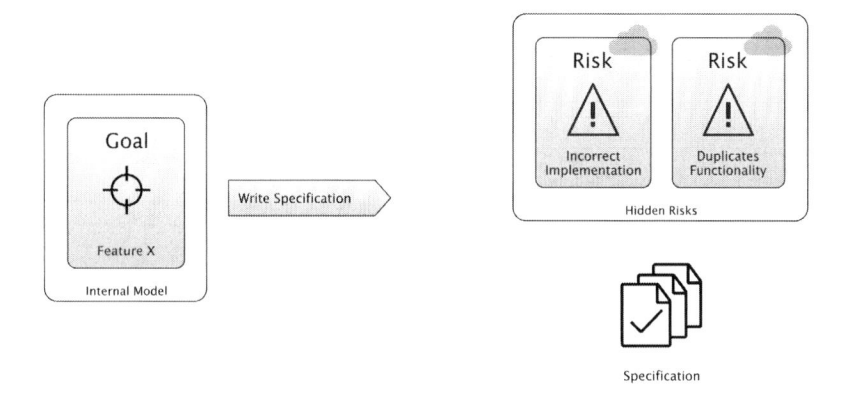

Figure 2.4: BA Specification: exposing Hidden Risks as soon as possible

This process of evolving the feature request into a requirement is the BA's job. From our Risk-First perspective, it is *taking an idea and making it Meet Reality*. Not the *full reality* of production (yet), but something more limited.

Code And Unit Test

The next stage for our feature, **Feature X** is that it gets coded and some tests get written. Let's look at how our Goal In Mind meets a new reality: this time it's the reality of a pre-existing codebase, which has it's own internal logic.

As the developer begins coding the feature in the software, they will start with an Internal Model of the software, and how the code fits into it. But, in the process of implementing it, they are likely to learn about the codebase, and their Internal Model will develop.

At this point, let's stop and discuss the visual grammar of the Risk-First Diagrams we've been looking at. A Risk-First diagram shows what you expect to happen when you Take Action. The action itself is represented by the shaded, sign-post-shaped box in the middle. On the left, we have the current state of the world, on the right is the anticipated state *after* taking the action.

The round-cornered rectangles represent our Internal Model, and these contain our view of Risk, whether the risks we face right now, or the Attendant Risks expected after taking the action. In Figure 2.5, taking the action of

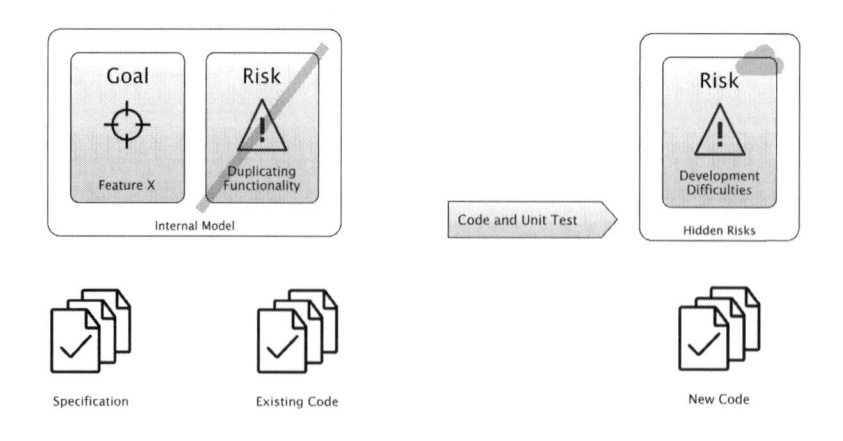

Figure 2.5: Coding Process: exposing more hidden risks as you code

"coding and unit testing" is expected to mitigate the risk of "Duplicating Functionality".

Beneath the internal models, we are also showing real-world tangible artifacts. That is, the physical change we would expect to see as a result of taking action. In Figure 2.5, the action will result in "New Code" being added to the project, needed for the next steps of the development process.

Integration

Integration is where we run *all* the tests on the project, and compile *all* the code in a clean environment, collecting together the work from the whole development team.

So, this stage is about meeting a new reality: the clean build.

At this stage, we might discover the Hidden Risk that we'd break **Feature Y**

User Acceptance Test

Next, User Acceptance Testing (UAT) is where our new feature meets another reality: *actual users*. I think you can see how the process works by now. We're just flushing out yet more Hidden Risks.

- Taking Action is the *only* way to create change in the world.
- It's also the only way we can *learn* about the world, adding to our Internal Model.

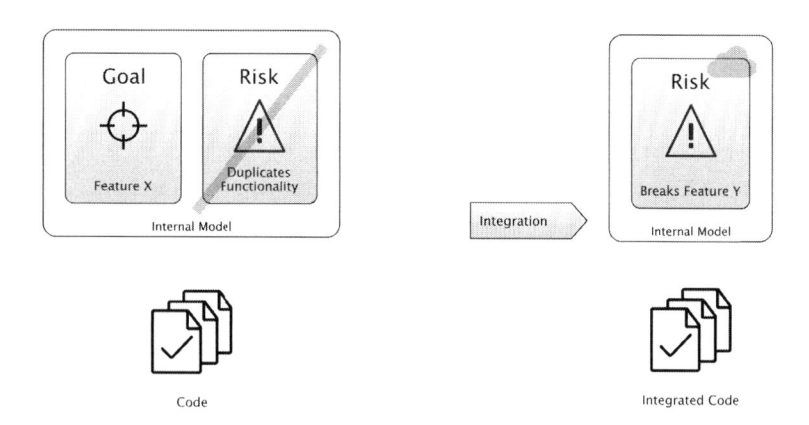

Figure 2.6: Integration testing exposes Hidden Risks before you get to production

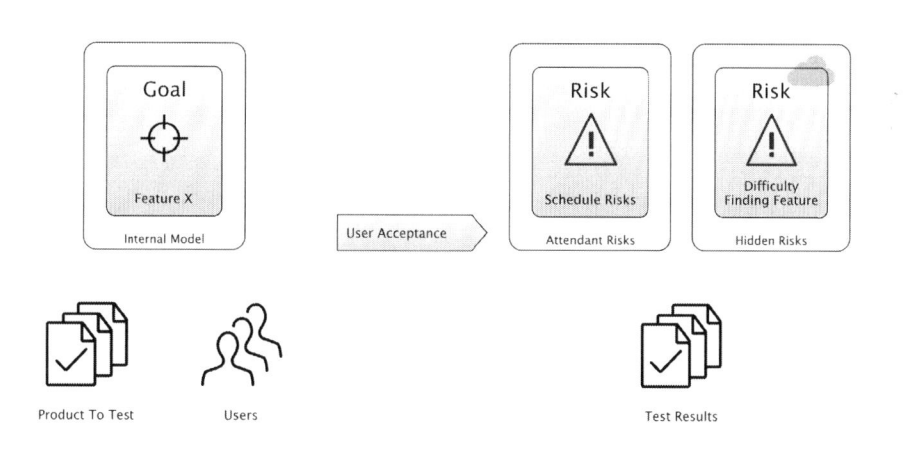

Figure 2.7: UAT - putting tame users in front of your software is better than real ones, where the risk is higher

- In this case, we discover a Hidden Risk: the user's difficulty in finding the feature. (The cloud obscuring the risk shows that it is hidden).
- In return, we can *expect* the process of performing the UAT to delay our release (this is an attendant schedule risk).

2.3 Observations

First, the people setting up the development process *didn't know* about these *exact* risks, but they knew the *shape that the risks take*. The process builds "nets" for the different kinds of Hidden Risks without knowing exactly what they are.

Second, are these really risks, or are they *problems we just didn't know about*? I am using the terms interchangeably, to a certain extent. Even when you know you have a problem, it's still a risk to your deadline until it's solved. So, when does a risk become a problem? Is a problem still just a schedule-risk, or cost-risk? We'll come back to this question presently.

Third, the real take-away from this is that all these risks exist because we don't know 100% how reality is. We don't (and can't) have a perfect view of the universe and how it'll develop. Reality is reality, *the risks just exist in our head*.

Fourth, hopefully you can see from the above that really *all this work is risk management*, and *all work is testing ideas against reality*.

In the next chapter, we're going to look at the concept of Meeting Reality in a bit more depth.

CHAPTER 3

Meeting Reality

In this chapter, we will look at how exposing your Internal Model to reality is in itself a good risk management technique.

3.1 Revisiting the Model

In A Simple Scenario, we looked at a basic model for how **Reality** and our Internal Model interacted with each other: we take action based on out Internal Model, hoping to **change Reality** with some positive outcome.

And, in Development Process we looked at how we can meet with reality in *different forms*: Analysis, Testing, Integration and so on, and saw how the model could work in each stage of a project.

It should be no surprise to see that there is a *recursive* nature about this: the actions we take each day have consequences, they expose new hidden risks which inform our Internal Model and at the same time change reality in some way. As a result, we then have to take *new actions* to deal with these new risks.

So, let's see how this kind of recursion looks on our model.

3.2 Navigating the "Risk Landscape"

Figure 3.1 shows *just one possible action*, in reality, you'll have choices. We often have multiple ways of achieving a Goal In Mind.

What's the best way?

I would argue that the best way is the one which mitigates the most existing risk while accruing the least attendant risk to get it done.

15

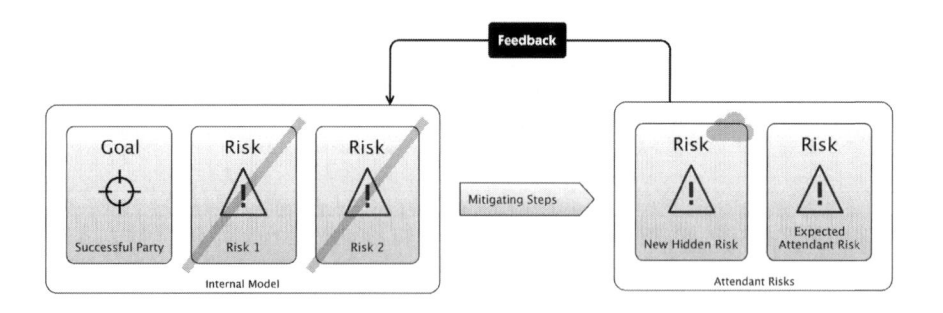

Figure 3.1: Taking actions changes reality, but changes your model of the risks too

Figure 3.2: Navigating The Risk Landscape

Ideally, when you take an action, you are trading off a big risk for a smaller one. Take Unit Testing for example. Clearly, writing Unit Tests adds to the amount of development work, so on its own, it adds Schedule Risk. However, if you write *just enough* of the right Unit Tests, you should be short-cutting the time spent finding issues in the User Acceptance Testing (UAT) stage, so you're hopefully trading off a larger Schedule Risk from UAT and adding a smaller Schedule Risk to Development. There are other benefits of Unit Testing too: once written, a suite of unit tests is almost cost-free to run repeatedly, whereas repeating a UAT is costly as it involves people's time.

You can think of Taking Action as moving your project on a "Risk Landscape": ideally, when you take an action, you move from some place with worse risk to somewhere more favourable.

Sometimes, you can end up somewhere *worse*: the actions you take to manage a risk will leave you with worse Attendant Risks afterwards. Almost certainly, this will have been a Hidden Risk when you embarked on the action, otherwise you'd not have chosen it.

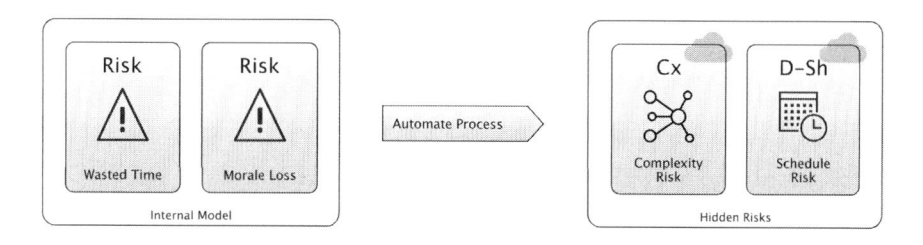

Figure 3.3: Hidden Risks of Automation

An Example: Automation

For example, *automating processes* is very tempting: it *should* save time, and reduce the amount of boring, repetitive work on a project. But sometimes, it turns into an industry in itself, and consumes more effort than it's worth.

Another Example: MongoDB

On a recent project in a bank, we had a requirement to store a modest amount of data and we needed to be able to retrieve it fast. The developer chose to use MongoDB[1] for this. At the time, others pointed out that other teams in the bank had had lots of difficulty deploying MongoDB internally, due to licensing issues and other factors internal to the bank.

Other options were available, but the developer chose MongoDB because of their *existing familiarity* with it: therefore, they felt that the Hidden Risks of MongoDB were *lower* than the other options, and disregarded the others' opinions.

This turned out to be a mistake: The internal bureaucracy eventually proved too great, and MongoDB had to be abandoned after much investment of time.

This is not a criticism of MongoDB: it's simply a demonstration that sometimes, the cure is worse than the disease. Successful projects are *always* trying to *reduce* Attendant Risks.

3.3 Payoff

We can't know in advance how well any action we take will work out. Therefore, Taking Action is a lot like placing a bet.

---

[1] https://www.mongodb.com

Payoff then is our judgement about whether we expect an action to be worthwhile: are the risks we escape *worth* the attendant risks we will encounter? We should be able to *weigh these separate risks in our hands* and figure out whether the Payoff makes a given Action worthwhile.

The fruits of this gambling are revealed when we meet reality, and we can see whether our bets were worthwhile.

3.4 The Cost Of Meeting Reality

Meeting reality *in full* is costly. For example, going to production can look like this:

- Releasing software
- Training users
- Getting users to use your system
- Gathering feedback

All of these steps take a lot of effort and time. But you don't have to meet the whole of reality in one go. But we can meet it in a limited way which is less expensive.

In all, to de-risk, you should try and meet reality:

- **Sooner**: so you have time to mitigate the hidden risks it uncovers.
- **More Frequently**: so the hidden risks don't hit you all at once.
- **In Smaller Chunks**: so you're not over-burdened by hidden risks all in one go.
- **With Feedback**: if you don't collect feedback from the experience of meeting reality, hidden risks *stay hidden*.

In Development Process, we performed a UAT in order to Meet Reality more cheaply and sooner. The *cost* of this is that we delayed the release to do it, adding risk to the schedule.

3.5 Practice 1: YAGNI

As a flavour of what's to come, let's look at YAGNI, an acronym for You Aren't Gonna Need It:

Figure 3.4: Testing flushes out Hidden Risk, but increases Schedule Risk

> YAGNI originally is an acronym that stands for "You Aren't Gonna Need It". It is a mantra from Extreme Programming that's often used generally in agile software teams. It's a statement that some capability we presume our software needs in the future should not be built now because "you aren't gonna need it".
> —YAGNI, *Martin Fowler*[2]

The idea makes sense: if you take on extra work that you don't need, *of course* you'll be accreting Attendant Risks.

But, there is always the opposite opinion: You *Are* Gonna Need It[3]. As a simple example, we often add log statements in our code as we write it (so we can trace what happened when things go wrong), though following YAGNI strictly says we shouldn't.

Which is right?

Now, we can say: do the work *if there is a worthwhile Payoff*.

- Logging statements are *good*, because otherwise, you're increasing the risk that in production, no one will be able to understand *how the software went wrong*.
- However, adding them takes time, which might introduce Schedule Risk.

So, it's a trade-off: continue adding logging statements so long as you feel that overall, the activity pays off reducing overall risk.

---

[2] https://www.martinfowler.com/bliki/Yagni.html
[3] http://wiki.c2.com/?YouAreGonnaNeedIt

3.6 Practice 2: Do The Simplest Thing That Could Possibly Work

Another mantra from Kent Beck (originator of the Extreme Programming methodology), is "Do The Simplest Thing That Could Possibly Work", which is closely related to YAGNI and is an excellent razor for avoiding over-engineering. At the same time, by adding "Could Possibly", Kent is encouraging us to go beyond straightforward iteration, and use our brains to pick apart the simple solutions, avoiding them if we can logically determine when they would fail.

Our risk-centric view of this strategy would be:

- Every action you take on a project has its own Attendant Risks.
- The bigger or more complex the action, the more Attendant Risk it'll have.
- The reason you're taking action *at all* is because you're trying to reduce risk elsewhere on the project
- Therefore, the biggest Payoff is likely to be the one with the least Attendant Risk.
- So, usually this is going to be the simplest thing.

So, "Do The Simplest Thing That Could Possibly Work" is really a helpful guideline for Navigating the Risk Landscape, but this analysis shows clearly where it's left wanting:

- *Don't* do the simplest thing if there are other things with a better Payoff available.

3.7 Summary

So, here we've looked at Meeting Reality, which basically boils down to taking actions to manage risk and seeing how it turns out:

- Each Action you take is a step on the Risk Landscape
- Each Action exposes new Hidden Risks, changing your Internal Model.
- Ideally, each action should reduce the overall Attendant Risk on the project (that is, puts it in a better place on the Risk Landscape

Could it be that *everything* you do on a software project is risk management? This is an idea explored in the next chapter.

CHAPTER 4

Just Risk

In this chapter, I am going to propose the idea that everything you do on a software project is Risk Management.

In the Development Process chapter, we observed that all the activities in a simple methodology had a part to play in exposing different risks. They worked to manage risk prior to them creating bigger problems in production.

Here, we'll look at one of the tools in the Project Manager's tool-box, the RAID Log[1], and observe how risk-centric it is.

4.1 RAID Log

Many project managers will be familiar with the RAID Log. It's simply four columns on a spreadsheet: **Risks**, **Actions**, **Issues** and **Decisions**.

Let's try and put the following Risk into the RAID Log:

> "Debbie needs to visit the client to get them to choose the logo to use on the product, otherwise we can't size the screen areas exactly."

- So, is this an **action**? Certainly. There's definitely something for Debbie to do here.
- Is it an **issue**? Yes, because it's holding up the screen-areas sizing thing.
- Is it a **decision**? Well, clearly, it's a decision for someone.
- Is it a **risk**? Probably. Debbie might go to the client and they *still* don't make a decision. What then?

---

[1] http://pmtips.net/blog-new/raid-logs-introduction

4.2 Let's Go Again

This is a completely made-up example, deliberately chosen to be hard to categorise. Normally, items are more one thing than another. But often, you'll have to make a choice between two categories, if not all four.

This *hints* at the fact that at some level it's all about risk:

4.3 Every Action Attempts to Mitigate Risk

The reason you are *taking* an action is to mitigate a risk. For example:

- If you're coding up new features in the software, this is mitigating Feature Risk (which we'll explore in more detail later).
- If you're getting a business sign-off for something, this is mitigating the risk of everyone not agreeing on a course of action (a Coordination Risk).
- If you're writing a specification, then that's mitigating the type of "Incorrect Implementation Risk" we saw in the last chapter.

4.4 Every Action Has Attendant Risk

- How do you know if the action will get completed?
- Will it overrun, or be on time?
- Will it lead to yet more actions?
- What Hidden Risk will it uncover?

Consider *coding a feature* (as we did in the earlier Development Process chapter). We saw here how the whole process of coding was an exercise in learning what we didn't know about the world, uncovering problems and improving our Internal Model. That is, flushing out the Attendant Risk of the Goal In Mind.

And, as we saw in the Introduction, even something *mundane* like the Dinner Party had risks.

4.5 An Issue is Just A Type of Risk

- Because issues need to be fixed...
- And fixing an issue is an action...
- Which, as we just saw also carries risk.

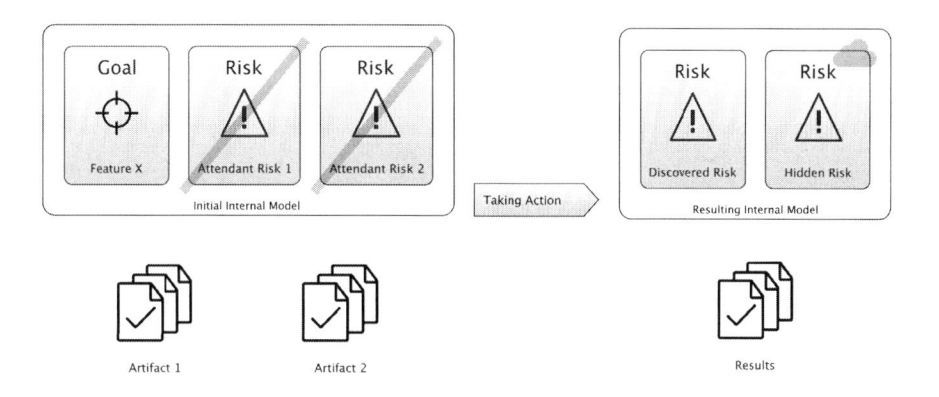

Figure 4.1: Risk-First Diagram Language

One retort to this might be to say: "an issue is a problem I have now, whereas a risk is a problem that *might* occur." I am going to try and break that mind-set in the coming pages, but I'll just start with this:

- Do you know *exactly* how much damage this will do?
- Can you be sure that the issue might not somehow go away?

Issues then, just seem more "definite" and "now" than *risks*, right? This classification is arbitrary: they're all just part of the same spectrum, they all have inherent uncertainty, so there should be no need to agonise over which column to put them in.

4.6 Goals Are Risks Too

In the previous chapters, we introduced something of a "diagram language" of risk. Let's review it:

Goals live inside our Internal Model, just like Risks. It turns out, that functionally, Goals and Risks are equivalent. For example, The Goal of "Implementing Feature X" is equivalent to mitigating "Risk of Feature X not being present".

Let's try and back up that assertion with a few more examples:

Goal	Restated As A Risk
Build a Wall	Mitigate the risk of something getting in / out

Goal	Restated As A Risk
Land a man on the moon	Mitigate the risk of looking technically inferior during the cold war
Move House	Mitigate the risks/problems of where you currently live

There is a certain "interplay" between the concepts of risks, actions and goals. After all, on the Risk Landscape they correspond to a starting point, a movement, and a destination. From a redundancy perspective, any one of these can be determined by knowing the other two.

Psychologically, humans are very goal-driven: they like to know where they're going, and are good at organising around a goal. However, by focusing on goals ("solutionizing") it's easy to ignore alternatives. By focusing on "Risk-First", we don't ignore the reasons we're doing something.

4.7 Every Decision is About Payoff

Sometimes, there will be multiple moves available on the Risk Landscape and you have to choose one.

- There's the risk you'll decide wrongly.
- And, making a decision takes time, which could add risk to your schedule.
- And what's the risk if the decision doesn't get made?

Let's take a hypothetical example: you're on a project and you're faced with the decision - release now or do more testing?

Obviously, in the ideal world, we want to get to the place on the Risk Landscape where we have a tested, bug-free system in production. But we're not there yet, and we have funding pressure to get the software into the hands of some paying customers. The table below shows an example:

Risk Managed	Action	Attendant Risk	Payoff
Funding Risk	Go Live	Reputational Risk, Operational Risk	MEDIUM
Implementation Risk	User Acceptance Test	Worse Funding Risk, Operational Risk	LOW

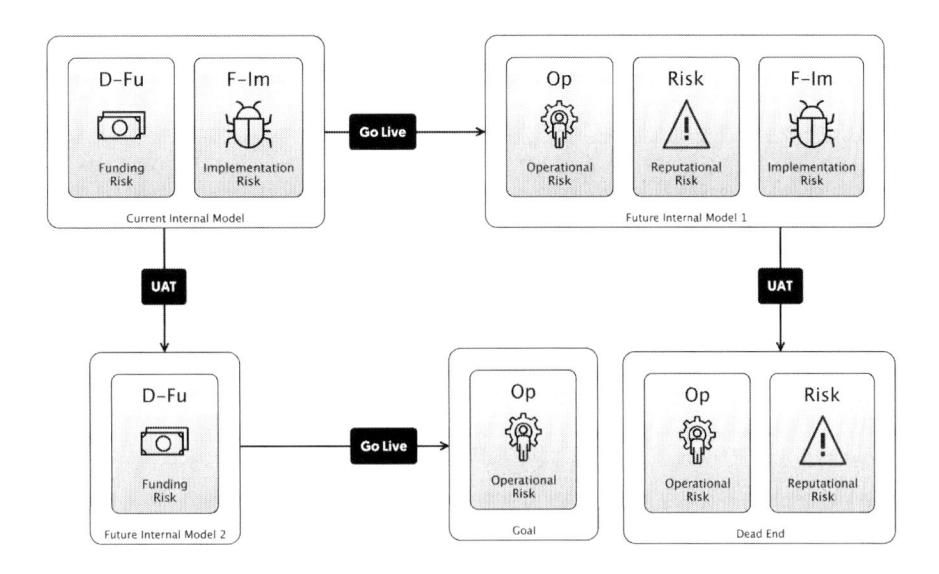

Figure 4.2: UAT or Go Live: where will you end up?

This is (a simplification of) the dilemma of lots of software projects - *test further*, to reduce the risk of users discovering bugs (Implementation Risk) which would cause us reputational damage, or *get the release done* and reduce our Funding Risk by getting paying clients sooner.

In the above table, it *appears* to be better to do the "Go Live" action, as there is a greater Payoff. The problem is, actions are not *commutative*, i.e. the order you do them in counts.

Figure 4.2 shows our decision as *moves on the Risk Landscape*. Whether you "Go Live" first, or "UAT" first makes a difference to where you will end up. Is there a further action you can take to get you from the "Dead End" to the "Goal"? Perhaps.

Failure

So, when we talk about a project "failing", what do we mean?

Usually, we mean we've failed to achieve a goal, and since *goals are risks*, it is simply the scenario where we are overwhelmed by Attendant Risks: there is *no* action to take that has a good-enough Payoff to get us out of our hole.

25

4.8 What To Do?

It makes it much easier to tackle the RAID log if there's only one list. But you still have to choose a *strategy*: do you tackle the *most important* risk on the list, or the *most urgent*, or take the action with the biggest Payoff and deal with it?

In the next chapter, Evaluating Risk we'll look at some approaches to choosing what to do.

CHAPTER 5

Evaluating Risk

Here, I am going to re-cap on some pre-existing risk management theory in order to set the scene for the next chapter which heads back to looking at risk on software projects.

5.1 Risk Registers

Most developers are familiar with recording issues in an issue tracker. For all of the same reasons, it's good practice to record the risks you face running a project or an operation in a Risk Register[1]. Typically, this will include for each risk:

- The **name** of the risk, or other identifier.
- A **categories** to which the risk belongs (this is the focus of the Risk Landscape chapter in Part 2).
- A **brief description** or name of the risk to make the risk easy to discuss.
- Some estimate for the **Impact**, **Probability** or **Risk Score** of the risk.
- Proposed actions and a log of the progress made to manage the risk.

Some points about this description:

A Continuum of Formality

Remember back to the Dinner Party example at the start: the Risk Register happened *entirely in your head*. There is a continuum all the way from "in your head" through "using a spreadsheet" to dedicated Risk Management software.

---

[1] https://en.wikipedia.org/wiki/Risk_register

It's also going to be useful *in conversation*, and this is where the value of the Risk-First approach is: providing a vocabulary to *talk about risks* with your team.

Probability And Impact

Probability is how likely something is to happen, whilst **Impact** is the cost (usually financial) when it does happen.

In a financial context (or a gambling one), we can consider the overall **Risk Score** as being the sum of the **Impact** of each outcome multiplied by its **Probability**. For example, if you buy a 1-Euro ticket in a raffle, there are two outcomes: win or lose. The impact of *winning* would be (say) a hundred Euros, but the **probability** might be 1 in 200. The impact of *losing* would be the loss of 1 Euro, with

Outcome	Impact	Probabilty	Risk Score
Win	+ 99 EUR	1 in 200	.5 EUR
Lose	- 1 EUR	199 in 200	-.99 EUR

Risk Management in the finance industry *starts* here and gets more complex. But often (especially on a software project), it's better to skip all this, and just figure out a Risk Score. This is because if you think about "impact", it implies a definite, discrete event occurring (or not occurring) and asks you then to consider the probability of that.

Risk-First takes a view that risks are a continuous quantity, more like *money* or *water*: by taking an action before delivering a project you might add a degree of Schedule Risk, but decrease the Operational Risk later on by a greater amount.

5.2 Risk Matrix

A risk matrix presents a graphical view on where risks exist. Figure 5.1 is an example, showing the risks from the dinner party in the A Simple Scenario chapter:

This type of graphic is *helpful* in deciding what to do next, although alternatively, you can graph the overall **Risk Score** against the Payoff. Easily mitigated risk (on the right), and worse risks (at the top) can therefore be dealt with first (hopefully).

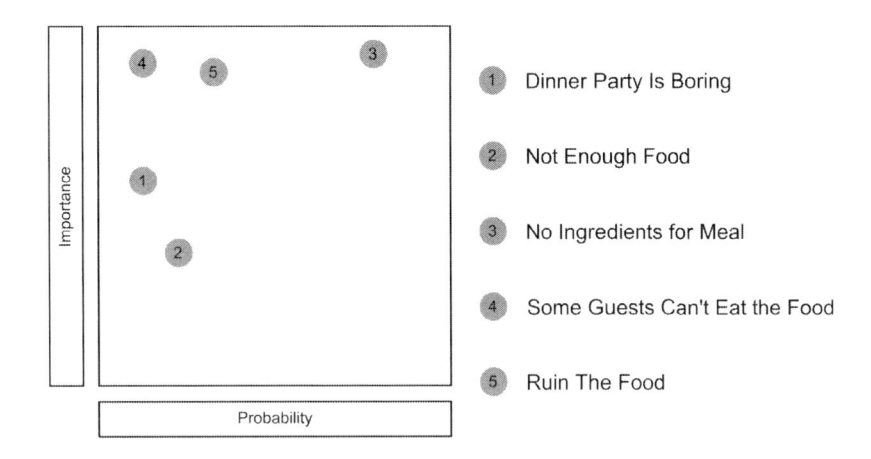

Figure 5.1: Risk Register of Dinner Party Risks

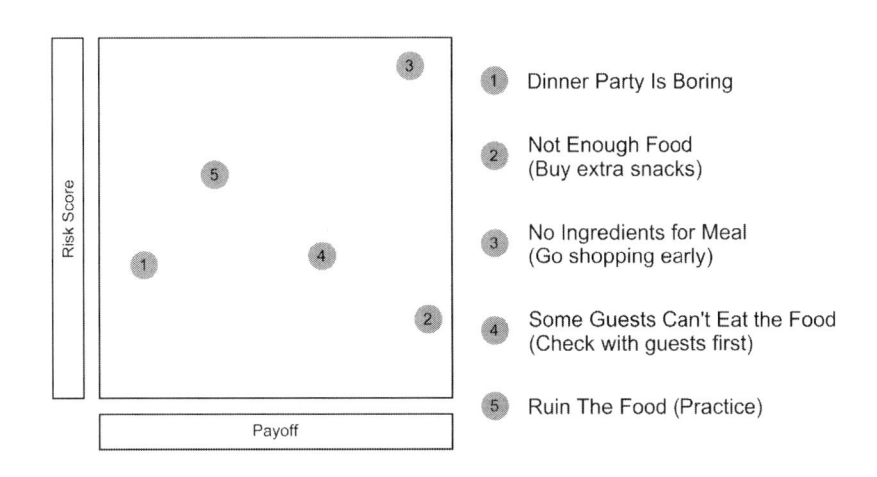

Figure 5.2: Risk Register of Dinner Party Risks, Considering Payoff

5.3 Unknown Unknowns

One of the criticisms of the Risk Register approach is that of mistaking the map for the territory. That is, mistakenly believing that what's on the Risk Register *is all there is*.

In the preceding discussions, I have been careful to point out the existence of Hidden Risks for that very reason. Or, to put another way:

> "What we don't know is what usually gets us killed"
> —Petyr Baelish, *Game of Thrones*[2]

Donald Rumsfeld's famous Known Knowns[3] is also a helpful conceptualisation:

- A *known* **unknown** is an Attendant Risk. i.e. something you are aware of, but where the precise degree of threat can't be established.
- An *unknown* **unknown** is a Hidden Risk. i.e a risk you haven't even thought to exist yet.

5.4 Risk And Uncertainty

Arguably, Risk-First uses the term 'Risk' wrongly: most literature suggests risk can be measured[4] whereas uncertainty represents things that cannot.

I am using **risk** everywhere because later we will talk about specific risks (e.g. Boundary Risk or Complexity Risk), and it doesn't feel grammatically correct to talk about those as **uncertainties**, especially given the pre-existing usage in Banking of terms like Operational Risk[5] or Reputational risk[6] which are also not really a-priori measurable.

5.5 The Opposite Of Risk Management

Let's look at a classic description of Risk Management:

> "Risk Management is the process of thinking out corrective actions before a problem occurs, while it's still an abstraction.

---

[2]https://medium.com/@TanyaMardi/petyr-baelishs-best-quotes-on-game-of-thrones-1ea92968db5c
[3]https://en.wikipedia.org/wiki/There_are_known_knowns
[4]https://keydifferences.com/difference-between-risk-and-uncertainty.html
[5]https://en.wikipedia.org/wiki/Operational_risk
[6]https://www.investopedia.com/terms/r/reputational-risk.asp

> The opposite of risk management is crisis management, trying to figure out what to do about the problem after it happens."
> —Waltzing With Bears, *De Marco, Lister*[7]

This is not how Risk-First sees it:

First, we have the notion that Risks are discrete events. Some risks *are* (like gambling on a horse race), but most *aren't*. In the Dinner Party, for example, bad preparation is going to mean a *worse* time for everyone, but how good a time you're having is a spectrum, it doesn't divide neatly into just "good" or "bad".

Second, the opposite of "Risk Management" (or trying to minimise the "Down-side") is either "Upside Risk Management", (trying to maximise the good things happening), or it's trying to make as many bad things happen as possible.

Third, Crisis Management is *still just Risk Management*: the crisis (Earthquake, whatever) has *happened*. You can't manage it because it's in the past. All you can do is Risk Manage the future (minimize further casualties and human suffering, for example).

Yes, it's fine to say "we're in crisis", but to assume there is a different strategy for dealing with it is a mistake: this is the Fallacy of Sunk Costs[8].

5.6 Invariances #1: Panic Invariance

You would expect that any methods for managing software delivery should be *invariant* to the degree of crisis in the project. If, for example, a project proceeds using Scrum[9] for eight months, and then the deadline looms and everyone agrees to throw Scrum out of the window and start hacking, then *this implies there is a problem with Scrum*, and that it is not **Panic Invariant**. In fact, many tools like Scrum don't consider this:

- If there is a production outage during the working week, we don't wait for the next Scrum Sprint to fix it.
- Although a 40-hour work-week *is a great idea*, this goes out of the window if the databases all crash on a Saturday morning.

In these cases, we (hopefully calmly) *evaluate the risks and Take Action*.

---
[7] http://amzn.eu/d/i0IDFA2
[8] https://en.wikipedia.org/wiki/Escalation_of_commitment
[9] https://en.wikipedia.org/wiki/Scrum_(software_development)

This is **Panic Invariance**: your methodology shouldn't need to change given the amount of pressure or importance on the table.

5.7 Invariances #2: Scale Invariance

We are used to the idea that physical laws work at *any scale*: if they don't apply equally to big and small scenarios then that implies something is wrong. For example, Newton's Laws of Motion work fine for artillery shells but fail to calculate the orbital period of Mercury, which led to Einstein trying to improve on them with the Theory of Relativity[10].

Ideally, a methodology should be applicable at *any* scale too:

- A single class or function.
- A collection of functions, or a library.
- A project team.
- A department.
- An entire organisation.

In practice, however, we usually find methodologies are tuned for certain scales. For example, Extreme Programming is designed for small, co-located teams. And, that's useful. But the fact it doesn't scale tells us something about it: chiefly, that it considers certain *kinds* of risk, while ignoring others. At small scales that works ok, but at larger scales other risks (such as team Coordination Risk) increase too fast for it to work.

If the methodology *fails at a particular scale* this tells you something about the risks that the methodology isn't addressing. One of the things Risk-First explores is trying to place methodologies and practices within a framework to say *when* they are applicable.

5.8 Value vs Speed

"Upside Risk"

"Upside Risk" isn't a commonly used term: industry tends to prefer "value", as in "Is this a value-add project?". There is plenty of theory surrounding **Value**, such as Porter's Value Chain[11] and Net Present Value[12]. This is all fine so long as we remember:

---

[10] https://en.wikipedia.org/wiki/Theory_of_relativity
[11] https://en.wikipedia.org/wiki/Value_chain
[12] https://en.wikipedia.org/wiki/Net_present_value

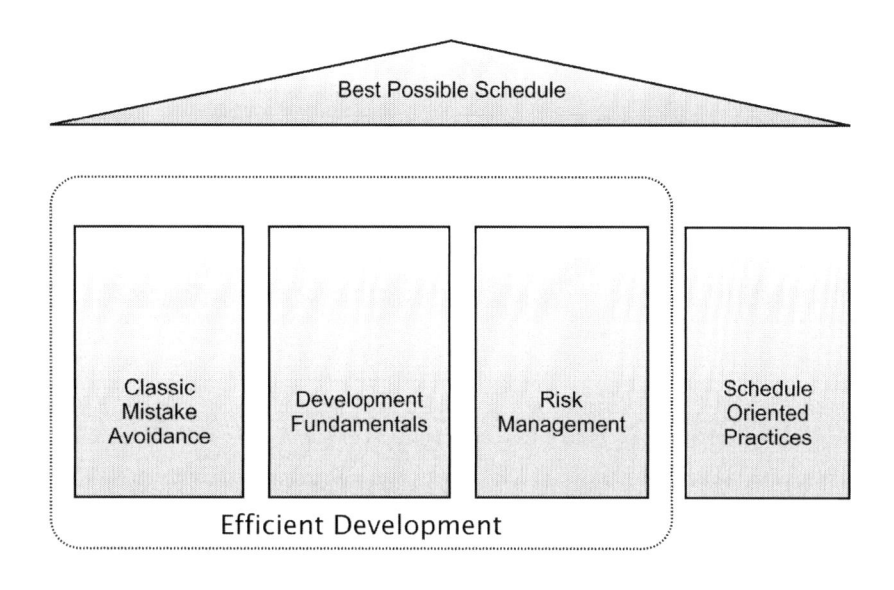

Figure 5.3: Pillars, From Rapid Development By Steve McConnell

- **The probability of Payoff is risky**. Since the value is created in the future, we can't be certain about it happening - we should never consider it a done-deal. **Future Value** is always at risk. In finance, for example, we account for this in our future cash-flows by discounting them according to the risk of default.
- **The Payoff amount is risky**. Additionally, whereas in a financial transaction (like a loan, say), we might know the size of a future payment, in IT projects we can rarely be sure that they will deliver a certain return. On some fixed-contract projects this sometimes is not true: there may be a date when the payment-for-delivery gets made, but mostly we'll be expecting an uncertain Payoff.
- Humans tend to be optimists (especially when there are lots of Hidden Risks), hence our focus on Downside Risk. Sometimes though, it's good to stand back and look at a scenario and think: am I capturing all the Upside Risk here?

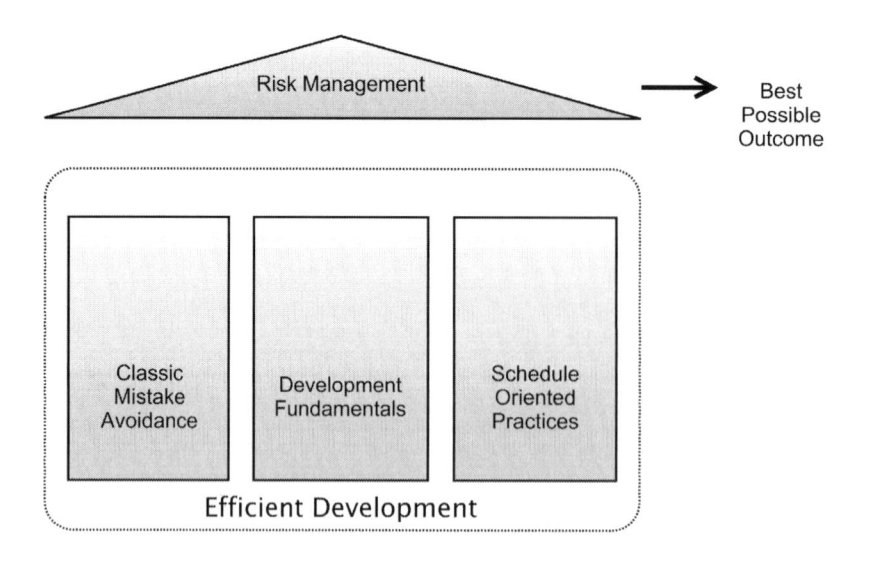

Figure 5.4: Pillars, re-arranged

Speed

Figure 5.3 reproduces a figure from Rapid Development[13] by Steve McConnell. This is *fine*: McConnell is structuring the process from the perspective of *delivering as quickly as possible*. However, here, I want to turn this on its head. Software Development from a risk-first perspective is an under-explored technique, and I believe it offers some useful insights. So the aim here is to present the case for viewing software development like this:

As we will see, *Speed* (or Schedule Risk as we will term it) is one risk amongst others that need to be considered from a risk-management perspective. There's no point in prioritising *speed* if the software fails in production due to Operational Risk issues and damages trust in the product.

Eisenhower's Box

Eisenhower's Box is a simple model allowing us to consider *two* aspects of risk at the same time:

- How valuable the work is (Importance, Value).

---
[13]http://a.co/d/ddWGTB2

	Urgent	**Not Urgent**
Important	Crying Baby Kitchen Fire Some Calls	Exercise Vocation Planning
Not Important	Interruptions Distractions Other Calls	Trivia Busy Work Time Wasters

Figure 5.5: A basic "Eisenhower box" to help evaluate urgency and importance. Items may be placed at more precise points within each quadrant. - Adapted From Time Management, **Wikipedia**[14]

- How soon it is needed (Urgency, Time, Speed).

The problem is, we now need to choose whether to do something that is *urgent* or something that is *important*.

5.9 Discounting

We can use Net Present Value to discount value in the future, which offers us a way to reconcile these two variables. The further in the future the value is realised, the bigger the discount. This is done because payment *now* is better than payment in the future: there is the risk that something will happen to prevent that future payment. This is why we have *interest rates* on loan payments.

In Figure 5.6, you can see two future payments: Payment **A** of £100 due in one year, and Payment **B** of £150 due in 10 years. By discounting at a given rate (here at a high rate of 20% per year) we can compare their worth *now*. At this discount rate, Payment **A** - arriving next year - has a far greater value.

Can we do the same thing with risk? Let's introduce the concept of **Net Present Risk**, or NPR:

> Net Present Risk is the *Impact* of a Future risk, discounted to a common level of *Urgency*.

Let's look at a quick example to see how this could work out. Let's say you had the following risks:

- Risk **A**, which will cost you £50 in 5 days' time.
- Risk **B**, which will cost you £70 in 8 days' time.

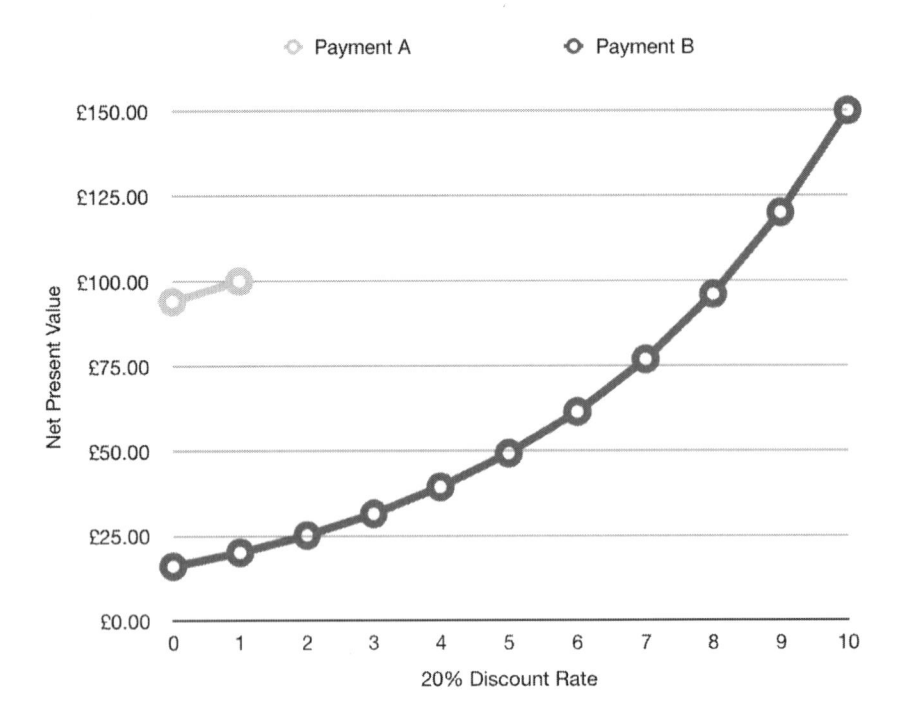

Figure 5.6: Net Present Value Discounting

Which has the biggest NPR? Well, it depends on the discount rate that you apply. Figure 5.7 assumes we are discounting at 6% per *day*. On this basis, the biggest NPR is **B**, at about £45.

However, Figure 5.8 increases the discount factor to 20% and we get a different result: Now, risk **A** is bigger.

Because this is *Net* Present Risk, we can also use it to make decisions about whether or not to mitigate risks. Let's assume the cost of mitigating any risk *right now* is £40. Under the 6% regime, only Risk **B** is worth mitigating today, because you spend £40 today to get rid of £45 of risk (today).

Under the 20% regime, neither are worth mitigating. The 20% Discount Rate may reflect that sometimes, future risks just don't materialise.

Discounting the Future To Zero

I have worked in teams sometimes where the blinkers go down, and the only thing that matters is *now*. Anything with a horizon over a week is irrelevant.

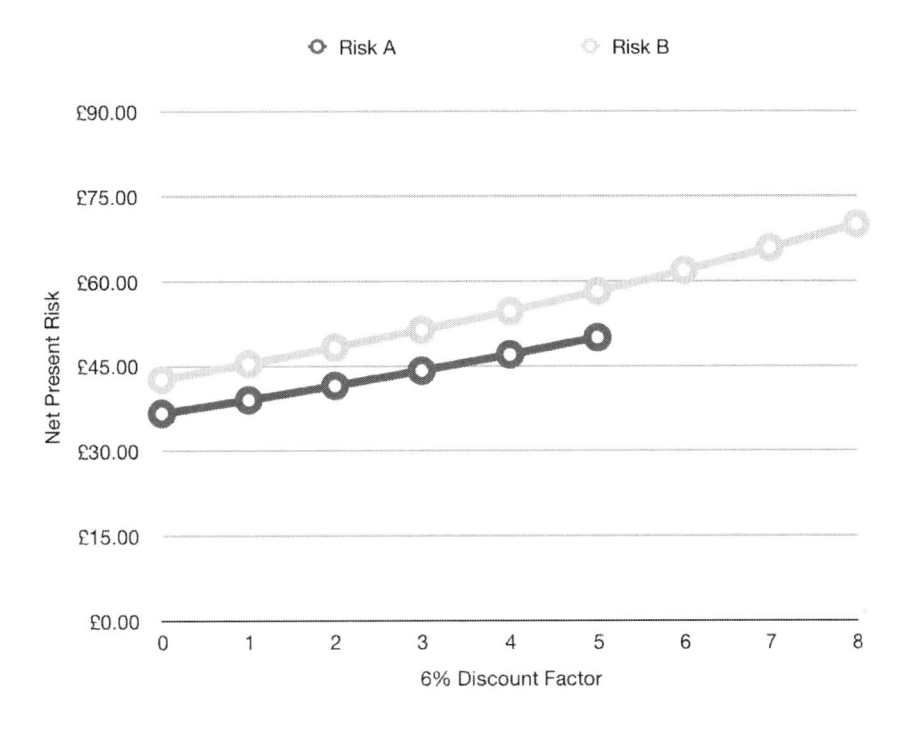

Figure 5.7: Net Present Risk, 6% Discount Rate

Regimes of such hyper-inflation[15] are a sure sign that something has *really broken down* within a project. Consider in this case a Discount Factor of 60% per day, and the following risks:

- Risk A, £10 cost, happening *tomorrow*
- Risk B, £70 cost, happening in *5 days*.

Risk B is almost irrelevant under this regime, as this graph shows:

Why do things like this happen? Often, the people involved are under incredible job-stress: usually they are threatened on a daily basis, and therefore feel they have to react. In a similar way, publicly-listed companies also often apply short-term focus, because they only care about the *next annual report*, which limits their horizons and ability to consider future risk.

Under these circumstances, we often see *Pooh-Bear Procrastination*:

---

[15]https://en.wikipedia.org/wiki/Hyperinflation

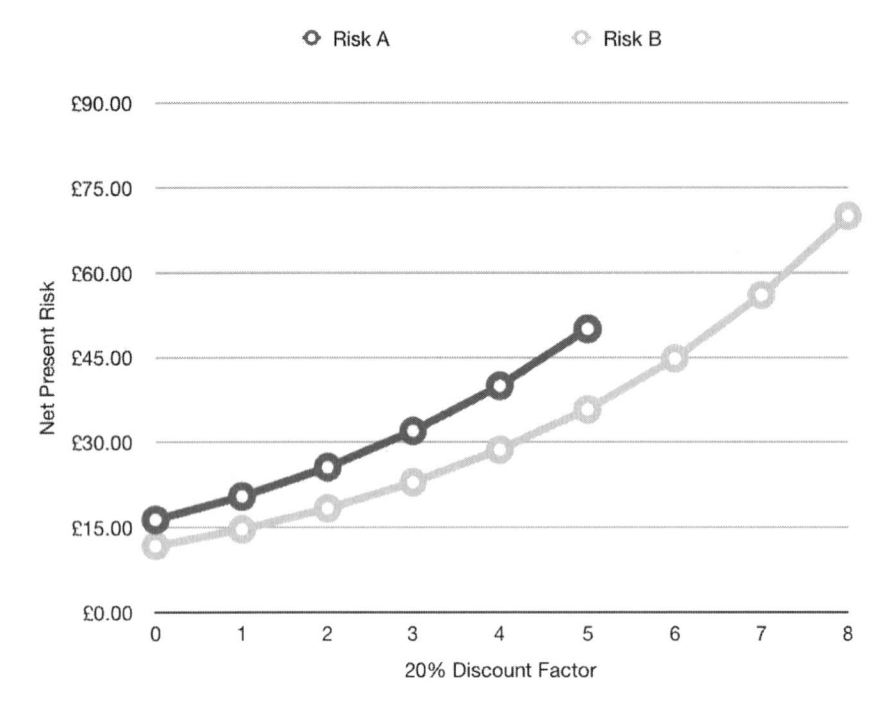

Figure 5.8: Net Present Risk, 20% Discount Rate

> "Here is Edward Bear coming downstairs now, bump, bump, bump, on the back of his head, behind Christopher Robin. It is, as far as he knows, the only way of coming downstairs, but sometimes he feels that there really is another way... if only he could stop bumping for a moment and think of it!"
> —A. A. Milne, *Winne-the-Pooh*[16]

5.10 Is This Scientific?

Enough with the numbers and the theory: we need a practical framework, rather than a scientifically rigorous analysis. For software development, you should probably *give up* on trying to compute risk numerically. You *can't* work out how long a software project will take based purely on an analysis of (say) *function points*. (Whatever you define them to be).

- First, there isn't enough scientific evidence for an approach like this.

---
[16] http://amzn.eu/d/acJ5a2j

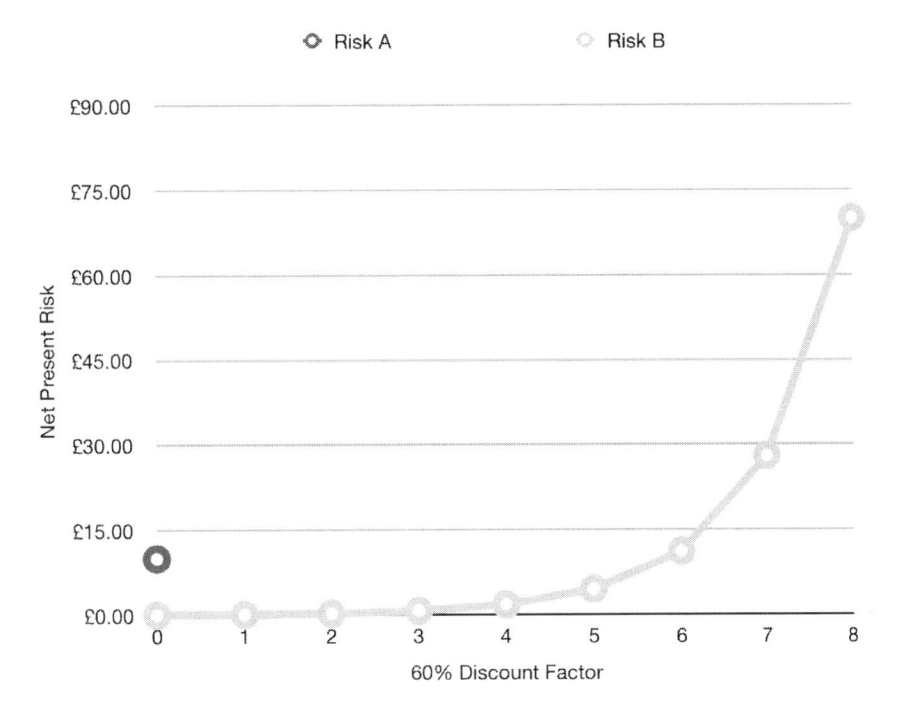

Figure 5.9: Net Present Risk, 60% Discount Rate

We *can* look at collected data about IT projects, but techniques and tools advance rapidly.
- Second, IT projects have too many confounding factors, such as experience of the teams, technologies used etc. That is, the risks faced by IT projects are *too diverse* and *hard to quantify* to allow for meaningful comparison from one to the next.
- Third, as soon as you *publish a date* it changes the expectations of the project (see Student Syndrome).
- Fourth, metrics get misused and gamed (as we will see in a later chapter).

Reality is messy. Dressing it up with numbers doesn't change that and you risk fooling yourself. If this is the case, is there any hope at all in what we're doing? Yes: *forget precision*. You should, with experience, be able to hold up two separate risks and answer the question, "is this one bigger than this one?"

With that in mind, let's look at how we can meet reality as fast and as often as possible.

CHAPTER 6

Cadence

Let's go back to the model again, introduced in Meeting Reality.

As you can see, it's an idealized **Feedback Loop**.

How *fast* should we go round this loop? The longer you leave your goal in mind, the longer it'll be before you find out how it really stacks up against reality.

Testing your goals in mind against reality early and safely is how you'll manage risk effectively, and to do this, you need to set up **Feedback Loops**. e.g.

- **Bug Reports and Feature Requests** tell you how the users are getting on with the software.
- **Monitoring Tools and Logs** allow you to find out how your software is doing in reality.

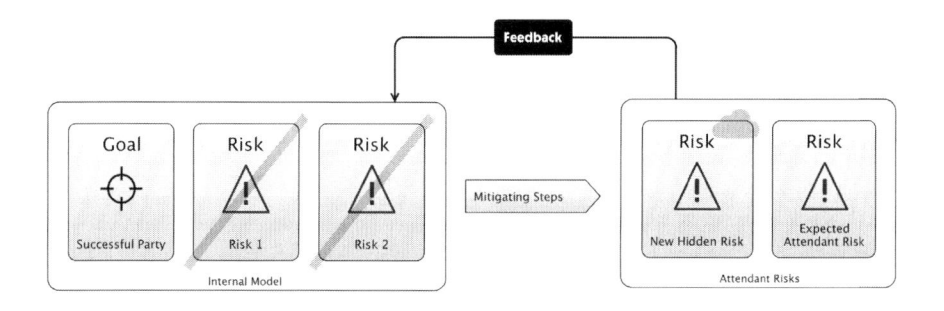

Figure 6.1: Meeting Reality: reality is changed and so is your internal model.

- **Dog-Fooding** i.e using the software you write yourself might be faster than talking to users.
- **Continuous Delivery**[1] is about putting software into production as soon as it's written.
- **Integration Testing** is a faster way of meeting *some* reality than continually deploying code and re-testing it manually.
- **Unit Testing** is a faster feedback loop than Integration Testing.
- **Compilation** warns you about logical inconsistencies in your code.

.. and so on.

Time / Reality Trade-Off

This list is arranged so that at the top, we have the most visceral, most *real* feedback loop, but at the same time, the slowest.

At the bottom, a good IDE can inform you about errors in your Internal Model in real time, by way of highlighting compilation errors . So, this is the fastest loop, but it's the most *limited* reality.

Imagine for a second that you had a special time-travelling machine. With it, you could make a change to your software, and get back a report from the future listing out all the issues people had faced using it over its lifetime, instantly.

That'd be neat, eh? If you did have this, would there be any point at all in a compiler? Probably not, right?

The whole *reason* we have tools like compilers is because they give us a short-cut way to get some limited experience of reality *faster* than would otherwise be possible. Because cadence is really important: the faster we test our ideas, the more quickly we'll find out if they're correct or not.

Development Cycle Time

Developers often ignore the fast feedback loops at the bottom of the list above because the ones nearer the top *will do*.

In the worst cases this means changing two lines of code, running the build script, deploying and then manually testing out a feature. And then repeating. Doing this over and over is a terrible waste of time because the feedback loop is so long and you get none of the benefit of a permanent suite of tests to run again in the future.

---
[1]https://en.wikipedia.org/wiki/Continuous_delivery

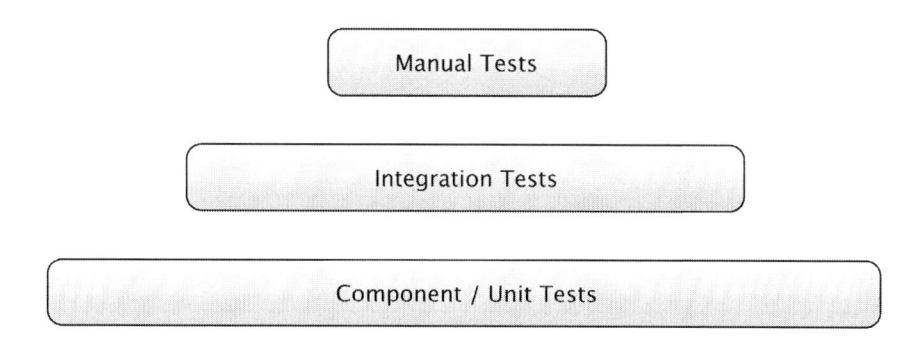

Figure 6.2: The Testing Pyramid

The Testing Pyramid[2] hints at this truth:

- **Unit Tests** have a *fast feedback loop*, so have *lots of them*.
- **Integration Tests** have a slightly *slower feedback loop*, so have *few of them*. Use them when you can't write unit tests (at the application boundaries).
- **Manual Tests** have a *very slow feedback loop*, so have *even fewer of them*. Use them as a last resort.

Production

You could take this chapter to mean that Continuous Delivery (CD) is always and everywhere a good idea. That's not a bad take-away, but it's clearly more nuanced than that.

Yes, CD will give you faster feedback loops, but even getting things into production is not the whole story: the feedback loop isn't complete until people have used the code, and reported back to the development team.

The right answer is to use multiple feedback loops, as shown in Figure 6.3.

In the next chapter De-Risking we're going to introduce a few more useful terms for thinking about risk.

---

[2]http://www.agilenutshell.com/episodes/41-testing-pyramid

Figure 6.3: Different actions have different feedback loops

CHAPTER 7

De-Risking

It's important not only to consider the Attendant Risks you're trying to mitigate, but the ones you're likely to pick up in the process. This means picking a careful path through the Risk Landscape. This is the essence of *De-Risking*.

> "To take steps to make (something) less risky or less likely to involve a financial loss."
>
> —De-Risk, *OxfordDictionaries.com*[1]

Some simple examples of this might be:

- **Safety-nets and ropes** de-risk climbing. But, the activity of climbing itself is otherwise much unchanged.
- **Backups and Source-Control** de-risk the development process by reducing the impact of computer failure. Our process is changed *slightly* by this imposition, but we're not massively inconvenienced.
- **Insurance** de-risks owning a house, going on holiday or driving a car. Usually, the payment is small enough not to impact us too much.
- **The National Health Service (NHS)** de-risks medical expense by pooling health-care costs across the entire population. If you were struck down with a debilitating illness, then at least you wouldn't also have to pay to get better.

Let's look at some common strategies for De-Risking.

---
[1] https://en.oxforddictionaries.com/definition/de-risk

7.1 Mitigate

Mitigating risk is taking steps towards minimising either its likelihood or impact (as we discussed in the Evaluating Risk chapter). Safety-nets, for example, mitigate the impact of hitting the ground. This is the main approach we will be looking at in Part 2. We'll break down risk into its different types and look at the general mitigations for each.

7.2 Avoid

Avoiding risk, means taking a route on the Risk Landscape *around* the risk. For example, if you are working in a team which has no experience of relational databases, then *storing data in files* might be a way to avoid the Learning Curve Risk associated with this technology.

Of course, you may pick up other, more serious Attendant Risks as a result: Relational Databases are software solutions to many kinds of Coordination Risk problem.

Not launching an online service *avoids* the Operational Risk involved in running one. Although you avoid the upsides too.

7.3 Transfer

Transferring risk means *making it someone else's problem.* For example, when I buy home insurance, the personal consequence of my house burning down is reduced. It hasn't gone away completely, but at least the financial element of it is handled by the insurance company.

In part 2, we'll see how **Transfer** of risk is an essential feature of Software-as-a-Service (SaaS). Inside organisations, **Transfer** of risk can become a political game:

> "... ownership results in 'one throat to choke' for audit functions [and] from ownership comes responsibility. A lot of the political footwork in an enterprise revolves around trying to not own technologies. Who wants to be responsible for Java usage across a technology function of dozens of thousands of staff, any of whom might be doing crazy stuff? You first, mate."
> —Why Are Enterprises So Slow?, *zwischenzugs.com*[2]

---

[2]https://zwischenzugs.com/2018/10/02/why-are-enterprises-so-slow/

7.4 Ignore / Accept

Accepting risk is to deal with it when it arises. One example is the Key Person Risk involved in having a super-star programmer on the team. Although there would be fallout if they left, they are often mitigating more risk than they cause.

Another example is using particular software dependencies: building a mobile application which requires a Facebook account to log in might give rise to the risk that people without Facebook accounts can't log in, but might simplify the software to such an extent that it's worthwhile.

Whereas **Accepting** a risk seems to imply an eyes-wide-open examination; **Ignoring** seems to imply that either the risk is so insignificant it doesn't warrant evaluation, or so daunting that it can't be stared down. Either way, **Ignoring** a risk amounts to the same thing as **Accepting** it, since you're not doing anything about it.

Accepting a risk has to occur *before* we can **Mitigate** it.

A Nice Problem To Have

Ignoring or **Accepting** risks is a lot less work than **Mitigating** them, and sometimes it can feel negligent to just add them to the backlog or risk-register without doing anything immediately about them. One useful test I have found is whether "This would be a nice problem to have". For example:

> "Running out of space in the database would be a nice problem to have, because it would mean we have lots of users"

> "Users complaining about lacking function X would be a nice problem to have, because it would mean they were using the system"

Applying this kind of logic at the start of a project leads you towards building a Minimum Viable Product[3].

---
[3] https://en.wikipedia.org/wiki/Minimum_viable_product

Learned Helplessness

Sometimes risks just go away on their own. Learned Helplessness[4], on the other hand, is where we *could* do something about the risk, but fail to see that as an option:

> "Learned helplessness is behaviour typical of animals, and in rare cases humans, that occurs when the subject endures repeatedly painful or otherwise aversive stimuli which it is unable to escape or avoid. After such experience, the organism often fails to learn or accept"escape" or "avoidance" in new situations where such behavior would likely be effective. "
>
> —Learned Helplessness, *Wikipedia*[5]

7.5 Contain

Containing risks means setting aside sufficient time or money to deal with them if they occur. This is an excellent approach for Hidden Risk or entire sets of minor Attendant Risks.

Whenever a project-manager builds slack into a project plan, this is **Containment**. "Time-Boxing" is also containment: this is where you give a piece of work a week (say) to prove itself. If it can't be done in this time, we move on and try a different approach.

In the chapter on Schedule Risk we are going to look in detail at how this works.

7.6 Exploit

Exploiting as a strategy usually means taking advantage of the upside of a risk. For example, ensuring enough stock is available to mitigate the risk of a rush on sales over the Christmas period, or ensuring your website has enough bandwidth to capture all the traffic headed towards it after it's featured on television.

Going back to the example of home insurance, the Insurance company is **exploiting** the risk of my house burning down by selling me insurance. This is a common pattern: wherever there is risk, there is likely to be a way to profit from it.

---

[4]https://en.wikipedia.org/wiki/Learned_helplessness
[5]https://en.wikipedia.org/wiki/Learned_helplessness

Later, in the chapter on Process Risk we'll be looking at how **exploiting risk** can happen organically within a company.

7.7 Re-cap

Let's look at the journey so far.

- In A Simple Scenario we looked at how risk pervades every goal we have in life, big or small. We saw that risk stems from the fact that our Internal Model of the world couldn't capture everything about reality, and so some things were down to chance.

- In the Development Process we looked at how common software engineering conventions like Unit Testing, User Acceptance Testing and Integration could help us manage the risk of taking an idea to production, by *gradually* introducing it to reality in stages.

- Then, generalizing the lessons of the Development Process article, we examined the idea that Meeting Reality frequently helps flush out Hidden Risks and improve your Internal Model.

- In Just Risk we took a leap of faith: could *everything* we do just be risk management? And we looked at the RAID log and thought that maybe it could be.

- Next, in A Software Project Scenario we looked at how you could treat the project-as-a-whole as a risk management exercise, and treat the goals from one day to the next as activities to manage risk.

- Evaluating Risk was an aside, looking at some terminology and the useful concept of a Risk Register.

- We looked at Cadence and how feedback loops allow you to navigate the Risk Landscape more effectively, by showing you more quickly when you're going wrong.

What this has been building towards is supplying us with a vocabulary with which to communicate to our team-mates about which Risks are important to us, which actions we believe are the right ones, and which tools we should use.

In the next chapter we will see an example of this in action.

CHAPTER 8

A Conversation

After so much theory, it seems like it's time to look at how we can apply these principles in the real world.

The following is based on a summary of a real issue around the time of writing. It's heavily edited and anonymized, and I've tried to add the Risk-First vocabulary along the way, but otherwise, it's real.

Some background: **Synergy** is an online service with an app-store, and **Eve** and **Bob** are developers working for **Large Corporation LTD**, which wants to have an application accepted into Synergy's app-store.

Synergy's release process means that the app-store submission must happen in a few weeks, so this is something of a hard deadline: if we miss it, the next opportunity for release will be four months away.

8.1 A Risk Conversation

Eve: We've got a problem with the Synergy security review.

Bob: Tell me.

Eve: Well, you know Synergy did their review and asked us to upgrade our Web Server to only allow TLS version 1.1 and greater?

Bob: Yes, I remember: we discussed it as a team and thought the simplest thing would be to change the security settings on the Web Server, but we all felt it was pretty risky. We decided that in order to flush out Hidden Risk, we'd upgrade our entire production site to use it *now*, rather than wait for the app launch.

Eve: Right, and it *did* flush out Hidden Risk: some of our existing software broke on Windows 7, which sadly we still need to support. So, we had to back it out.

Bob: Ok, well I guess it's good we found out *now*. It would have been a disaster to discover this after the app had gone live on Synergy's app-store.

Eve: Yes. So, what's our next-best action to mitigate this?

Bob: Well, we could go back to Synergy and ask them for a reprieve, but I think it'd be better to mitigate this risk now if we can... they'll definitely want it changed at some point.

Eve: How about we run two web-servers? One for the existing content, and one for our new Synergy app? We'd have to get a new external IP address, handle DNS setup, change the firewalls, and then deploy a new version of the Web Server software on the production boxes.

Bob: This feels like there'd be a lot of Attendant Risk: we're adding Complexity Risk to our estate, and all of this needs to be handled by the Networking Team, so we're picking up a lot of Process Risk. I'm also worried that there are too many steps here, and we're going to discover loads of Hidden Risks as we go.

Eve: Well, you're correct on the first one. But, I've done this before not that long ago for a Chinese project, so I know the process - we shouldn't run into any new Hidden Risk.

Bob: OK, fair enough. But isn't there something simpler we can do? Maybe some settings in the Web Server?

Eve: Well, if we were using Apache, yes, it would be easy to do this. But, we're using Baroque Web Server, and it *might* support it, but the documentation isn't very clear.

Bob: OK, and upgrading to Apache is a *big* risk, right? We'd have to migrate all of our configuration...

Eve: Yes, let's not go there. So, *changing* the settings on Baroque, we have the risk that it's not supported by the software and we're back where we started. Also, if we isolate the Synergy app stuff now, we can mess around with it at any point in future, which is a big win in case there are other Hidden Risks with the security changes that we don't know about yet.

Bob: OK, I can see that buys us something, but time is really short and we have holidays coming up.

Eve: Yes. How about for now, we go with the isolated server, and review next week? If it's working out, then great, we continue with it. Otherwise, if we're not making progress next week, then it'll be because our isolation solution is meeting more risk than we originally thought. In that case, we can attempt the settings change instead.

Bob: Fair enough, it sounds like we're managing the risk properly, and because we can hand off a lot of this to the Networking Team, we can get on with mitigating our biggest risk on the project, the authentication problem, in the meantime.

Eve: Right. I'll check in with the Networking Team each day and make sure it doesn't get forgotten.

8.2 Isn't It Obvious?

At this point, you might be wondering what all the fuss is about. This stuff is all obvious! It's what we do anyway! Perhaps. Risk management *is* what we do anyway:

> "We've survived 200,000 years as humans. Don't you think there's a reason why we survived? We're good at risk management." - Nassim Nicholas Taleb, author of *The Black Swan*[1]

The problem is that although all this *is* obvious, it appears to have largely escaped codification within the literature, practices and methodologies of software development. Further, while it is obvious, there is a huge hole: successful De-Risking depends heavily on individual experience and talent.

In the next chapter, we are going to briefly look at software methodology, and how it comes up short in when addressing risk.

---

[1] https://www.zerohedge.com/news/2018-03-13/taleb-best-thing-society-bankruptcy-goldman-sachs

CHAPTER 9

One Size Fits No-One

Why are Software Methodologies[1] all different?

Previously, we made the case that any action you take on a software project is to do with managing risk, and the last chapter, A Conversation was an example of this happening.

Therefore, it stands to reason that software methodologies are all about handling risk too. Since they are prescribing a particular day-to-day process, or set of actions to take, they are also prescribing a particular approach to managing the risks on software projects.

9.1 Methodologies Surface Hidden Risks...

Back in the Development Process chapter we introduced a toy software methodology that a development team might follow when building software. It included steps like *analysis*, *coding* and *testing*. We looked at how the purpose of each of these actions was to manage risk in the software delivery process. For example, it doesn't matter if a developer doesn't know that he's going to break "Feature Y", because the *Integration Testing* part of the methodology will expose this hidden risk in the testing stage, rather than in let it surface in production (where it becomes more expensive).

9.2 ... But Replace Judgement

But, following a methodology means that you are trusting something *other* than your own judgement to make decisions on what actions to take: perhaps

---

[1] https://en.wikipedia.org/wiki/Software_development_process

Requirements Capture → Specification → Implementation → Verification → Delivery / Operations → Sign Offs

Figure 9.1: Waterfall Actions

the methodology recommends some activity which wastes time, money or introduces some new risk?

Following a software methodology is therefore an act of *trust*:

- Why should we place trust in any *one* methodology, given there are so many alternatives?
- Should there not be more agreement between them, and if not, why not?
- How can a methodology *possibly* take into account the risks on *my* project?

In this chapter, we're going to have a brief look at some different software methodologies, and try to explain *why* they are different. Let's start with Waterfall.

9.3 Waterfall

> "The waterfall development model originated in the manufacturing and construction industries; where the highly structured physical environments meant that design changes became prohibitively expensive much sooner in the development process. When first adopted for software development, there were no recognized alternatives for knowledge-based creative work."
>
> —Waterfall Model, *Wikipedia*[2]

Waterfall is a family of methodologies advocating a linear, stepwise approach to the processes involved in delivering a software system. The basic idea behind Waterfall-style methodologies is that the software process is broken into distinct stages, as shown in Figure 9.1. These usually include:

- Requirements Capture
- Specification

---

[2] https://en.wikipedia.org/wiki/Waterfall_model

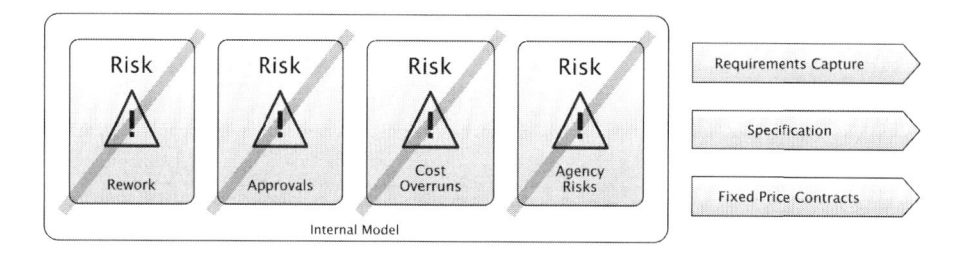

Figure 9.2: Waterfall, Specifications and Requirements Capture

- Implementation
- Verification
- Delivery and Operations
- Sign Offs at each stage

Because Waterfall methodologies are borrowed from *the construction industry*, they manage the risks that you would care about in a construction project, specifically, minimising the risk of rework, and the risk of costs spiralling during the physical phase of the project. For example, pouring concrete is significantly easier than digging it out again after it sets.

Construction projects are often done by tender which means that the supplier will bid for the job of completing the project, and deliver it to a fixed price. This is a risk-management strategy for the client: they are transferring the risk of construction difficulties to the supplier, and avoiding the Agency Risk that the supplier will "pad" the project and take longer to implement it than necessary, charging them more in the process. In order for this to work, both sides need to have a fairly close understanding of what will be delivered, and this is why a specification is created.

The Wrong Risks?

In construction this makes a lot of sense. But *software projects are not the same as building projects*. There are two key criticisms of the Waterfall approach when applied to software:

> "1. Clients may not know exactly what their requirements are before they see working software and so change their requirements, leading to redesign, redevelopment, and re-testing, and increased costs."

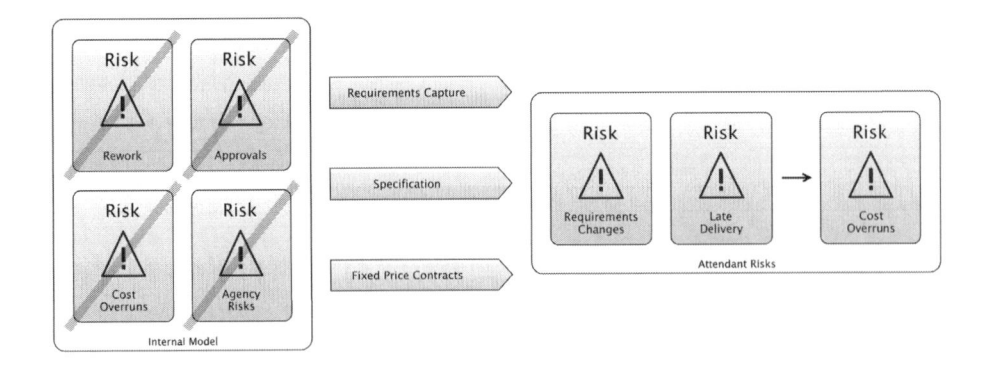

Figure 9.3: Waterfall, Applied to a Software Project

"2. Designers may not be aware of future difficulties when designing a new software product or feature."
—Waterfall Model, *Wikipedia*[3]

So, the same actions Waterfall prescribes to mitigate rework and cost-overruns in the building industry do not address (and perhaps exacerbate) the two issues raised above when applied to software.

As you can see in Figure 9.3, some of the risks on the left *are the same* as the ones on the right: the actions taken to manage them made no difference (or made things worse). The inability to manage these risks led to the identification of a "Software Crisis", in the 1970's:

> "Software crisis is a term used in the early days of computing science for the difficulty of writing useful and efficient computer programs in the required time... The software crisis was due to the rapid increases in computer power and the complexity of the problems that could not be tackled."
> —Software Crisis, *Wikipedia*[4]

9.4 Agile

The Software Crisis showed that, a lot of the time, up-front requirements-capture, specification and fixed-price bids did little to manage cost and schedule risks on software projects. So it's not surprising that by the 1990's, various

---

[3] https://en.wikipedia.org/wiki/Waterfall_model#Supporting_arguments
[4] https://en.wikipedia.org/wiki/Software_crisis

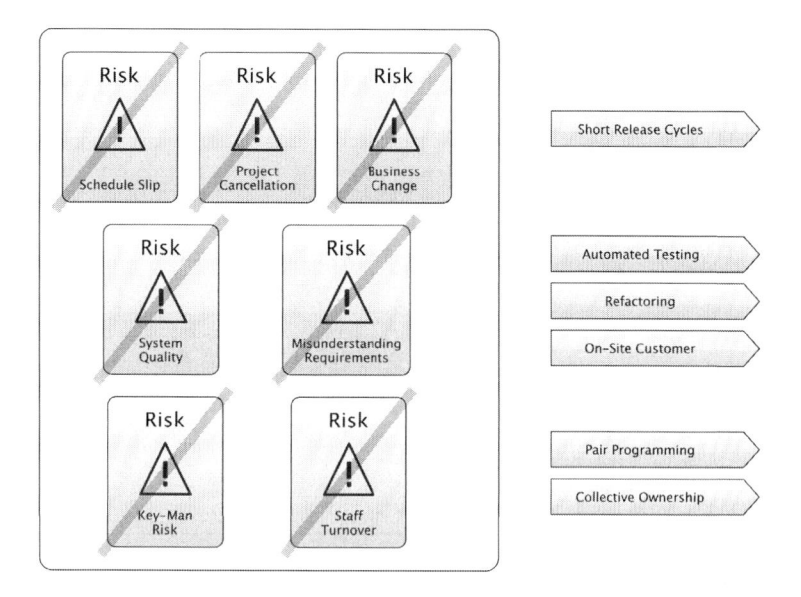

Figure 9.4: Risks, and the practices that manage them in Extreme Programming

different groups of software engineers were advocating "Agile" techniques which did away with those actions.

In Extreme Programming Explained[5], Kent Beck breaks down his methodology, 'Extreme Programming', listing the risks he wants to address and the actions with which he proposes to address them. Figure 9.4 summarises the main risks and actions he talks about. These are *different* risks to those addressed by Waterfall, so unsurprisingly, they lead to different actions.

9.5 Different Methodologies For Different Risks

Here are some high-level differences we see in some other popular methodologies:

- **Lean Software Development**[6]. While Waterfall borrows from risk management techniques in the construction industry, Lean Software Development applies the principles from Lean Manufacturing[7], which was developed at Toyota in the last century. Lean takes the view that the biggest risk in manufacturing is from *waste*, where waste is inventory,

---
[5]http://amzn.eu/d/1vSqAWa
[6]https://en.wikipedia.org/wiki/Lean_software_development
[7]https://en.wikipedia.org/wiki/Lean_manufacturing

over-production, work-in-progress, time spent waiting or defects in production. Applying this approach to software means minimising work-in-progress, frequent releases and continuous improvement.

- **Project Management Body Of Knowledge (PMBoK)**[8]. This is a formalisation of traditional project management practice. It prescribes best practices for managing scope, schedule, resources, communications, dependencies, stakeholders etc. on a project. Although "risk" is seen as a separate entity to be managed, all of the above areas are sources of risk within a project, as we will see in Part 2.

- **Scrum**[9]. Is a popular Agile methodology. Arguably, it is less "extreme" than Extreme Programming, as it promotes a limited set, more achievable set of agile practices, such as frequent releases, daily meetings, a product owner and retrospectives. This simplicity arguably makes it simpler to learn and adapt to and probably contributes to Scrum's popularity over XP.

- **DevOps**[10]. Many software systems struggle at the boundary between "in development" and "in production". DevOps is an acknowledgement of this, and is about more closely aligning the feedback loops between the developers and the production system. It champions activities such as continuous deployment, automated releases and automated monitoring.

While this is a limited set of examples, you should be able to observe that the actions promoted by a methodology are contingent on the risks it considers important.

9.6 Effectiveness

> "All methodologies are based on fear. You try to set up habits to prevent your fears from becoming reality."
> —Extreme Programming Explained, *Kent Beck*[11]

The promise of any methodology is that it will help you manage certain Hidden Risks. But this comes at the expense of the *effort* you put into the practices of the methodology.

---

[8]https://en.wikipedia.org/wiki/Project_Management_Body_of_Knowledge

[9]https://en.wikipedia.org/wiki/Scrum

[10]https://en.wikipedia.org/wiki/DevOps

[11]http://amzn.eu/d/1vSqAWa

A methodology offers us a route through the Risk Landscape, based on the risks that the designers of the methodology care about. When we use the methodology, it means that we are baking into our behaviour actions to avoid those risks.

Methodological Failure

When we take action according to a methodology, we expect the Payoff, and if this doesn't materialise, then we feel the methodology is failing us. It could just be that it is inappropriate to the *type of project* we are running. Our Risk Landscape may not be the one the designers of the methodology envisaged. For example:

- NASA don't follow an agile methodology[12] when launching space craft: there's no two-weekly launch that they can iterate over, and the the risks of losing a rocket or satellite are simply too great to allow for iteration in production. The risk profile is just all wrong: you need to manage the risk of *losing hardware* over the risk of *requirements changing*.

- Equally, regulatory projects often require big, up-front, waterfall-style design: keeping regulators happy is often about showing that you have a well-planned path to achieving the regulation. Often, the changes need to be reviewed and approved by regulators and other stakeholders in advance of their implementation. This can't be done with an approach of "iterate for a few months".

- At the other end of the spectrum, Facebook used to have[13] an approach of "move fast and break things". This may have been optimal when they were trying mitigate the risk of being out-innovated by competitors within the fast-evolving sphere of social networking. *Used to have*, because now they have modified this to "move fast with stable infrastructure"[14], perhaps as a reflection of the fact that their biggest risk is no longer competition, but bad publicity.

9.7 Choosing A Methodology

There is value in adopting a methodology as a complete collection of processes: choosing a methodology (or any process) reduces the amount of

---

[12]https://standards.nasa.gov/standard/nasa/nasa-std-87398
[13]https://mashable.com/2014/04/30/facebooks-new-mantra-move-fast-with-stability/?europe=true
[14]https://www.cnet.com/news/zuckerberg-move-fast-and-break-things-isnt-how-we-operate-anymore/

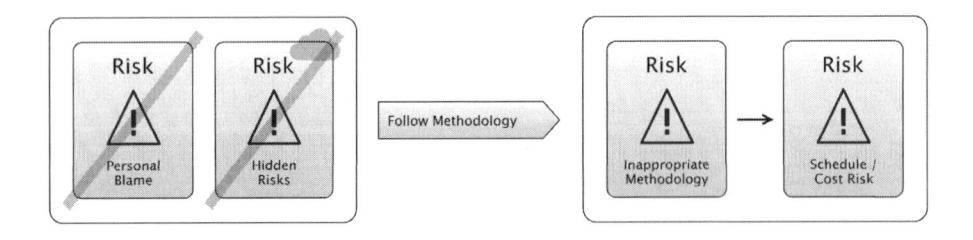

Figure 9.5: Inappropriate Methodologies create their own risks

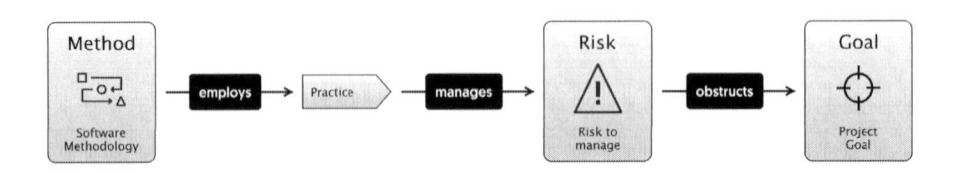

Figure 9.6: Methodologies, Actions, Risks, Goals

thinking individuals have to do, and it becomes *the process* that is responsible for failure, not the individual (as shown in Figure 9.5).

It's nice to lay the blame somewhere else. But, if we genuinely care about our projects, then it's critical that we match the choice of methodology to the risk profile of the project. We need to understand exactly what risks our methodology will help us with, which it won't, where it is appropriate, and where it isn't.

> "Given any rule, however 'fundamental' or 'necessary' for science, there are always circumstances when it is advisable not only to ignore the rule, but to adopt its opposite."
>
> Paul Feyerabend[15]

An off-the-shelf methodology is unlikely to fit the risks of any project exactly. Sometimes, we need to break down methodologies into their component practices, and apply just the practices we need. This requires a much more fine-grained understanding of how the individual practices work, and what they bring.

As Figure 9.6 shows, different methodologies advocate different practices, and different practices manage different risks. If we want to understand

---

[15] https://www.azquotes.com/author/4773-Paul_Feyerabend

methodologies, or choose practices from one, we really need to understand the *types of risks* we face on software projects. This is where we go next in Part 2.

Part II

The Risk Landscape

CHAPTER 10

The Risk Landscape

In the previous chapter, we saw how *Lean Software Development* owed its existence to production-line manufacturing techniques developed at Toyota. And we saw that the *Waterfall* approach originally came from engineering. If Risk-First is anything, it's about applying the techniques of *Risk Management* to the discipline of *Software Development* (there's nothing new under the sun, after all).

One key activity of Risk Management we haven't discussed yet is *categorizing* risks. Thus, Part 2 of Risk-First is all about developing categories of risks for use in Software Development.

10.1 The Risk Landscape Again

In Meeting Reality, we looked at the concept of the Risk Landscape, and how a software project tries to *navigate* across this landscape, testing the way as it goes, and trying to get to a position of *more favourable risk*.

It's tempting to think of our Risk Landscape as being like a Fitness Landscape[1]. That is, you have a "cost function" which is your height above the landscape, and you try and optimise by moving downhill in a Gradient Descent[2] fashion.

However, there's a problem with this: as we said in Evaluating Risk, we don't have a cost function. We can only *guess* at what risks there are. We have to go on our *experience*. For this reason, I prefer to think of the Risk Landscape as a terrain which contains *fauna* and *obstacles* (or, specifically *Boundaries*).

---

[1] https://en.wikipedia.org/wiki/Fitness_landscape
[2] https://en.wikipedia.org/wiki/Gradient_descent

Just as I can tell you that the landscape outside your window will probably will have some trees, fields and buildings, and that the buildings are likely to be joined together by roads, we can make generalisations about risks too.

10.2 Why Should We Categorise The Risks?

A lot of knowledge and understanding of the world starts by naming and categorising things.

If we were studying insects, this might be a guide giving you a description and a picture of each insect, telling you where to find it and how it lives. That doesn't mean that this is *all* there is to know. Just as a scientist could spend an entire lifetime studying a particular species of bee, each of the risks we'll look at really has a whole sub-discipline of Computer Science attached to it, which we can't possibly hope to cover in any great depth.

As software developers, we can't hope to know the specifics of the whole discipline of Complexity Theory[3], or Concurrency Theory[4]. But, we're still required to operate in a world where these things exist. So, we may as well get used to them and ensure that we respect their primacy. We are operating in *their* world, so we need to know the rules.

Once we can spot and name different types of risk we can then think about their characteristics and how to manage or avoid them. Over the following pages, we're going to take a tour of various different categories of risks, exploring their characteristics and sometimes suggesting actions to take to deal with them. But foremost, this is a "spotters' guide" to software risks and where to find them.

10.3 Our Tour Itinerary

Below is a table outlining the different risks we'll see. There *is* an order to this: the later risks are written assuming a familiarity with the earlier ones. Hopefully, you'll stay to the end and see everything, but you're free to choose your own tour if you want to.

---

[3]https://en.wikipedia.org/wiki/Complexity_theory
[4]https://en.wikipedia.org/wiki/Concurrency_(computer_science)

Risk	Description
Feature Risk	When you haven't built features the market needs, or the features you have built contain bugs, or the market changes underneath you.
Communication Risk	Risks associated with getting messages heard and understood.
Complexity Risk	Your software is so complex it makes it hard to change, understand, or run.
Dependency Risk	Risks of depending on other people, products, software, functions, etc. This is a general look at dependencies, before diving into specifics like...
Scarcity Risk	Risks associated with having limited time, money or some other resource.
Deadline Risk	The risk of having a date to hit.
Software Dependency Risk	The risk of depending on a software library, service or function.
Process Risk	When you depend on a business process, or human process to give you something you need.
Boundary Risk	Risks due to making decisions that limit your choices later on. Sometimes, you go the wrong way on the Risk Landscape and it's hard to get back to where you want to be.
Agency Risk	Risks that staff have their own Goals, which might not align with those of the project or team.
Coordination Risk	Risks due to the fact that systems contain multiple agents, which need to work together.
Map And Territory Risk	Risks due to the fact that people don't see the world as it really is. (After all, they're working off different, imperfect Internal Models.)

Risk	Description
Operational Risk	Software is embedded in a system containing people, buildings, machines and other services. Operational risk considers this wider picture of risk associated with running a software service or business in the real world.

After the last stop on the tour, in Staging and Classifying we'll have a recap about what we've seen and make some guesses about how things fit together.

10.4 Causation & Correlation

Although we're going to try and categorise the kinds of things we see on this Risk Landscape, this isn't going to be perfect, because:

- One risk can "blend" into another just like sometimes a "field" is also a "car-park", or a building might contain some trees (but isn't a forest).
- As we know from Part 1, mitigating one risk probably means accepting another.
- There can be *causation* and *correlation* between different risks: one risk may cause another, or two risks might have the same underlying cause.

Risk is messy. It's not always easy to tease apart the different components of risk and look at them individually. Let's look at a high-profile recent example to see why.

The Financial Crisis

In the Financial Services[5] industry, whole departments exist to calculate different risks like:

- **Market Risk**[6], the risk that the amount some asset is going to change in value.

---

[5] https://en.wikipedia.org/wiki/Financial_services
[6] https://en.wikipedia.org/wiki/Market_risk

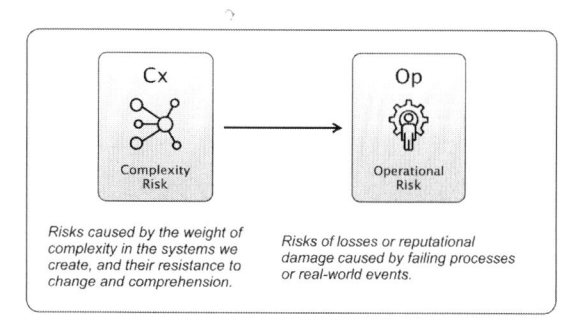

Figure 10.1: Causation shown on a Risk-First Diagram. More complexity is likely to lead to more Operational Risk

- **Credit Risk**[7], the risk that someone who owes you a payment at a specific point in time might not pay it back.
- **Liquidity Risk**[8], the risk that you can't find a market to sell/buy something, usually leading to a shortage of ready cash.

In the financial crisis of 2007, these models of risk didn't turn out to be much use. Although there are lots of conflicting explanations of what happened, one way to look at it is this:

- Liquidity difficulties (i.e. amount of cash you have for the day-to-day running of the bank) caused some banks to not be able to cover their short term payment obligations.
- This caused credit defaults (the thing that Credit Risk measures were meant to guard against) even though the banks *technically* were solvent.

- Once credit defaults started, this worried investors in the banks, which had massive Market Risk impacts that none of the models foresaw.

All the Risks were correlated[9]. That is, they were affected by the *same underlying events*, or *each other*.

It's like this with software risks, too, sadly. For example, Operational Risk is going to be heavily correlated with Complexity Risk: the more complex your operation, the more risky it will be. In the Risk-First diagrams, we will sometimes show correlation or causation with an arrow, like in Figure 10.1.

---

[7]https://en.wikipedia.org/wiki/Credit_risk
[8]https://en.wikipedia.org/wiki/Liquidity_risk
[9]https://www.investopedia.com/terms/c/correlation.asp

10.5 We're all Naturalists Now

Just as naturalists are able to head out and find new species of insects and plants, we should expect to do the same. Risk-First is by no means a complete picture - it's barely a sketch.

It's a big, crazy, evolving world of software. Help to fill in the details. Report back what you find.

So, let's get started with Feature Risk.

CHAPTER 11

Feature Risk

Feature Risks are risks to do with functionality that you need to have in the software you're building.

As a simple example, if your needs are served perfectly by Microsoft Excel, then it doesn't have any Feature Risk. However, the day you find Microsoft Excel wanting, and decide to build an Add-On is the day when you first appreciate some Feature Risk. Now *you're* a customer: does the Add-On you build satisfy the requirements you have?

Feature Risk is very fundamental: if your project has *no* Feature Risk it would be perfect!

As we will explore below, Feature Risk exists in the gaps between what users *want*, and what they *are given*.

Not considering Feature Risk means that you might be building the wrong functionality, for the wrong audience or at the wrong time. And eventually, this will come down to lost money, business, acclaim, or whatever you are doing your project for. So let's unpack this concept into some of its variations.

11.1 Feature Fit Risk

This is the one we've just discussed above - the feature that clients want to use in the software *isn't there*.

- This might manifest itself as complete *absence* of something you need, e.g "Why is there no word count in this editor?"
- It could be that the implementation isn't complete enough, e.g "why can't I add really long numbers in this calculator?"

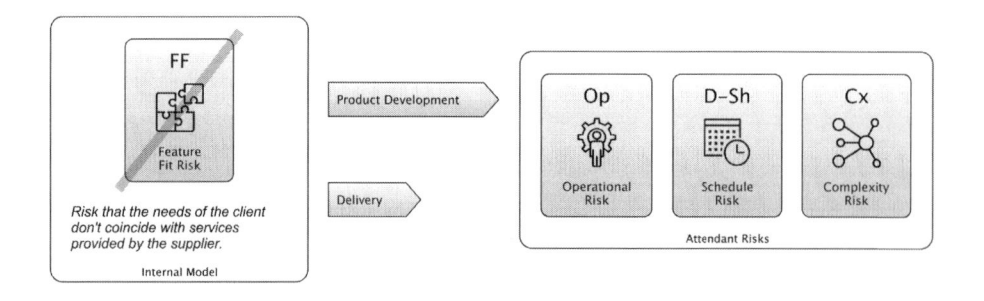

Figure 11.1: Feature Fit Risk

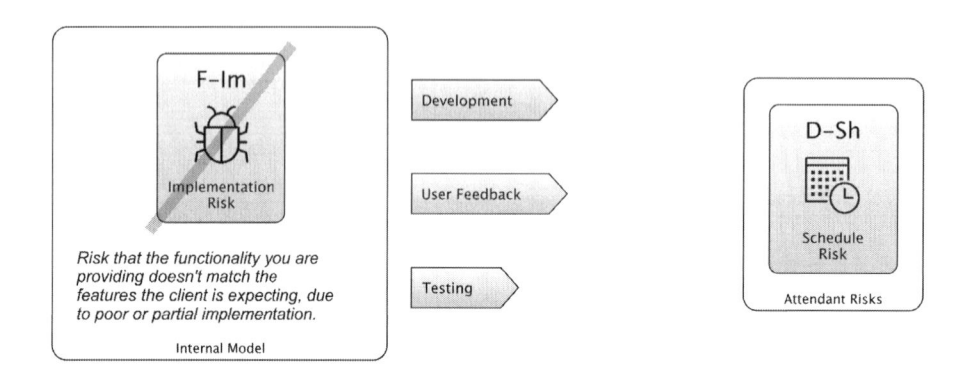

Figure 11.2: Implementation Risk

Feature Fit Risks are mitigated by talking to clients and building things (as shown in Figure 11.1). But that leads on to...

11.2 Implementation Risk

Feature Risk also includes things that don't work as expected, that is to say, bugs[1]. Although the distinction between "a missing feature" and "a broken feature" might be worth making in the development team, we can consider these both the same kind of risk: *the software doesn't do what the user expects*. As shown in Figure 11.2, we can mitigate this risk with *feedback* from users, as well as further *development* and *testing*.

It's worth pointing out that sometimes, *the user expects the wrong thing*. This is a different but related risk, which could be down to training, documentation

---

[1]https://en.wikipedia.org/wiki/Software_bug

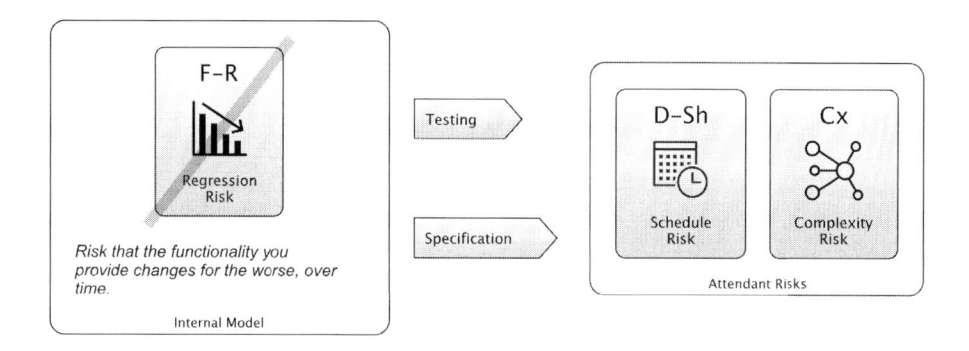

Figure 11.3: Regression Risk

or simply a poor user interface (and we'll look at that more in Communication Risk.)

11.3 Regression Risk

Regression Risk is the risk of breaking existing features in your software when you add new ones. As with the previous risks, the eventual result is the same: customers don't have the features they expect. This can become a problem as your code-base gains Complexity and as it becomes impossible to keep a complete Internal Model of the whole thing in your head.

Delivering new features can delight your customers, breaking existing ones will annoy them. This is something we'll come back to in Operational Risk.

11.4 Conceptual Integrity Risk

Sometimes users *swear blind* that they need some feature or other, but it runs at odds with the design of the system, and plain *doesn't make sense*. Often the development team can spot this kind of conceptual failure as soon as it enters the Backlog. Usually it's in coding that this becomes apparent.

Sometimes it can go for a lot longer. I once worked on some software that was built as a score-board within a chat application. However, after we'd added much-asked-for commenting and reply features to our score-board, we realised we'd implemented a chat application *within a chat application*, and had wasted our time enormously.

Feature Phones[2] are a real-life example: although it *seemed* like the market

---
[2]https://en.wikipedia.org/wiki/Feature_phone

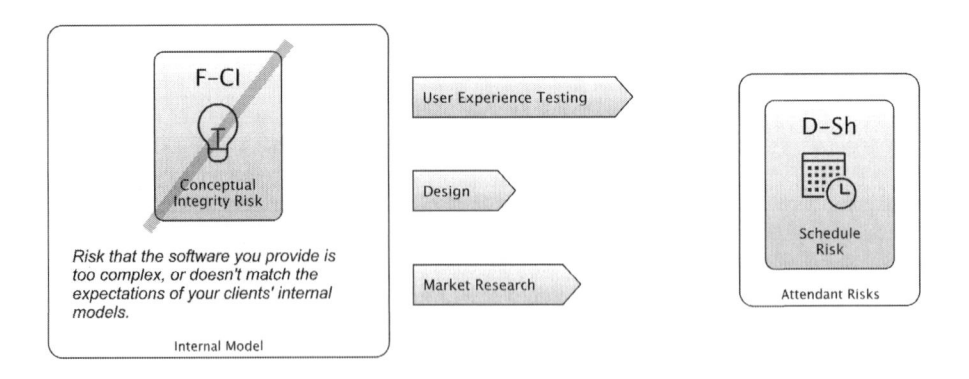

Figure 11.4: Conceptual Integrity Risk

wanted more and more features added to their phones, Apple's iPhone[3] was able to steal huge market share by presenting a much more enjoyable, more coherent user experience, despite being more expensive and having fewer features. Feature Phones had been drowning in increasing Conceptual Integrity Risk without realising it.

This is a particularly pernicious kind of Feature Risk which can only be mitigated by good Design. Human needs are fractal in nature: the more you examine them, the more complexity you can find. The aim of a product is to capture some needs at a *general* level: you can't hope to anticipate everything.

Conceptual Integrity Risk is the risk that chasing after features leaves the product making no sense, and therefore pleasing no-one.

11.5 Feature Access Risk

Sometimes features can work for some people and not others: this could be down to Accessibility[4] issues, language barriers or localisation.

You could argue that the choice of *platform* is also going to limit access: writing code for XBox-only leaves PlayStation owners out in the cold. This is *largely* Feature Access Risk, though Dependency Risk is related here.

In marketing terms, minimising Feature Access Risk is all about Segmentation[5]: trying to work out *who* your product is for, and tailoring it to that

---

[3] https://en.wikipedia.org/wiki/IPhone
[4] https://en.wikipedia.org/wiki/Accessibility
[5] https://en.wikipedia.org/wiki/Market_segmentation

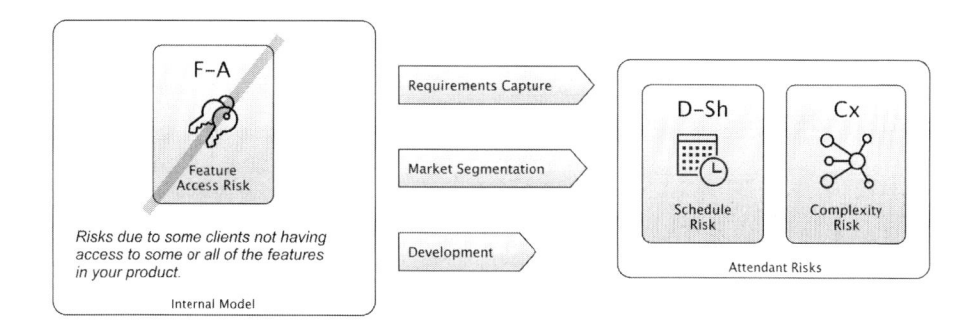

Figure 11.5: Feature Access Risk

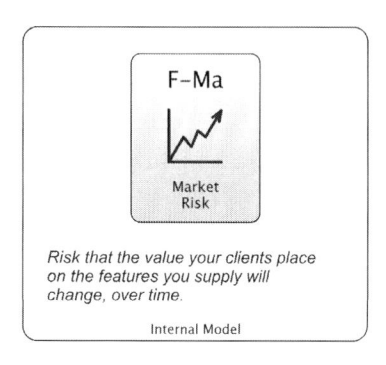

Figure 11.6: Market Risk

particular market. As shown in Figure 11.5, mitigating Feature Access Risk means increasing complexity: you have to deliver the software on more platforms, localised in more languages, with different configurations of features. It also means increased development effort.

11.6 Market Risk

Feature Access Risk is related to Market Risk, which I introduced in the Risk Landscape chapter as being the value that the market places on a particular asset.

> "Market risk is the risk of losses in positions arising from movements in market prices." - Market Risk, *Wikipedia*

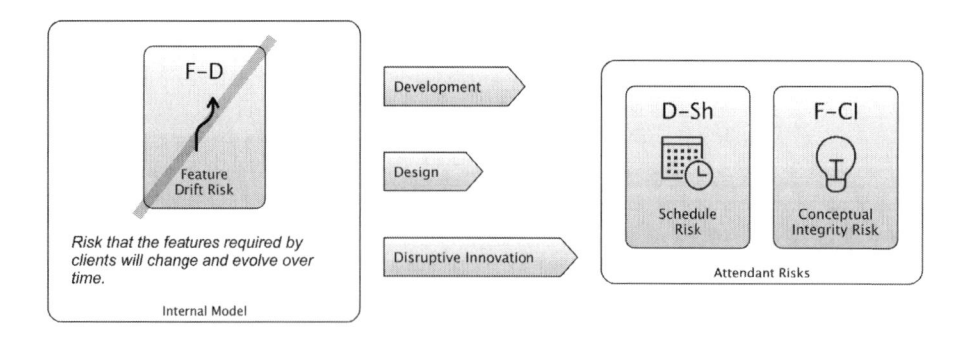

Figure 11.7: Feature Drift Risk

I face market risk when I own (i.e. have a *position* in) some Apple[6] stock. Apple's stock price will decline if a competitor brings out an amazing product, or if fashions change and people don't want their products any more.

Since the product you are building is your asset, it makes sense that you'll face Market Risk on it: the *market* decides what it is prepared to pay and it tends to be outside your control.

11.7 Feature Drift Risk

Feature Drift is the tendency that the features people need *change over time*. For example, at one point in time, supporting IE6 was right up there for website developers, but it's not really relevant anymore. The continual improvements we see in processor speeds and storage capacity of our computers is another example: the Wii[7] was hugely popular in the early 2000's, but expectations have moved on now.

The point is: Requirements captured *today* might not make it to *tomorrow*, especially in the fast-paced world of IT, partly because the market *evolves* and becomes more discerning. This happens in several ways:

- Features present in competitors' versions of the software become *the baseline*, and they're expected to be available in your version.
- Certain ways of interacting become the norm (e.g. querty[8] keyboards, or the control layout in cars: these don't change with time).

---

[6] http://apple.com
[7] https://en.wikipedia.org/wiki/Wii
[8] https://en.wikipedia.org/wiki/QWERTY

- Features decline in usefulness: *Printing* is less important now than it was, for example.

Feature Drift Risk is *not the same thing* as **Requirements Drift**, which is the tendency projects have to expand in scope as they go along. There are lots of reasons they do that, a key one being the Hidden Risks uncovered on the project as it progresses.

11.8 Fashion

Fashion plays a big part in IT. By being *fashionable*, web-sites are communicating: *this is a new thing, this is relevant, this is not terrible*. All of which is mitigating a Communication Risk. Users are all-too-aware that the Internet is awash with terrible, abandon-ware sites that are going to waste their time. How can you communicate that you're not one of them to your users?

11.9 Delight

If this breakdown of Feature Risk seems reductive, then try not to think of it that way: the aim *of course* should be to delight users, and turn them into fans.

Consider Feature Risk from both the down-side and the up-side:

- What are we missing?
- How can we be *even better*?

11.10 Analysis

So far in this chapter, we've simply seen a bunch of different types of Feature Risk. But we're going to be relying heavily on Feature Risk as we go on in order to build our understanding of other risks, so it's probably worth spending a bit of time up front to classify what we've found.

The Feature Risks identified here basically exist in a space with at least 3 dimensions:

- **Fit**: how well the features fit for a particular client.
- **Audience**: the range of clients (the *market*) that may be able to use this feature.

- **Evolution**: the way the fit and the audience changes and evolves as time goes by.

Let's examine each in turn.

Fit

> "This preservation, during the battle for life, of varieties which possess any advantage in structure, constitution, or instinct, I have called Natural Selection; and Mr. Herbert Spencer has well expressed the same idea by the Survival of the Fittest" - Charles Darwin (Survival of the Fittest), *Wikipedia*[9].

Darwin's conception of fitness was not one of athletic prowess, but how well an organism worked within the landscape, with the goal of reproducing itself.

Feature Fit Risk, Conceptual Integrity Risk and Implementation Risk all hint at different aspects of this "fitness". We can conceive of them as the gaps between the following entities:

- **Perceived Need**, what the developers *think* the users want.
- **Expectation**, what the user *expects*.
- **Reality**, what they actually *get*.

For further reading, you can check out The Service Quality Model[10] which Figure 11.8 is derived from. This model analyses the types of *quality gaps* in services and how consumer expectations and perceptions of a service arise.

In the Staging And Classifying chapter we'll come back and build on this model further.

Fit and Audience

Two risks, Feature Access Risk and Market Risk, consider *fit* for a whole *audience* of users. They are different: just as it's possible to have a small audience, but a large revenue, it's possible to have a product which has low Feature Access Risk (i.e lots of users can access it without difficulty) but high Market Risk (i.e. the market is highly volatile or capricious in it's demands). *Online services* often suffer from this Market Risk roller-coaster, being one moment highly valued and the next irrelevant.

---

[9] https://en.wikipedia.org/wiki/Survival_of_the_fittest
[10] http://en.wikipedia.org/SERVQUAL

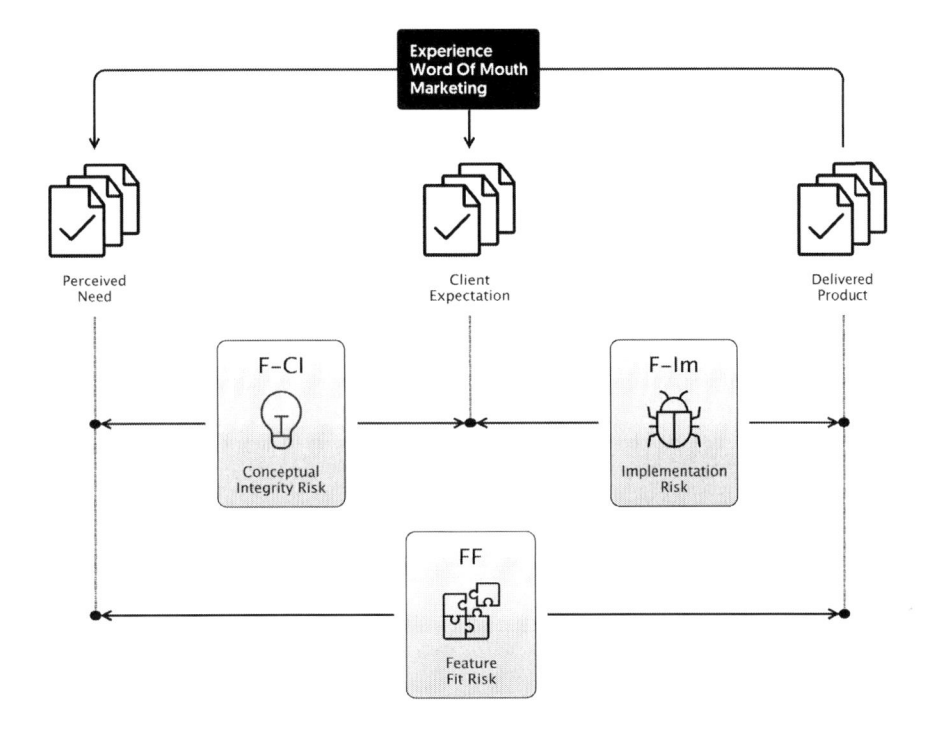

Figure 11.8: Feature Risks Assembled. Fit Risks, shown as **gaps**, *as in the* **Service Quality Model**

- **Market Risk** is therefore risk to *income* from the market changing.
- **Feature Access Risk** is risk to *audience* changing.

Fit, Audience and Evolution

Two risks further consider how the **fit** and **audience** *change*: Regression Risk and Feature Drift Risk. We call this *evolution* in the sense that:

- Our product's features *evolve* with time and the changes made by the development team.
- Our audience changes and evolves as it is exposed to our product and competing products.
- The world as a whole is an evolving system within which our product exists.

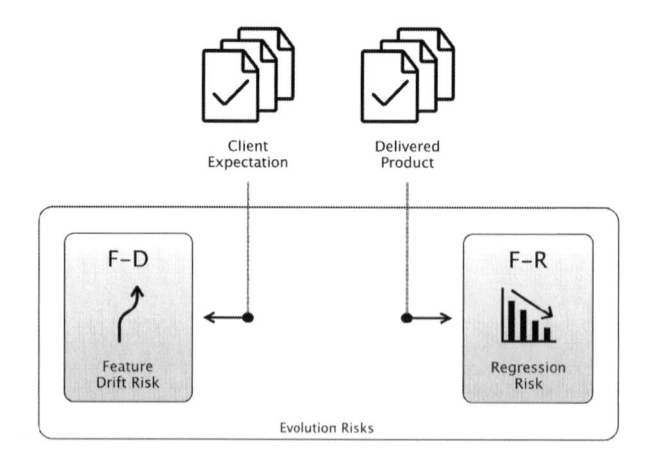

Figure 11.9: Risks of Evolution/Change either of the product or the expectations of clients.

11.11 Applying Feature Risk

Next time you are grooming the backlog, why not apply this:

- Can you judge which tasks mitigate the most Feature Risk?
- Are you delivering features that are valuable across a large audience? Or of less value across a wider audience?
- How does writing a specification mitigate Fit Risk? For what other reasons are you writing specifications?
- Does the audience *know* that the features exist? How do you communicate feature availability to them?

In the next chapter, we are going to unpack this last point further. Somewhere between "what the customer wants" and "what you give them" is a *dialogue*. In using a software product, users are engaging in a *dialogue* with its features. If the features don't exist, hopefully they will engage in a dialogue with the development team to get them added.

These dialogues are prone to risk and this is the subject of the next chapter, Communication Risk.

CHAPTER 12

Communication Risk

If we all had identical knowledge, there would be no need to do any communicating at all, and therefore no Communication Risk.

But people are not all-knowing oracles. We rely on our *senses* to improve our Internal Models of the world. There is Communication Risk here - we might overlook something vital (like an on-coming truck) or mistake something someone says (like "Don't cut the green wire").

12.1 A Model Of Communication

In 1948, Claude Shannon proposed this definition of communication:

> "The fundamental problem of communication is that of reproducing at one point, either exactly or approximately, a message

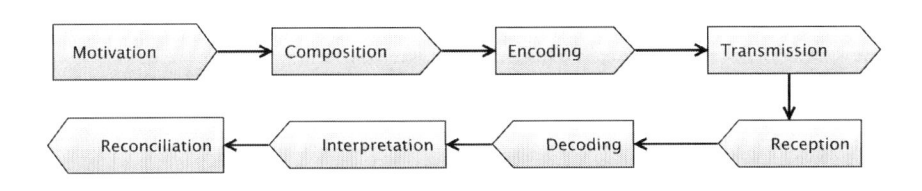

Figure 12.1: Shannon's Communication Model

selected at another point."

—A Mathematical Theory Of Communication, *Claude Shannon*[1]

And from this same paper we get Figure 12.1: we move from top-left ("I want to send a message to someone"), clockwise to bottom left where we hope the message has been understood and believed. (I've added this last box to Shannon's original diagram.)

One of the chief concerns in Shannon's paper is the risk of error between **Transmission** and **Reception**. He creates a theory of *information* (measured in *bits*), sets the upper-bounds of information that can be communicated over a channel, and describes ways in which Communication Risk between these processes can be mitigated by clever **Encoding** and **Decoding** steps.

But it's not just transmission. Communication Risk exists at each of these steps. Let's imagine a human example, where someone, **Alice** is trying to send a simple message to **Bob**.

Step	Potential Risk
Motivation	**Alice** might be **motivated** to send a message to tell **Bob** something, only to find out that *he already knew it*.
Composition	**Alice** might mess up the *intent* of the message: instead of "Please buy chips" she might say, "Please buy chops".
Encoding	**Alice** might not speak clearly enough to be understood.
Transmission	**Alice** might not say it *loudly* enough for **Bob** to hear.
Reception	**Bob** doesn't hear the message clearly (maybe there is background noise).
Decoding	**Bob** might not decode what was said into a meaningful sentence.
Interpretation	Assuming **Bob** *has* heard, will he correctly **interpret** which type of chips (or chops) **Alice** was talking about?
Reconciliation	Does **Bob** believe the message? Will he **reconcile** the information into his Internal Model and act on it? Perhaps not, if **Bob** thinks that there are chips at home already.

---

[1] https://en.wikipedia.org/wiki/A_Mathematical_Theory_of_Communication

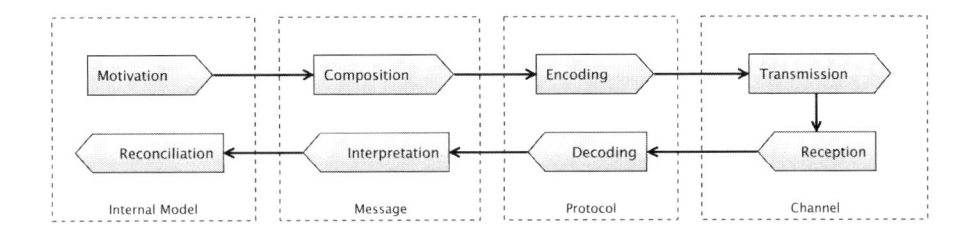

Figure 12.2: Communication Risk, broken into four areas

12.2 Approach To Communication Risk

There is a symmetry about the steps going on in Figure 12.1, and we're going to exploit this in order to break down Communication Risk into its main types.

To get inside Communication Risk, we need to understand **Communication** itself, whether between *machines*, *people* or *products*: we'll look at each in turn. In order to do that, we're going to examine four basic concepts in each of these settings:

- **Channels**[2]: the medium via which the communication is happening.
- **Protocols**[3]: the systems of rules that allow two or more entities of a communications system to transmit information.
- **Messages**[4]: the information we want to convey.
- **Internal Models**: the sources and destinations for the messages. Updating internal models (whether in our heads or machines) is the reason why we're communicating.

And, as we look at these four areas, we'll consider the Attendant Risks of each.

12.3 Channels

There are lots of different types of media for communicating (e.g. TV, Radio, DVD, Talking, Posters, Books, Phones, The Internet, etc.) and they all have different characteristics. When we communicate via a given medium, it's called a *channel*.

---

[2] https://en.wikipedia.org/wiki/Communication_channel
[3] https://en.wikipedia.org/wiki/Communication_protocol
[4] https://en.wikipedia.org/wiki/Message

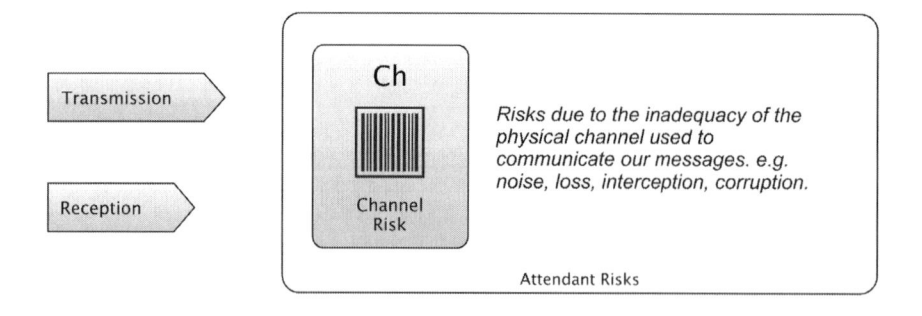

Figure 12.3: Communication Channel Risk

The channel *characteristics* depend on the medium then. Some obvious ones are cost, utilisation, number of people reached, simplex or duplex (parties can transmit and receive at the same time), persistence (a play vs a book, say), latency (how long messages take to arrive) and bandwidth (the amount of information that can be transmitted in a period of time).

Channel characteristics are important: in a high-bandwidth, low-latency situation, **Alice** and **Bob** can *check* with each other that the meaning was transferred correctly. They can discuss what to buy, they can agree that **Alice** wasn't lying or playing a joke.

The channel characteristics also imply suitability for certain *kinds* of messages. A documentary might be a great way of explaining some economic concept, whereas an opera might not be.

12.4 Channel Risk

Shannon discusses that no channel is perfect: there is always the **risk of noise** corrupting the signal. A key outcome from Shannon's paper is that there is a tradeoff: within the capacity of the channel (the **Bandwidth**), you can either send lots of information with *higher* risk that it is wrong, or less information with *lower* risk of errors.

But channel risk goes wider than just this mathematical example: messages might be delayed or delivered in the wrong order, or not be acknowledged when they do arrive. Sometimes, a channel is just an inappropriate way of communicating. When you work in a different time-zone to someone else on your team, there is *automatic* Channel Risk, because instantaneous communication is only available for a few hours a day.

When channels are **poor-quality**, less communication occurs. People will try to communicate just the most important information. But, it's often impossible to know a-priori what constitutes "important". This is why Extreme Programming recommends the practice of Pair Programming[5] and siting all the developers together: although you don't know whether useful communication will happen, you are mitigating Channel Risk by ensuring high-quality communication channels are in place.

At other times, channels are crowded, and can contain so much information that we can't hope to receive all the messages. In these cases, we don't even observe the whole channel, just parts of it.

Marketing Communications

When we are talking about a product or a brand, mitigating Channel Risk is the domain of Marketing Communications[6]. How do you ensure that the information about your (useful) project makes it to the right people? How do you address the right channels?

This works both ways. Let's looks at some of the **Channel Risks** from the point of view of a hypothetical software tool, **D**, which would really useful in my software:

- The concept that there is such a thing as **D** which solves my problem isn't something I'd even considered.
- I'd like to use something like **D**, but how do I find it?
- There are multiple implementations of **D**, which is the best one for the task?
- I know **D**, but I can't figure out how to solve my problem in it.
- I've chosen **D**, I now need to persuade my team that **D** is the correct solution...
- ... and then they also need to understand **D** to do their job too.

Internal Models don't magically get populated with the information they need: they fill up gradually, as shown in Figure 12.4. Popular products and ideas *spread*, by word-of-mouth or other means. Part of the job of being a good technologist is to keep track of new **Ideas**, **Concepts** and **Options**, so as to use them as Dependencies when needed.

---

[5] https://en.wikipedia.org/wiki/Pair_programming
[6] https://en.wikipedia.org/wiki/Marketing_communications

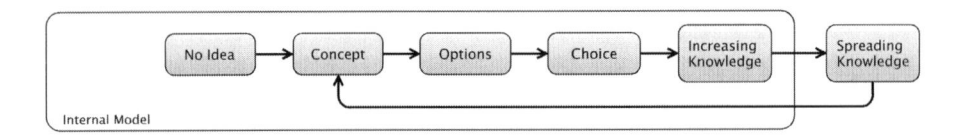

Figure 12.4: Marketing Communication

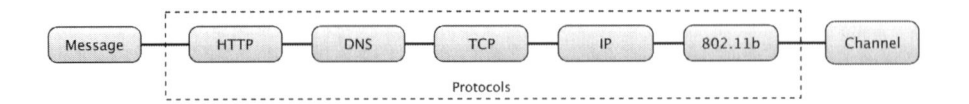

Figure 12.5: Protocol Stack

12.5 Protocols

> "A communication protocol is a system of rules that allow two or more entities of a communications system to transmit information."
>
> Communication Protocol, Wikipedia[7]

In this chapter I want to examine the concept of Communication Protocols and how they relate to Abstraction, which is implicated over and over again in different types of risk we will be looking at.

Abstraction means separating the *definition* of something from the *use* of something. It's a widely applicable concept, but our example below will be specific to communication, and looking at the abstractions involved in loading a web page.

First we need to broaden our terminology. Although so far we've talked about **Senders** and **Receivers**, we now need to talk from the point of view of who-depends-on-who. That is, Clients and Suppliers.

- If you're *depended on*, then you're a **"Supplier"** (or a **"Server"**, when we're talking about actual hardware).
- If you require communication with something else, you're a **"Client"**.

---

[7] https://en.wikipedia.org/wiki/Communication_protocol

In order that a web browser (a **client**) can load a web-page from a **server**, they both need to communicate with shared protocols. In this example, this is going to involve (at least) six separate protocols, as shown in Figure 12.5.

Let's examine each protocol in turn when I try to load the web page at the following address using a web browser:

`http://google.com/preferences`

1. DNS - Domain Name System

The first thing that happens is that the name `google.com` is *resolved* by DNS. This means that the browser looks up the domain name `google.com` and gets back an IP address.

This is some Abstraction: instead of using the machine's IP Address[8] on the network, `216.58.204.78`, I can use a human-readable address, `google.com`.

The address `google.com` doesn't necessarily resolve to that same address each time: *They have multiple IP addresses for `google.com`*, but as a user, I don't have to worry about this detail.

2. IP - Internet Protocol

But this hints at what is beneath the abstraction: although I'm loading a web-page, the communication to the server happens by IP Protocol[9] - it's a bunch of discrete "packets" (streams of binary digits). You can think of a packet as being like a real-world parcel or letter.

Each packet consists of two things:

- An **IP Address**, which tells the network components (such as routers and gateways) where to send the packet, much like you'd write the address on the outside of a parcel.
- The **Payload**, the stream of bytes for processing at the destination, like the contents of the parcel.

But even this concept of "packets" is an Abstraction. Although all the components of the network understand this protocol, we might be using Wired Ethernet cables, or WiFi, 4G or *something else* beneath that.

---

[8] https://en.wikipedia.org/wiki/IP_address
[9] https://en.wikipedia.org/wiki/Internet_Protocol

3. 802.11 - WiFi Protocol

I ran this at home using WiFi, which uses IEEE 802.11 Protocol[10], which is another standard abstraction allowing my laptop to communicate with the router wirelessly. But even *this* isn't the bottom, because this is likely using MIMO-OFDM[11], a specification about frequencies of microwave radiation, antennas, multiplexing, error-correction codes and so on.

And WiFi is just the first hop. After the WiFi receiver, there will be protocols for delivering the packets via the telephony system.

4. TCP - Transmission Control Protocol

Another Abstraction going on here is that my browser believes it has a "connection" to the server. This is provided by the TCP protocol.

But this is a fiction - my "connection" is built on the IP protocol, which as we saw above is just packets of data on the network. So there are lots of packets floating around which say "this connection is still alive" and "I'm message 5 in the sequence" and so on in order to maintain this fiction.

This all means that the browser can forget about all the details of packet ordering and work with the fictional abstraction of a connection.

5. HTTP - Hypertext Transfer Protocol

If we examine what is being sent on the TCP connection, we see something like this:

```
> GET /preferences HTTP/1.1
> Host: google.com
> Accept: */*
>
```

This is now the HTTP protocol proper, and these 4 lines are sending information *over the connection* to the `google.com` server, to ask it for the page. Finally, the server gets to respond:

```
< HTTP/1.1 301 Moved Permanently
< Location: http://www.google.com/preferences
...
```

---

[10]https://en.wikipedia.org/wiki/IEEE_802.11
[11]https://en.wikipedia.org/wiki/MIMO-OFDM

In this case, the server is telling us that the web page has changed address. The `301` is a status code meaning the page has moved: instead of `http://google.com/preferences`, we want `http://www.google.com/preferences`.

Summary

By having a stack of protocols we are able to apply Separation Of Concerns[12], each protocol handling just a few concerns:

Protocol	Abstractions
HTTP	URLs, error codes, pages.
DNS	Names of servers to IP Addresses.
TCP	The concept of a "connection" with guarantees about ordering and delivery.
IP	"Packets" with addresses and payloads.
WiFi	"Networks", 802.11 flavours, Transmitters, Antennas, error correction codes.

HTTP "stands on the shoulders of giants": not only does it get to use pre-existing protocols like TCP and DNS to make its life easier, it got WiFi "for free" when this came along and plugged into the existing IP protocol. This is the key value of abstraction: you get to piggy-back on *existing* patterns, and use them yourself.

12.6 Protocol Risk

Hopefully, the above example gives an indication of the usefulness of protocols within software. But for every protocol we use, we have Protocol Risk. While this is a problem in human communication protocols, it's really common in computer communication because we create protocols *all the time* in software.

For example, as soon as we define a Javascript function (called **b** here), we are creating a protocol for other functions (**a** here) to use it:

```
function b(a, b, c) {
    return a+b+c;
}
```

---

[12] https://en.wikipedia.org/wiki/Separation_of_concerns

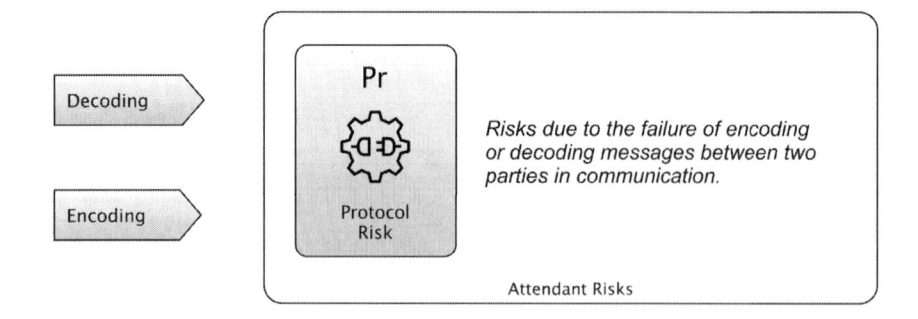

Figure 12.6: Communication Protocols Risks

```
function a() {
    var bOut = b(1,2,3);
    return "something "+bOut;        // returns "something 6"
}
```

If function **b** then changes, say:

```
function b(a, b, c, d /* new parameter */) {
    return a+b+c+d;
}
```

Then, **a** will instantly have a problem calling it and there will be an error of some sort.

Protocol Risk also occurs when we use Data Types[13]: whenever we change the data type, we need to correct the usages of that type. Note above, I've given the `JavaScript` example, but I'm going to switch to `TypeScript` now:

```
interface BInput {
    a: string,
    b: string,
    c: string,
    d: string
}
```

---

[13]https://en.wikipedia.org/wiki/Data_type

```
function b(in: BInput): string {
    return in.a + in.b + in.c + in.d;
}

function a() {
    var bOut = b({a: 1, b: 2, c: 3}); // new parameter d missing
    return "something "+bOut;
}
```

By using a static type checker[14], we can identify issues like this, but there is a trade-off: we mitigate Protocol Risk, because we define the protocols *once only* in the program, and ensure that usages all match the specification. But the tradeoff is (as we can see in the TypeScript code) more *finger-typing*, which means Codebase Risk in some circumstances.

Nevertheless, static type checking is so prevalent in software that clearly in most cases, the trade-off has been worth it: even languages like Clojure[15] have been retro-fitted with type checkers[16].

Let's look at some further types of Protocol Risk.

Protocol Incompatibility Risk

The people you find it *easiest* to communicate with are your friends and family, those closest to you. That's because you're all familiar with the same protocols. Someone from a foreign country, speaking a different language and having a different culture, will essentially have a completely incompatible protocol for spoken communication to you.

Within software there are also competing, incompatible protocols for the same things, which is maddening when your protocol isn't supported. For example, although the world seems to be standardising, there used to be *hundreds* of different image formats. Photographs often use TIFF[17], RAW[18] or JPEG[19], whilst we also have SVG[20] for vector graphics, GIF[21] for images and animations and PNG[22] for other bitmap graphics.

---

[14] https://en.wikipedia.org/wiki/Type_system#Static_type_checking
[15] https://clojure.org
[16] http://clojure-doc.org/articles/ecosystem/core_typed/home.html
[17] https://en.wikipedia.org/wiki/TIFF
[18] https://en.wikipedia.org/wiki/Raw_image_format
[19] https://en.wikipedia.org/wiki/JPEG
[20] https://en.wikipedia.org/wiki/Scalable_Vector_Graphics
[21] https://en.wikipedia.org/wiki/GIF
[22] https://en.wikipedia.org/wiki/Portable_Network_Graphics

Protocol Versioning Risk

Even when systems are talking the same protocol there can be problems. When we have multiple, different systems owned by different parties, on their own upgrade cycles, we have **Protocol Versioning Risk**: the risk that either client or supplier could start talking in a version of the protocol that the other side hasn't learnt yet. There are various mitigating strategies for this. We'll look at two now: **Backwards Compatibility** and **Forwards Compatibility**.

Backward Compatibility

Backwards Compatibility mitigates Protocol Versioning Risk. This means supporting the old protocol until it falls out of use. If a supplier is pushing for a change in protocol it either must ensure that it is Backwards Compatible with the clients it is communicating with, or make sure they are upgraded concurrently. When building web services[23], for example, it's common practice to version all API's so that you can manage the migration. Something like this:

- Supplier publishes /api/v1/something.
- Clients use /api/v1/something.
- Supplier publishes /api/v2/something.
- Clients start using /api/v2/something.
- Clients (eventually) stop using /api/v1/something.
- Supplier retires /api/v1/something API.

Forward Compatibility

HTML and HTTP provide "graceful failure" to mitigate Protocol Risk: while it's expected that all clients can parse the syntax of HTML and HTTP, it's not necessary for them to be able to handle all of the tags, attributes and rules they see. The specification for both these standards is that if you don't understand something, ignore it. Designing with this in mind means that old clients can always at least cope with new features, but it's not always possible.

JavaScript *can't* support this: because the meaning of the next instruction will often depend on the result of the previous one.

Do human languages support this? To some extent! New words are added to our languages all the time. When we come across a new word, we can either ignore it, guess the meaning, ask or look it up. In this way, human language has **Forward Compatibility** features built in.

---

[23]https://en.wikipedia.org/wiki/Web_service

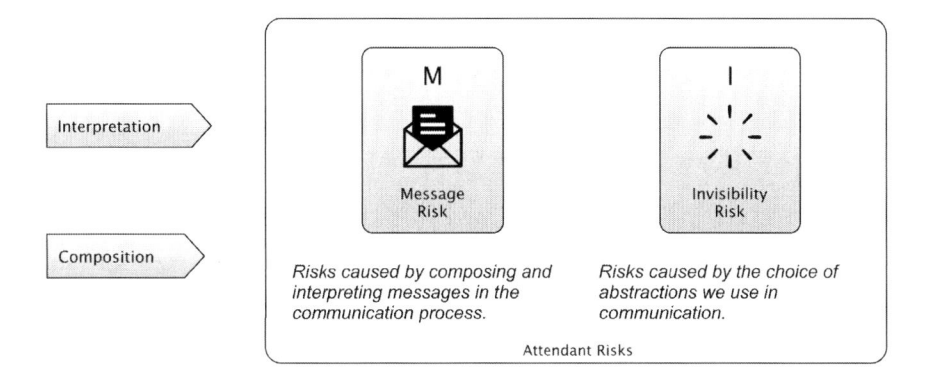

Figure 12.7: Message Risk

Protocol Implementation Risk

A second aspect of Protocol Risk exists in heterogeneous computing environments where protocols have been independently implemented based on standards. For example, there are now so many different browsers, all supporting variations of HTTP, HTML and JavaScript that it becomes impossible to test comprehensively over all the different versions. To mitigate as much Protocol Risk as possible, generally we test web sites in a subset of browsers, and use a lowest-common-denominator approach to choosing protocol and language features.

12.7 Messages

Although Shannon's Communication Theory is about transmitting **Messages**, messages are really encoded **Ideas** and **Concepts**, from an **Internal Model**. Let's break down some of the risks associated with this:

Internal Model Risk

When we construct messages in a conversation, we have to make judgements about what the other person already knows. For example, if I talk to you about a new JDBC Driver[24], this presumes that you know what JDBC is. The message has a dependency on prior knowledge. Or, when talking to children it's often hard work because they *assume* that you have knowledge of everything they do.

---

[24]https://en.wikipedia.org/wiki/JDBC_driver

This is called Theory Of Mind[25]: the appreciation that your knowledge is different to other people's, and adjusting you messages accordingly. When teaching, this is called The Curse Of Knowledge[26]: teachers have difficulty understanding students' problems *because they already understand the subject*.

Message Risk

A second, related problem is actually Dependency Risk, which is covered more thoroughly in a later chapter. Often, to understand a new message, you have to have followed everything up to that point already.

The same **Message Dependency Risk** exists for computer software: if there is replication going on between instances of an application and one of the instances misses some messages, you end up with a "Split Brain[27]" scenario, where later messages can't be processed because they refer to an application state that doesn't exist. For example, a message saying:

```
Update user 53's surname to 'Jones'
```

only makes sense if the application has previously processed the message

```
Create user 53 with surname 'Smith'
```

Misinterpretation Risk

For people, nothing exists unless we have a name for it. The world is just atoms, but we don't think like this. *The name is the thing.*

> "The famous pipe. How people reproached me for it! And yet, could you stuff my pipe? No, it's just a representation, is it not? So if I had written on my picture "This is a pipe", I'd have been lying!"
> —Rene Magritte, of *The Treachery of Images*[28]

People don't rely on rigorous definitions of abstractions like computers do; we make do with fuzzy definitions of concepts and ideas. We rely on Abstraction to move between the name of a thing and the *idea of a thing*.

---

[25]https://en.wikipedia.org/wiki/Theory_of_mind
[26]https://en.wikipedia.org/wiki/Curse_of_knowledge
[27]https://en.wikipedia.org/wiki/Split-brain_(computing)
[28]https://en.wikipedia.org/wiki/The_Treachery_of_Images

This brings about Misinterpretation Risk: names are not *precise*, and concepts mean different things to different people. We can't be sure that other people have the same meaning for a name that we have.

Invisibility Risk

Another cost of Abstraction is Invisibility Risk. While abstraction is a massively powerful technique, (as we saw above, Protocols allow things like the Internet to happen) it lets the function of a thing hide behind the layers of abstraction and become invisible.

Invisibility Risk In Conversation

Invisibility Risk is risk due to information not sent. Because humans don't need a complete understanding of a concept to use it, we can cope with some Invisibility Risk in communication and this saves us time when we're talking. It would be *painful* to have conversations if, say, the other person needed to understand everything about how cars worked in order to discuss cars.

For people, Abstraction is a tool that we can use to refer to other concepts, without necessarily knowing how the concepts work. This divorcing of "what" from "how" is the essence of abstraction and is what makes language useful.

The debt of Invisibility Risk comes due when you realise that *not* being given the details *prevents* you from reasoning about it effectively. Let's think about this in the context of a project status meeting, for example:

- Can you be sure that the status update contains all the details you need to know?
- Is the person giving the update wrong or lying?
- Do you know enough about the details of what's being discussed in order to make informed decisions about how the project is going?

Invisibility Risk In Software

Invisibility Risk is everywhere in software. Let's consider what happens when, in your program, you create a new function, **f**:

- First, by creating **f**, you have *given a piece of functionality a name*, which is abstraction.
- Second, **f** *supplies* functionality to clients, so we have created a client-supplier relationship.

- Third, these parties now need to communicate, and this will require a protocol. In a programming language, this protocol dictates the arguments passed to **f** and the response *back* from **f**.

But something else also happens: by creating **f**, you are saying "I have this operation, the details of which I won't mention again, but from now on it's called **f**" Suddenly, the implementation of "**f**" hides and it is working invisibly. Things go on in **f** that people don't necessarily understand.

Referring to f is a much simpler job than understanding f.

We try to mitigate this via documentation but this is a terrible deal: documentation is necessarily a simplified explanation of the abstraction, so will still suffer from Invisibility Risk.

Invisibility Risk is mainly Hidden Risk. (Mostly, *you don't know what you don't know*.) But you can carelessly *hide things from yourself* with software:

- Adding a thread to an application that doesn't report whether it worked, failed, or is running out of control and consuming all the cycles of the CPU.
- Redundancy can increase reliability, but only if you know when servers fail, and fix them quickly. Otherwise, you only see problems when the last server fails.
- When building a web-service, can you assume that it's working for the users in the way you want it to?

When you build a software service, or even implement a thread, ask yourself: "How will I know next week that this is working properly?" If the answer involves manual work and investigation, then your implementation has just cost you in Invisibility Risk.

12.8 Internal Models

The communication process so far has been fraught with risks, but now let's look at risks specific to our internal models.

Trust & Belief Risk

Although protocols can sometimes handle security features of communication (such as Authentication[29] and preventing man-in-the-middle attacks[30]),

---
[29] https://en.wikipedia.org/wiki/Authentication
[30] https://en.wikipedia.org/wiki/Man-in-the-middle_attack

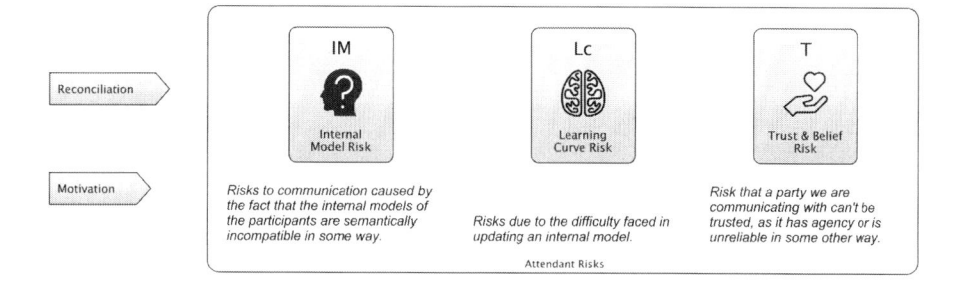

Figure 12.8: Internal Model Risks

trust goes further than this, it is the flip-side of Agency Risk, which we will look at later: can you be sure that the other party in the communication is acting in your best interests?

Even if the receiver trusts the communicator, they may not believe the message. Let's look at some reasons for that:

- **Weltanschauung (World View)**[31]: the ethics, values and beliefs in the receiver's Internal Model may be incompatible to those from the sender.
- **Relativism**[32] is the concept that there are no universal truths. Every truth is from a frame of reference. For example, what constitutes *offensive language* is dependent on the listener.
- **Psycholinguistics**[33] is the study of how humans acquire languages. There are different languages, dialects, and *industry dialects*. We all understand language in different ways, take different meanings and apply different contexts to the messages.

From the point-of-view of Marketing Communications, choosing the right message is part of the battle. You are trying to communicate your idea in such a way as to mitigate Trust & Belief Risk.

Learning Curve Risk

If the messages we are receiving force us to update our Internal Model too much, we can suffer from the problem of "too steep a Learning Curve[34]" or

---

[31]https://en.wikipedia.org/wiki/World_view
[32]https://en.wikipedia.org/wiki/Relativism
[33]https://en.wikipedia.org/wiki/Psycholinguistics
[34]https://en.wikipedia.org/wiki/Learning_curve

"Information Overload[35]", where the messages force us to adapt our Internal Model too quickly for our brains to keep up.

Commonly, the easiest option is just to ignore the information channel completely in these cases.

Reading Code

It has often been said that code is *harder to read than to write*:

> "If you ask a software developer what they spend their time doing, they'll tell you that they spend most of their time writing code. However, if you actually observe what software developers spend their time doing, you'll find that they spend most of their time trying to understand code." - When Understanding Means Rewriting, *Coding Horror*[36]

By now it should be clear that it's going to be *both* quite hard to read and write: the protocol of code is actually designed for the purpose of machines communicating, not primarily for people to understand. Making code human readable is a secondary concern to making it machine readable.

But now we should be able to see the reason why it's harder to read than write too:

- When reading code, you are having to shift your Internal Model to wherever the code is, accepting decisions that you might not agree with and accepting counter-intuitive logical leaps. i.e. Learning Curve Risk. (*cf. Principle of Least Surprise*[37])
- There is no Feedback Loop between your Internal Model and the Reality of the code, opening you up to Misinterpretation Risk. When you write code, your compiler and tests give you this.
- While reading code *takes less time* than writing it, this also means the Learning Curve is steeper.

12.9 Communication Risk Wrap Up

In this chapter, we've looked at Communication Risk itself and broken it down into six sub-types of risk as shown in Figure 12.9. Again, we are

---

[35] https://en.wikipedia.org/wiki/Information_overload
[36] https://blog.codinghorror.com/when-understanding-means-rewriting/
[37] https://en.wikipedia.org/wiki/Principle_of_least_astonishment

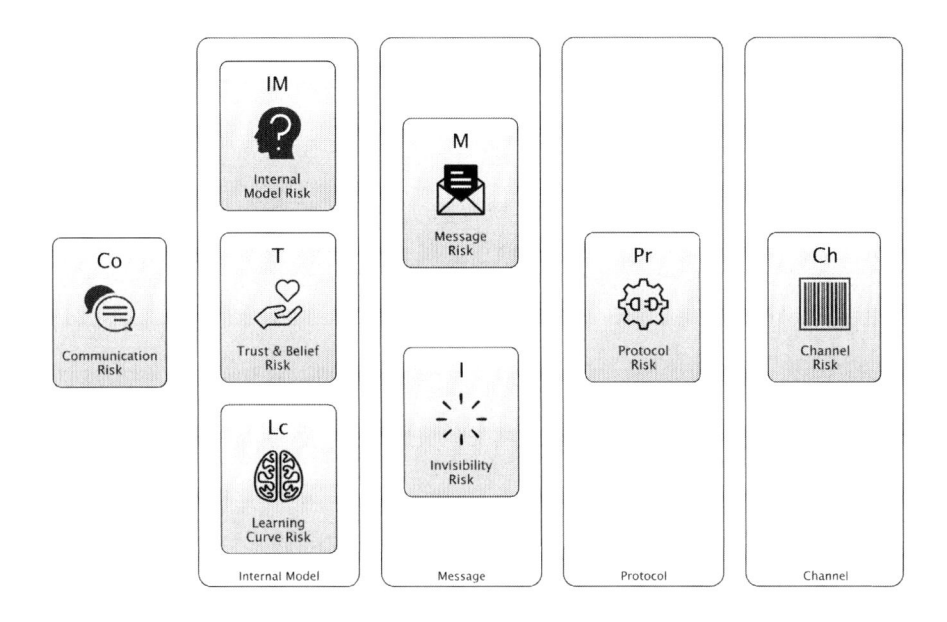

Figure 12.9: Communication Risks, Summarised

calling out *patterns* here. You could classify communication risks in other ways, but concepts like Learning Curve Risk and Invisibility Risk we will be using again in again in Risk-First.

In the next chapter we will address complexity head-on and understand how Complexity Risk manifests in software projects.

CHAPTER 13

Complexity Risk

Complexity Risk is the risks to your project due to its underlying "complexity". This chapter will break down exactly what we mean by complexity, and where it can hide on a software project, and look at some ways in which we can manage this important risk.

13.1 Codebase Risk

We're going to start by looking at *code you write*: the size of your code-base, the amount of code, the number of modules, the interconnectedness of the modules and how well-factored the code is.

You could think of this as Codebase Risk, being a specific type of Complexity Risk. We'll look at two measures of codebase complexity before talking about Technical Debt and Feature Creep.

13.2 Kolmogorov Complexity

The standard Computer-Science definition of complexity is Kolmogorov Complexity[1]. This is:

> "...the length of the shortest computer program (in a predetermined programming language) that produces the object as output."
>
> Kolmogorov Complexity, Wikipedia[2]

---
[1] https://en.wikipedia.org/wiki/Kolmogorov_complexity
[2] https://en.wikipedia.org/wiki/Kolmogorov_complexity

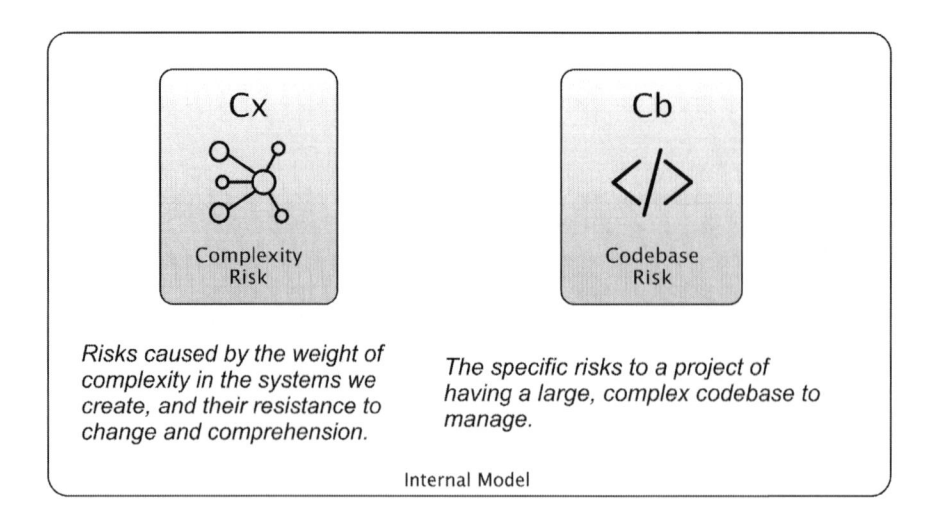

Figure 13.1: Complexity Risk and Codebase Risk

This is a fairly handy definition for us as it means that in writing software to solve a problem there is a lower bound on the size of the software we write. While in practice this is pretty much impossible to quantify, that doesn't really matter: here I want to focus on the techniques for *moving towards that minimum*.

Let's say we wanted to write a JavaScript program to output this string:

abcdabcdabcdabcdabcdabcdabcdabcdabcd

We might choose this representation:

```
function out() {                                              (7 )
    return "abcdabcdabcdabcdabcdabcdabcdabcdabcd" (45)
}                                                              (1 )
```

The numbers in brackets indicate how many symbols each line contains. In total, this code block contains **53 symbols** if you count `function`, `out` and `return` as one symbol each.

But, if we write it like this:

104

```
const ABCD="ABCD";                                          (11)

function out() {                                            (7 )
    return ABCD+ABCD+ABCD+ABCD+ABCD+ABCD+ABCD+              (16)
        ABCD+ABCD+ABCD;                                     (6 )
}                                                           (1 )
```

With this version, we now have **41 symbols** (ABCD is a single symbol - it's just a name). And with this version:

```
const ABCD="ABCD";                                          (11)

function out() {                                            (7 )
    return ABCD.repeat(10)                                  (7 )
}                                                           (1 )
```

... we have **26 symbols**.

Abstraction

What's happening here is that we're *exploiting a pattern*: we noticed that abcd occurs several times, so we defined it a single time and then used it over and over, like a stamp. This is called abstraction.

By applying abstraction, we can improve in the direction of the Kolmogorov lower bound. By allowing ourselves to say that *symbols* (like out and ABCD) are worth one complexity point, we've allowed that we can be descriptive in naming function and const. Naming things is an important part of abstraction, because to use something, you have to be able to refer to it.

Trade-Off

Generally, the more complex a piece of software is, the more difficulty users will have understanding it, and the more work developers will have changing it. We should prefer the third version of our code over either the first or second because of its brevity.

But we could go further down into Code Golf[3] territory. The following javascript program plays FizzBuzz[4] up to 100, but is less readable than you might hope.

---
[3]https://en.wikipedia.org/wiki/Code_golf
[4]https://en.wikipedia.org/wiki/Fizz_buzz

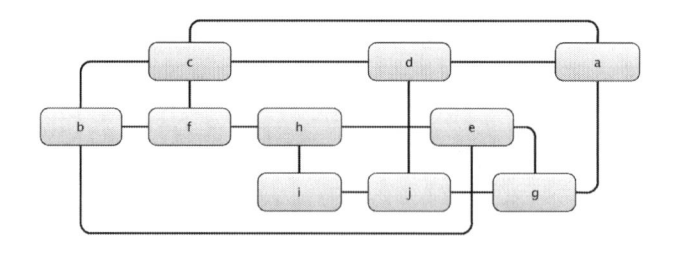

Figure 13.2: Graph 1, 2-Connected

```
for(i=0;i<100;)document.write(((++i%3?'':'Fizz')+
(i%5?'':'Buzz')||i)+"<br>")                           (62)
```

So there is at some point a trade-off to be made between Complexity Risk and Communication Risk. That is, after a certain point, reducing Kolmogorov Complexity further risks making the program less intelligible.

13.3 Connectivity

A second, useful measure of complexity comes from graph theory, and that is the connectivity of a graph:

> "... the minimum number of elements (nodes or edges) that need to be removed to disconnect the remaining nodes from each other"
>
> —Connectivity, *Wikipedia*[5])

To see this in action, have a look at Figure 13.2. It has 10 vertices, labelled **a** to **j**, and it has 15 edges (or links) connecting the vertices together. If any single edge were removed from Figure 13.2, the 10 vertices would still be linked together. Because of this, we can say that the graph is *2-connected*. That is, to disconnect any single vertex, you'd have to remove *at least* two edges.

As a slight aside, let's consider the **Kolmogorov Complexity** of this graph, by inventing a mini-language to describe graphs. It could look something like this:

---

[5]https://en.wikipedia.org/wiki/Connectivity_(graph_theory

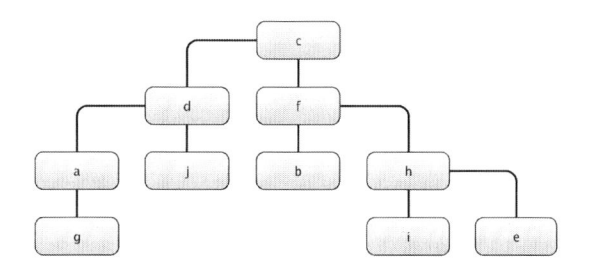

Figure 13.3: Graph 2, 1-Connected

```
<item> : [<item>,]* <item>    # Indicates that the item
                              # before the colon
                              # has a connection to all
                              # the items after the colon
```

So our graph could be defined like this:

```
a: b,c,d
b: c,f,e
c: f,d
d: j
e: h,j
f: h
g: j
h: i
i: j
```
(39)

In Figure 13.3, I've removed 6 of the edges. Now, we're in a situation where if any single edge is removed, the graph becomes *unconnected*. That is, it's broken into distinct chunks. So, it is *1-connected*.

The second graph is clearly simpler than the first. And, we can show this by looking at the **Kolmogorov Complexity** in our little language:

```
a: d,g
b: f
c: d,f
d: j
```

```
f: h
e: h
h: i
```
(25)

For defining our graphs, **Connectivity** is also **Complexity**. And this carries over into software too: heavily connected code is more complex than less-connected code. It's also harder to reason about and work with because changing one module potentially impacts many others. Let's dig into this further.

13.4 Hierarchies and Modularisation

In Figure 13.3, I've arranged it as a hierarchy which I can do trivially now that it's only 1-connected. For 10 vertices, we need 9 edges to connect everything up. It's always:

```
edges = vertices - 1
```

Note that I could pick any hierarchy here: I don't have to start at **c** (although it has the nice property that it has two roughly even sub-trees attached to it).

How does this help us? Imagine if **a** - **j** were modules of a software system, and the edges of the graph showed communications between the different sub-systems. In the first graph, we're in a worse position:

- Who's in charge? What deals with what?
- Can I isolate a component and change it safely?
- What happens if one component disappears?

But, in the second graph, it's easier to reason about, because of the reduced number of connections and the new hierarchy of organisation.

On the down-side, perhaps our messages have farther to go now: in the original, **i** could send a message straight to **j**, but now we have to go all the way via **c**. But this is the basis of Modularisation[6] and Hierarchy[7].

As a tool to battle complexity, we don't just see this in software, but everywhere in our lives: societies, business, and living organisms. For example in our bodies we have:

---
[6]https://en.wikipedia.org/wiki/Modular_programming
[7]https://en.wikipedia.org/wiki/Hierarchy

- **Organelles** - such as Mitochondria[8], contained in...
- **Cells** - such as blood cells, nerve cells, skin cells in the Human Body[9], inside...
- **Organs** - like hearts livers, brains etc, held within...
- **Organisms** - like you and me.

The great complexity-reducing mechanism of modularisation is that *you only have to consider your local environment*.

So, we've looked at some measures of software structure complexity. We can say "this is more complex than this" for a given piece of code or structure. We've also looked at two ways to manage it: Abstraction and Modularisation. However, we've not really said why complexity entails Risk. So let's address that now by looking at two analogies, Mass and Technical Debt.

13.5 Complexity is Mass

The first way to look at complexity is as **Mass** : a software project with more complexity has greater mass than one with less complexity. Newton's Second Law states:

$$F = m\mathbf{a}, \ (\text{Force} = \text{Mass} \times \text{Acceleration})$$

That is, in order to move your project *somewhere new*, and make it do new things, you need to give it a push, and the more mass it has, the more **Force** you'll need to move (accelerate) it.

You could stop here and say that the more lines of code a project contains, the greater its mass. And, that makes sense, because in order to get it to do something new, you're likely to need to change more lines.

But there is actually some underlying sense in which this is true in the real, physical world too, as discussed in a Veritasium[10] video. To paraphrase:

> "Most of your mass you owe due to $E = mc^2$, you owe to the fact that your mass is packed with energy because of the **interactions** between these quarks and gluon fluctuations in the

---

[8]https://en.wikipedia.org/wiki/Mitochondrion
[9]https://en.wikipedia.org/wiki/List_of_distinct_cell_types_in_the_adult_human_body
[10]https://www.youtube.com/user/1veritasium

gluon field... what we think of as ordinarily empty space... that turns out to be the thing that gives us most of our mass."
—Your Mass is NOT From the Higgs Boson, *Veritasium*[11]

I'm not an expert in physics *at all*, and so there is every chance that I am pushing this analogy too hard. But, by substituting quarks and gluons for pieces of software we can (in a very handwaving-y way) say that more connected software has more **interactions** going on, and therefore has more mass than simple software.

If we want to move *fast* we need simple codebases.

At a basic level, Complexity Risk heavily impacts on Schedule Risk: more complexity means you need more force to get things done, which takes longer.

13.6 Technical Debt

The most common way we talk about Complexity Risk in software is as Technical Debt:

> "Shipping first time code is like going into debt. A little debt speeds development so long as it is paid back promptly with a rewrite... The danger occurs when the debt is not repaid. Every minute spent on not-quite-right code counts as interest on that debt. Entire engineering organisations can be brought to a standstill under the debt load of an unconsolidated implementation, object-oriented or otherwise."
> —Ward Cunningham, 1992, *Wikipedia, Technical Debt*[12]

Building a low-complexity first-time solution is often a waste: in the first version, we're usually interested in reducing Feature Risk as fast as possible. That is, putting working software in front of users to get feedback. We would rather carry Complexity Risk than take on more attendant Schedule Risk.

So a quick-and-dirty, over-complex implementation mitigates the same Feature Risk and allows you to Meet Reality faster.

But having mitigated the Feature Risk this way, you are likely exposed to more Complexity Risk than you necessarily need. As Figure 13.4 shows, one

---
[11] https://www.youtube.com/watch?annotation_id=annotation_3771848421&feature=iv&src_vid=Xo232kyTsO0&v=Ztc6QPNUqls
[12] https://en.wikipedia.org/wiki/Technical_debt

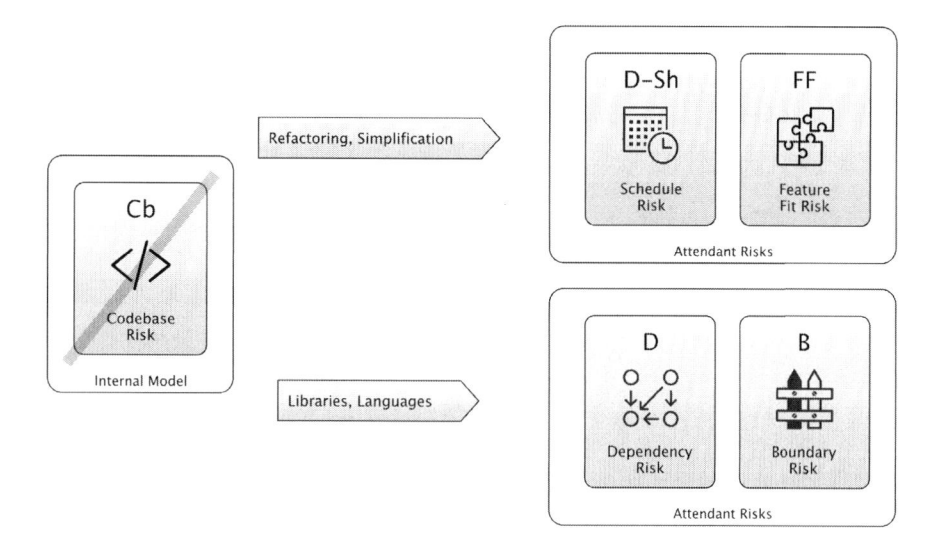

Figure 13.4: Complexity Risk and some mitigations

of the ways to mitigate Complexity Risk is by Refactoring[13] the software, which means using the tools of abstraction and modularisation.

13.7 Kitchen Analogy

It's often hard to make the case for minimising Technical Debt: it often feels that there are more important priorities, especially when technical debt can be "swept under the carpet" and forgotten about until later. (See Discounting.)

One helpful analogy I have found is to imagine your code-base is a kitchen. After preparing a meal (i.e. delivering the first implementation), *you need to tidy up the kitchen*. This is just something everyone does as a matter of *basic sanitation*.

Now of course, you could carry on with the messy kitchen. When tomorrow comes and you need to make another meal, you find yourself needing to wash up saucepans as you go, or working around the mess by using different surfaces to chop on.

It's not long before someone comes down with food poisoning.

---

[13]https://en.wikipedia.org/wiki/Code_refactoring

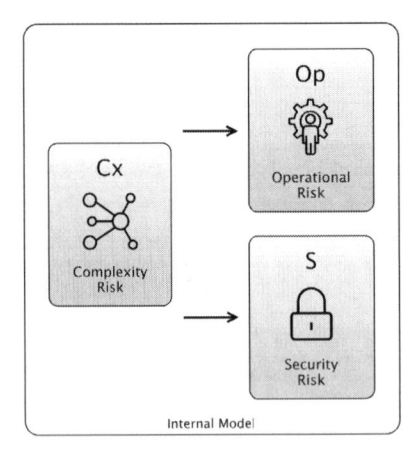

Figure 13.5: Complexity Risk and its implications

We wouldn't tolerate this behaviour in a restaurant kitchen, so why put up with it in a software project? This state-of-affairs is illustrated in Figure 13.5: Complexity Risk can be a cause of Operational Risks and Security Risks.

13.8 Feature Creep

In Brooks' essay "No Silver Bullet - Essence and Accident in Software Engineering", a distinction is made between:

- **Essence**: *the difficulties inherent in the nature of the software.*

- **Accident**: *those difficulties that attend its production but are not inherent.*

—Fred Brooks, *No Silver Bullet*[14]

The problem with this definition is that we are accepting features of our software as *essential*.

Applying Risk-First, if you want to mitigate some Feature Risk then you have to pick up Complexity Risk as a result. But, that's a *choice you get to make*.

---

[14]https://en.wikipedia.org/wiki/No_Silver_Bullet

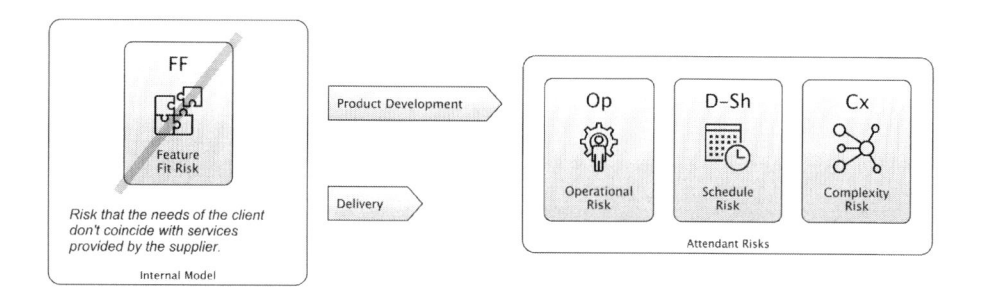

Figure 13.6: Mitigating Feature Fit Risk (from Feature Risk)

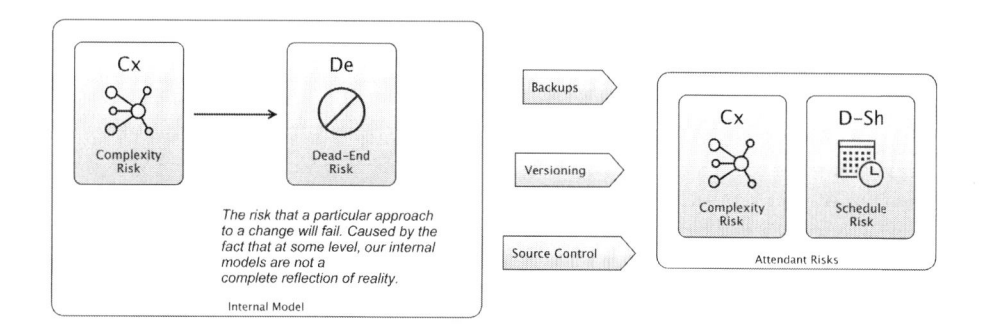

Figure 13.7: Dead-End Risk

Therefore, Feature Creep[15] (or Gold Plating[16]) is a failure to observe this basic equation: instead of considering this trade off, you're building *every feature possible*. This will impact on Complexity Risk.

Sometimes, feature-creep happens because either managers feel they need to keep their staff busy, or the staff decide on their own that they need to keep themselves busy. This is something we'll return to in Agency Risk.

13.9 Dead-End Risk

Dead-End Risk is where you take an action that you *think* is useful, only to find out later that actually it was a dead-end and your efforts were wasted. Here, we'll see that Complexity Risk is a big cause of this (as Figure 13.7 shows).

---

[15]https://en.wikipedia.org/wiki/Feature_creep

[16]https://en.wikipedia.org/wiki/Gold_plating_(software_engineering)

For example, imagine a complex software system composed of many sub-systems. Let's say that the Accounting sub-system needed password protection (so you built this). Then the team realised that you needed a way to *change the password* (so you built that). Then, you needed to have more than one user of the Accounting system so they would all need passwords (OK, fine).

Finally, the team realises that actually authentication would be something that all the sub-systems would need, and that it had already been implemented more thoroughly by the Approvals sub-system.

At this point, you realise you're in a **Dead End**:

- **Option 1: Continue.** You carry on making minor incremental improvements to the accounting authentication system (carrying the extra Complexity Risk of the duplicated functionality).
- **Option 2: Merge.** You rip out the accounting authentication system and merge in the Approvals authentication system, consuming lots of development time in the process, due to the difficulty in migrating users from the old to new way of working. There is Implementation Risk here.
- **Option 3: Remove.** You start again, trying to take into account both sets of requirements at the same time, again, possibly surfacing new hidden Complexity Risk due to the combined approach. Rewriting code can *seem* like a way to mitigate Complexity Risk but it usually doesn't work out too well. As Joel Spolsky says:

> There's a subtle reason that programmers always want to throw away the code and start over. The reason is that they think the old code is a mess. And here is the interesting observation: they are probably wrong. The reason that they think the old code is a mess is because of a cardinal, fundamental law of programming: *It's harder to read code than to write it.*
> —Things You Should Never Do, Part 1, *Joel Spolsky*[17]

Whichever option you choose, this is a Dead End because with hindsight, it would probably have been better to do authentication in a common way *once*. But it's hard to see these dead-ends up-front because of the complexity of the system in front of you.

Sometimes, the path across the Risk Landscape will take you to dead ends, and the only benefit to be gained is experience. No one deliberately chooses

---

[17] https://www.joelonsoftware.com/2000/04/06/things-you-should-never-do-part-i/

a dead end - often you can take an action that doesn't pay off, but frequently the dead end appears from nowhere: it's a Hidden Risk. The source of a lot of this hidden risk is the complexity of the risk landscape.

Version Control Systems[18] like Git[19] are a useful mitigation of Dead-End Risk, because using them means that at least you can *go back* to the point where you made the bad decision and go a different way. Additionally, they provide you with backups against the often inadvertent Dead-End Risk of someone wiping the hard-disk.

13.10 Where Complexity Hides

So far, we've focused mainly on Codebase Risk, but this isn't the only place complexity appears in software. We're going to cover a few of these areas now, but be warned, this is not a complete list by any means:

- Algorithmic (Space and Time) Complexity
- Memory Management
- Protocols / Types
- Concurrency / Mutability
- Networks / Security
- The Environment

Space and Time Complexity

There is a whole branch of complexity theory devoted to how the software *runs*, namely Big O Complexity[20].

Once running, an algorithm or data structure will consume space or runtime dependent on its performance characteristics, which may well have an impact on the Operational Risk of the software. Using off-the-shelf data structures and algorithms helps, but you still need to know their performance characteristics.

The Big O Cheat Sheet[21] is a wonderful resource to investigate this further.

Memory Management

Memory Management (and more generally, all resource management in software) is another place where Complexity Risk hides:

---

[18] https://en.wikipedia.org/wiki/Version_control
[19] https://en.wikipedia.org/wiki/Git
[20] https://en.wikipedia.org/wiki/Big_O_notation
[21] http://bigocheatsheet.com

> "Memory leaks are a common error in programming, especially when using languages that have no built in automatic garbage collection, such as C and C++."
>
> —Memory Leak, *Wikipedia*[22]

Garbage Collectors[23] (as found in Javascript or Java) offer you the deal that they will mitigate the Complexity Risk of you having to manage your own memory, but in return perhaps give you fewer guarantees about the *performance* of your software. Again, there are times when you can't accommodate this Operational Risk, but these are rare and usually only affect a small portion of an entire software-system.

Protocols And Types

As we saw in Communication Risk, whenever two components of a software system need to interact, they have to establish a protocol for doing so. As systems become more complex, and the connectedness increases, it becomes harder to manage the risk around versioning protocols. This becomes especially true when operating beyond the edge of the compiler's domain.

Although type-checking helps mitigate Protocol Risk, when software systems grow large it becomes hard to communicate intent and keep connectivity low. You can end up with "The Big Ball Of Mud":

> "A big ball of mud is a software system that lacks a perceivable architecture. Although undesirable from a software engineering point of view, such systems are common in practice due to business pressures, developer turnover and code entropy."
>
> —Big Ball Of Mud, *Wikipedia*[24]

Concurrency / Mutability

Although modern languages include plenty of concurrency primitives (such as the java.util.concurrent[25] libraries), concurrency is *still* hard to get right.

Race conditions[26] and Deadlocks[27] abound in over-complicated concurrency designs: complexity issues are magnified by concurrency concerns, and are also hard to test and debug.

---

[22] https://en.wikipedia.org/wiki/Memory_leak
[23] https://en.wikipedia.org/wiki/Garbage_collection_(computer_science)
[24] https://en.wikipedia.org/wiki/Big_ball_of_mud
[25] https://docs.oracle.com/javase/9/docs/api/java/util/concurrent/package-summary.html
[26] https://en.wikipedia.org/wiki/Race_condition
[27] https://en.wikipedia.org/wiki/Deadlock

Recently, languages such as Clojure have introduced persistent collections[28] to alleviate concurrency issues. The basic premise is that any time you want to *change* the contents of a collection, you get given back a *new collection*. So, any collection instance is immutable once created. The trade-off is again speed to mitigate Complexity Risk.

An important lesson here is that choice of language can reduce complexity: and we'll come back to this in Software Dependency Risk.

Networking / Security

There are plenty of Complexity Risk perils in *anything* to do with networked code, chief amongst them being error handling and (again) protocol evolution.

In the case of security considerations, exploits *thrive* on the complexity of your code, and the weaknesses that occur because of it. In particular, Schneier's Law says, never implement your own cryptographic scheme:

> "Anyone, from the most clueless amateur to the best cryptographer, can create an algorithm that he himself can't break. It's not even hard. What is hard is creating an algorithm that no one else can break, even after years of analysis."
>
> Bruce Schneier, 1998[29]

Luckily, most good languages include cryptographic libraries that you can include to mitigate these Complexity Risks from your own code-base.

This is a strong argument for the use of libraries. But when should you use a library and when should you code-your-own? This is again covered in the chapter on Software Dependency Risk.

The Environment

The complexity of software tends to reflect the complexity of the environment it runs in, and complex software environments are more difficult to reason about, and more susceptible to Operational Risk and Security-Risk.

In particular, when we talk about the environment, we are talking about the number of dependencies that the software has, and the risks we face when relying on those dependencies.

So the next stop in the tour is a closer look at Dependency Risk.

---

[28] https://en.wikipedia.org/wiki/Persistent_data_structure
[29] https://en.wikipedia.org/wiki/Bruce_Schneier#Cryptography

CHAPTER 14

Dependency Risk

Dependency Risk is the risk you take on whenever you have a dependency on something (or someone) else.

One simple example could be that the software service you write might depend on hardware to run on: if the server goes down, the service goes down too. In turn, the server depends on electricity from a supplier, as well as a network connection from a provider. If either of these dependencies aren't met, the service is out of commission.

Dependencies can be on *events*, *people*, *teams*, *work*, *processes*, *software*, *services*, *money* and pretty much *any resource*, and while every project will need some of these, they also *add risk* to any project because the reliability of the project itself is now a function involving the reliability of the dependency.

In order to avoid repetition, and also to break down this large topic, we're going to look at this over 7 chapters:

- This first chapter will look at dependencies *in general*, and some of the variations of Dependency Risk.
- Next, we'll look at Scarcity Risk, because time, money and staff are scarce resources in every project.
- We'll cover Deadline Risk, and discuss the purpose of Events and Deadlines, and how they enable us to coordinate around dependency use.

- Then, we'll move on to look specifically at Software Dependency Risk, covering using libraries, software services and building on top of the work of others.
- Then, we'll take a look at Process Risk, which is still Dependency Risk, but we'll be considering more organisational factors and how bureaucracy comes into the picture.

- After that, we'll take a closer look at Boundary Risk and Dead-End Risk. These are the risks you face in making choices about what to depend on.
- Finally, we'll wrap up this analysis with a look at some of the specific problems around depending on other people or businesses in Agency Risk.

14.1 Why Have Dependencies?

Luckily for us, the things we depend on in life are, for the most part, abundant: water to drink, air to breathe, light, heat and most of the time, food for energy.

This isn't even lucky though: life has adapted to build dependencies on things that it can *rely* on.

Although life exists at the bottom of the ocean around hydrothermal vents[1], it is a very different kind of life to ours and has a different set of dependencies given its circumstances.

This tells us a lot about Dependency Risk right here:

- On the one hand, *depending on something* is very often helpful, and quite often essential. (For example, all life seem to depend on water).
- Successful organisms *adapt* to the dependencies available to them (like the thermal vent creatures).
- However, as soon as you have dependencies, you need to take into account their *reliability*. (Living near a river or stream gives you access to fresh water, for example). So, dependencies are a trade-off. They give with one hand and take with the other. Our modern lives are full of dependency (just think of the chains of dependency needed for putting a packet of biscuits on a supermarket shelf, for example), but we accept this risk because it makes life *easier*.
- There is likely to be *competition* for a dependency when it is scarce (think of droughts and famine).

Let's look at four types of risk that apply to every dependency: Fit, Reliability, Invisibility and Complexity.

14.2 Fit Risk

In order to illustrate some of the different Dependency Risks, let's introduce a running example: trying to get to work each day. There are probably a few

---
[1] https://en.wikipedia.org/wiki/Hydrothermal_vent

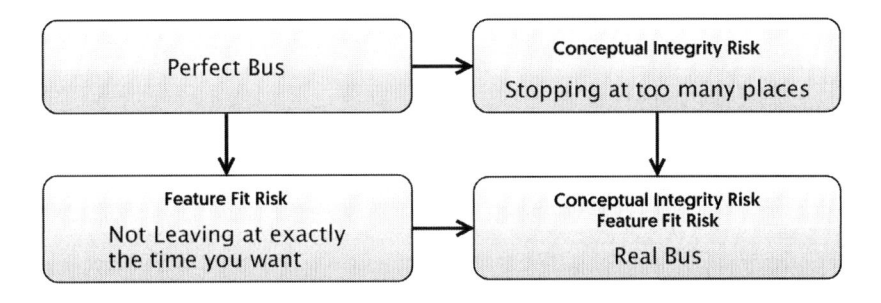

Figure 14.1: Two-Dimensions of Feature Fit for the bus-ride

alternative ways to make your journey each day, such as *by car*, *walking* or *by bus*. These are all alternative dependencies but give you the same *feature*: they'll get you there.

Normally, we'll use the same dependency each day. This speaks to the fact that each of these approaches has different Feature Fit Risk. Perhaps you choose going by bus over going by car because of the risk that owning the car is expensive, or that you might not be able to find somewhere to park it.

But there are a couple of problems with buses you don't have with your own car, as shown in Figure 14.1. A bus might take you to lots of in-between places you *didn't* want to go, which is Conceptual Integrity Risk and we saw this already in the chapter on Feature Risk. Also, it might not go at the time you want it to, which is Feature-Fit-Risk.

What this shows us is that Fit Risks are as much a problem for the suppliers of the dependency (the people running the bus service) as they are for the people (like you or I) *using* the dependency.

14.3 Reliability Risk

This points to the problem that when we use an external dependency, we are at the mercy of its reliability.

> "... Reliability describes the ability of a system or component to function under stated conditions for a specified period of time."
> —Reliability Engineering, *Wikipedia*[2]

---
[2]https://en.m.wikipedia.org/wiki/Reliability_engineering

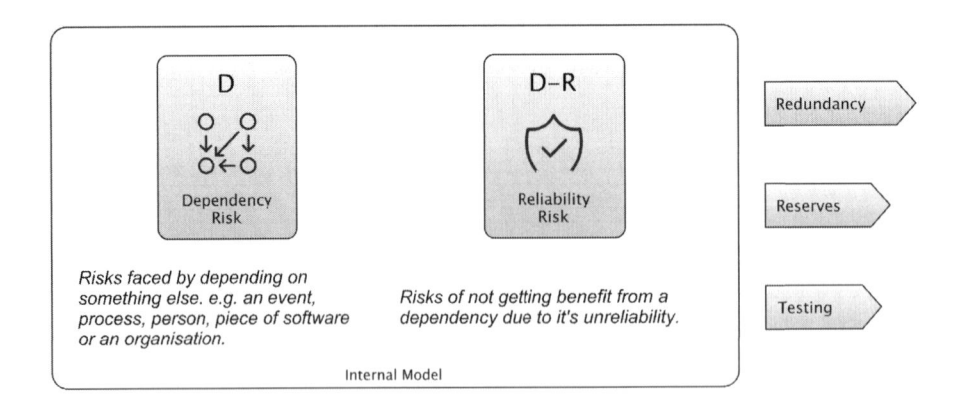

Figure 14.2: Reliability Risk

It's easy to think about reliability for something like a bus: sometimes, it's late due to weather, or cancelled due to driver sickness, or the route changes unexpectedly due to road works.

In software, it's no different: *unreliability* is the flip-side of Feature Implementation Risk. It's caused in the gap between the real behaviour of the software and the expectations for it.

There is an upper bound on the reliability of the software you write, and this is based on the dependencies you use and (in turn) the reliability of those dependencies:

- If a component **A** depends on component **B**, unless there is some extra redundancy around **B**, then **A** *can't* be more reliable than **B**.
- Is **A** or **B** a Single Point Of Failure[3] in a system?
- Are there bugs in **B** that are going to prevent it working correctly in all circumstances?

This kind of stuff is encapsulated in the science of Reliability Engineering[4]. For example, Failure Mode and Effects Analysis (FEMA)[5]:

> "...was one of the first highly structured, systematic techniques for failure analysis. It was developed by reliability engi-

---

[3]https://en.wikipedia.org/wiki/Single_point_of_failure
[4]https://en.wikipedia.org/wiki/Reliability_engineering
[5]https://en.wikipedia.org/wiki/Failure_mode_and_effects_analysis

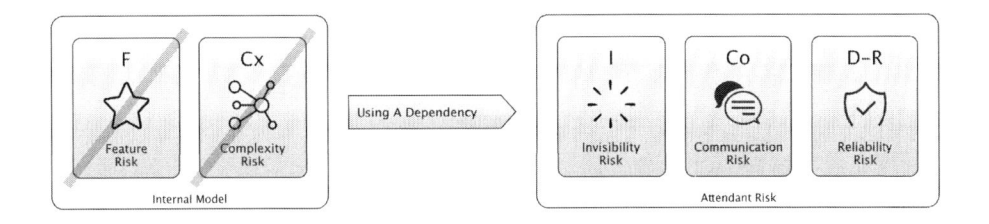

Figure 14.3: Dependencies help with complexity risk, but come with their own attendant risks

neers in the late 1950s to study problems that might arise from malfunctions of military systems."

—FEMA, *Wikipedia*[6]

This was applied on NASA missions, and then in the 1970's to car design following the Ford Pinto exploding car[7] affair. But establishing the reliability of software dependencies like this would be *hard* and *expensive*. We are more likely to mitigate Reliability Risk in software using *testing*, *redundancy* and *reserves*, as shown in Figure 14.2.

Additionally, we often rely on *proxies for reliability*. We'll look at these proxies (and the way in which software projects signal their reliability) in much more detail in the chapter on Software Dependency Risk.

14.4 Invisibility Risk

Dependencies (like the bus) make life simpler for you by taking on complexity for you.

In software, dependencies are a way to manage Complexity Risk. The reason for this is that a dependency gives you an abstraction: you no longer need to know *how* to do something, (that's the job of the dependency), you just need to interact with the dependency properly to get the job done. Buses are *perfect* for people who can't drive, after all.

But (as shown in Figure 14.3) this means that all of the issues of abstractions that we covered in Communication Risk apply. For example, there is Invisibility Risk because you probably don't have a full view of what the dependency is doing. Nowadays, bus stops have a digital "arrivals" board which gives you details of when the bus will arrive, and shops publish their

---
[6] https://en.wikipedia.org/wiki/Failure_mode_and_effects_analysis
[7] https://en.wikipedia.org/wiki/Ford_Pinto#Design_flaws_and_ensuing_lawsuits

opening hours online. But, abstraction always means the loss of detail (the bus might be two minutes away but could already be full).

14.5 Dependencies And Complexity

In Rich Hickey's talk, Simple Made Easy[8] he discusses the difference between *simple* software systems and *easy* (to use) ones, heavily stressing the virtues of simple over easy. It's an incredible talk and well worth watching.

But: living systems are not simple. Not anymore. They evolved in the direction of increasing complexity because life was *easier* that way. In the "simpler" direction, life is first *harder* and then *impossible*, and then an evolutionary dead-end.

Depending on things makes *your job easier*. But the Complexity Risk hasn't gone away: it's just *transferred* to the dependency. It's just division of labour[9] and dependency hierarchies, as we saw in Complexity Risk.

Our economic system and our software systems exhibit the same tendency-towards-complexity. For example, the television in my house now is *vastly more complicated* than the one in my home when I was a child. But, it contains much more functionality and consumes much less power and space.

14.6 Managing Dependency Risk

Arguably, managing Dependency Risk is *what Project Managers do*. Their job is to meet the project's Goal by organising the available dependencies into some kind of useful order.

There are some tools for managing dependency risk: Gantt Charts[10] for example, arrange work according to the capacity of the resources (i.e. dependencies) available, but also the *dependencies between the tasks*. If task **B** requires the outputs of task **A**, then clearly task **A** comes first and task **B** starts after it finishes. We'll look at this more in Process Risk.

We'll look in more detail at project management in Part 3, later. But now, let's get into specifics with Scarcity Risk.

---

[8] https://www.infoq.com/presentations/Simple-Made-Easy
[9] https://en.wikipedia.org/wiki/Division_of_labour
[10] https://en.wikipedia.org/wiki/Gantt_chart

CHAPTER 15

Scarcity Risk

While Reliability Risk (which we met in the previous chapter) considers what happens when a *single dependency* is unreliable, scarcity is about *quantities* of a dependency, and specifically, *not having enough*.

In the previous chapter we talked about the *reliability* of the bus: it will either arrive or it wont. But what if, when it arrives, it's already full of passengers? There is a *scarcity of seats*: you don't much care which seat you get on the bus, you just need one. Let's term this Scarcity Risk, *the risk of not being able to access a dependency in a timely fashion due to its scarcity*.

Any resource (such as disk space, oxygen, concert tickets, time or pizza) that you depend on can suffer from *scarcity*, and here, we're going to look at five particular types, relevant to software.

15.1 Funding Risk

On a lot of software projects you are "handed down" deadlines from above and told to deliver by a certain date or face the consequences. But sometimes you're given a budget instead, which really just adds another layer of abstraction to the Schedule Risk. That is, do I have enough funds to cover the team for as long as I need them?

This grants you some leeway as now you have two variables to play with: the *size* of the team, and *how long* you can run it for. The larger the team, the shorter the time you can afford to pay for it.

In startup circles, this "amount of time you can afford it" is called the "Runway"[1]: you have to get the product to "take-off" (become profitable) before the runway ends.

---

[1]https://en.wiktionary.org/wiki/runway

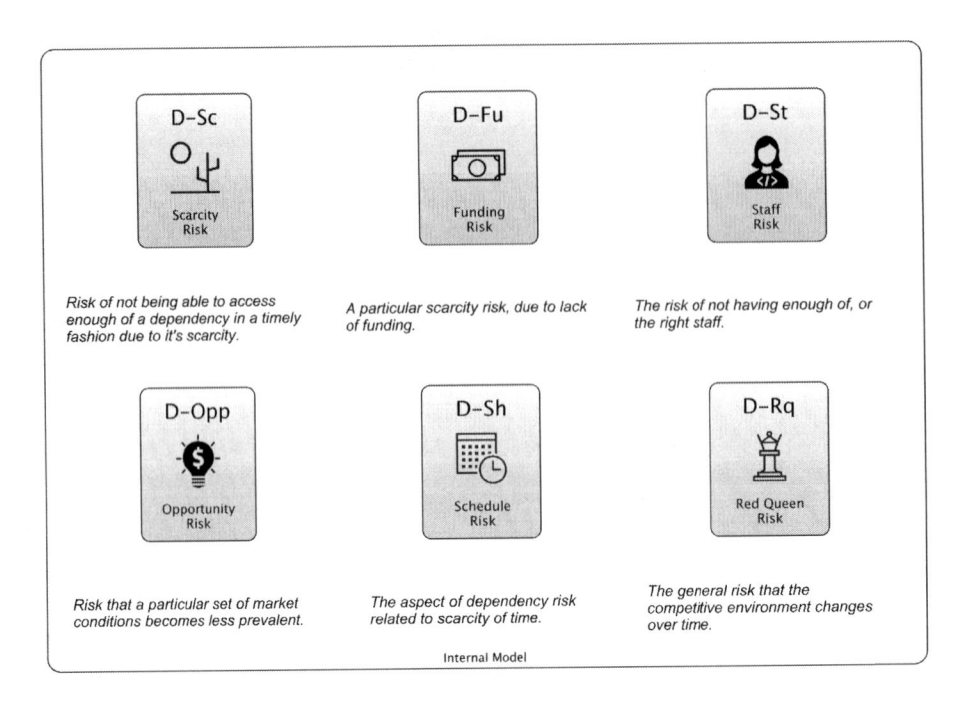

Figure 15.1: Scarcity Risk and its variations

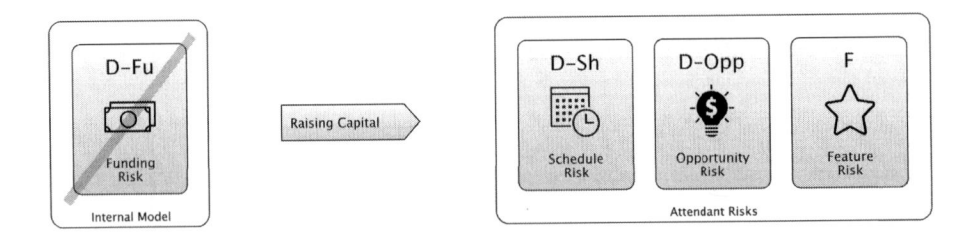

Figure 15.2: Funding Risk

Startups often spend a lot of time courting investors in order to get funding and mitigate this type of Schedule Risk. But, as shown in Figure 15.2, this activity usually comes at the expense of Opportunity Risk and Feature Risk, as usually the same people are diverted into raise funds instead of building the project itself.

15.2 Staff Risk

Since staff are a scarce resource, it stands to reason that if a startup has a "Runway", then the chances are that the founders and staff do too, as this article by Entrepreneur.com explores[2]. It identifies the following risks:

- **Company Cash**: the **Runway** of the startup itself
- **Founder Cash**: the **Runway** for a founder, before they run out of money and can't afford their rent.
- **Team Cash**: the **Runway** for team members, who may not have the same appetite for risk as the founders do.

You need to consider how long your staff are going to be around, especially if you have Key Person Risk[3] on some of them. People like to have new challenges, move on to live in new places, or simply get bored. Replacing staff can be highly risky.

The longer your project goes on for, the more Staff Risk you will have to endure, and you can't rely on getting the best staff for failing projects.

15.3 Schedule Risk

Schedule Risk is very pervasive, and really underlies *everything* we do. People *want* things, but they *want them at a certain time*. We need to eat and drink every day, for example. We might value having a great meal, but not if we have to wait three weeks for it.

And let's go completely philosophical for a second: were you to attain immortality, you'd probably not feel the need to buy *anything*. You'd clearly have no *needs*. Anything you wanted, you could create yourself within your infinite time-budget. *Rocks don't need money*, after all.

In the chapter on Feature Risk we looked at Market Risk, the idea that the value of your product is itself at risk from the whims of the market, share

---

[2]https://www.entrepreneur.com/article/223135
[3]https://en.wikipedia.org/wiki/Key_person_insurance#Key_person_definition

prices being the obvious example of that effect. In Finance, we measure this using *price*, and we can put together probability models based on how much *money* you might make or lose.

With Schedule Risk, the underlying measure is *time*:

- "If I implement feature X, I'm picking up something like 5 days of Schedule Risk."
- "If John goes travelling that's going to hit us with lots of Schedule Risk while we train up Anne."

... and so on. Clearly, in the same way as you don't know exactly how much money you might lose or gain on the stock-exchange, you can't put precise numbers on Schedule Risk either.

Student Syndrome

Student Syndrome[4] is, according to Wikipedia:

> "Student syndrome refers to planned procrastination, when, for example, a student will only start to apply themselves to an assignment at the last possible moment before its deadline." - *Wikipedia*

Arguably, there is good psychological, evolutionary and risk-based reasoning behind procrastination: if there is apparently a lot of time to get a job done, then Schedule Risk is low. If we're only ever mitigating our *biggest risks*, then managing Schedule Risk in the future doesn't matter so much. Putting efforts into mitigating future risks that *might not arise* is wasted effort.

Or at least, that's the argument: if you're Discounting the Future To Zero then you'll be pulling all-nighters in order to deliver any assignment.

So, the problem with Student Syndrome is that the *very mitigation* for Schedule Risk (allowing more time) is an Attendant Risk that *causes* Schedule Risk: you'll work within the more generous time allocation more slowly and you'll end up revealing Hidden Risk *later*. And, discovering these hidden risks later causes you to end up being late because of them.

---

[4]https://en.wikipedia.org/wiki/Student_syndrome

15.4 Opportunity Risk

Opportunity Risk is really the concern that whatever we do, we have to do it *in time*. If we wait too long, we'll miss the Window Of Opportunity[5] for our product or service.

Any product idea is necessarily of its time: the Goal In Mind will be based on observations from a particular Internal Model, reflecting a view on reality at a specific *point in time*.

How long will that remain true for? This is your *opportunity*: it exists apart from any deadlines you set yourself, or funding options. It's purely, "how long will this idea be worth doing?"

With any luck, decisions around *funding* your project will be tied into this, but it's not always the case. It's very easy to under-shoot or overshoot the market completely and miss the window of opportunity.

The iPad

For example, let's look at the iPad[6], which was introduced in 2010 and was hugely successful.

This was not the first tablet computer. Apple had already tried to introduce the Newton[7] in 1989, and Microsoft had released the Tablet PC[8] in 1999. But somehow, they both missed the Window Of Opportunity. Possibly, the window existed because Apple had changed the market with their release of the iPhone, which left people open to the idea of a tablet being "just a bigger iPhone".

But maybe now, the iPad's window is closing? We have more *wearable computers* like the Apple Watch[9], and voice-controlled devices like Alexa[10] or Siri[11]. Peak iPad was in 2014 (according to this graph at statista.com[12]).

So, it seems Apple timed the iPad to hit the peak of the Window of Opportunity.

But, even if you time the Window Of Opportunity correctly, you might still have the rug pulled from under your feet due to a different kind of Scarcity Risk, such as...

---

[5] https://en.wikipedia.org/wiki/Window_of_opportunity
[6] https://en.wikipedia.org/wiki/History_of_tablet_computers
[7] https://en.wikipedia.org/wiki/Apple_Newton
[8] https://en.wikipedia.org/wiki/Microsoft_Tablet_PC
[9] https://en.wikipedia.org/wiki/Apple_Watch
[10] https://en.wikipedia.org/wiki/Amazon_Alexa
[11] https://en.wikipedia.org/wiki/Siri
[12] https://www.statista.com/statistics/269915/global-apple-ipad-sales-since-q3-2010/

Figure 15.3: Red Queen Risk

15.5 Red-Queen Risk

A more specific formulation of Schedule Risk is Red Queen Risk, which is that whatever you build at the start of the project will go slowly more-and-more out of date as the project goes on.

This is named after the Red Queen quote from Alice in Wonderland:

> "My dear, here we must run as fast as we can, just to stay in place. And if you wish to go anywhere you must run twice as fast as that."
>
> —Lewis Carroll, *Alice in Wonderland*[13]

The problem with software projects is that tools and techniques change *really fast*. In 2011, 3DRealms released Duke Nukem Forever after 15 years in development[14], to negative reviews:

> "... most of the criticism directed towards the game's long loading times, clunky controls, offensive humor, and overall aging and dated design." - *Duke Nukem Forever, Wikipedia*

Now, they didn't *deliberately* take 15 years to build this game (lots of things went wrong). But, the longer it took, the more their existing design and code-base were a liability rather than an asset.

Personally, I have suffered the pain on project teams where we've had to cope with legacy code and databases because the cost of changing them was too high. This is shown in Figure 15.3: mitigating Red Queen Risk (by *keeping*

---

[13]https://www.goodreads.com/quotes/458856-my-dear-here-we-must-run-as-fast-as-we
[14]https://en.wikipedia.org/wiki/Duke_Nukem_Forever

up-to-date) has the Attendant Risk of costing time and money, which might not seem worth it. Any team who is stuck using Visual Basic 6.0[15] is here.

It's possible to ignore Red Queen Risk for a time, but this is just another form of Technical Debt which eventually comes due.

15.6 Mitigations

Here are a selection of mitigations for Scarcity Risk in general:

- **Buffers**: smoothing out peaks and troughs in utilisation.
- **Reservation Systems**: giving clients information *ahead* of the dependency usage about whether the resource will be available to them.
- **Graceful degradation**: ensuring *some* service in the event of oversubscription. It would be no use allowing people to cram onto the bus until it can't move.
- **Demand Management**: having different prices during busy periods helps to reduce demand. Having "first class" seats means that higher-paying clients can get service even when the train is full. Uber[16] adjust prices in real-time by so-called Surge Pricing[17]. This is basically turning Scarcity Risk into a Market Risk problem.
- **Queues**: these provide a "fair" way of dealing with scarcity by exposing some mechanism for prioritising use of the resource. Buses operate a first-come-first-served system, whereas emergency departments in hospitals triage according to need.
- **Pools**: reserving parts of a resource for a group of customers, and sharing within that group.
- **Horizontal Scaling**: allowing a scarce resource to flexibly scale according to how much demand there is. (For example, putting on extra buses when the trains are on strike, or opening extra check-outs at the supermarket.)

Much like Reliability Risk, there is science for it:

- **Queue Theory**[18] is all about building mathematical models of buffers, queues, pools and so forth.

---

[15]https://en.wikipedia.org/wiki/Visual_Basic
[16]https://www.uber.com
[17]https://www.uber.com/en-GB/drive/partner-app/how-surge-works/
[18]https://en.wikipedia.org/wiki/Queueing_theory

- **Logistics**[19] is the practical organisation of the flows of materials and goods around things like Supply Chains[20],
- and **Project Management**[21] is in large part about ensuring the right resources are available at the right times.

In this chapter, we've looked at various risks to do with scarcity of time, as a quantity we can spend like money. But frequently, we have a dependency on a specific *event*. On to Deadline Risk.

---

[19]https://en.wikipedia.org/wiki/Logistics
[20]https://en.wikipedia.org/wiki/Supply_chain
[21]https://en.wikipedia.org/wiki/Project_management

CHAPTER 16

Deadline Risk

Let's examine dependencies on *events*.

We rely on events occuring all the time in our lives, and event dependencies are simple to express: usually, a *time* and a *place*. For example:

- "The bus to work leaves at 7:30am" or
- "I can't start shopping until the supermarket opens at 9am".

In the first example, you can't *start* something until a particular event happens. In the latter example, you must *be ready* for an event at a particular time.

16.1 Events Mitigate Risk...

Having an event occur in a fixed time and place is mitigating risk:

- By taking the bus, we are mitigating our own Schedule Risk: we're (hopefully) reducing the amount of time we're going to spend on the activity of getting to work. It's not entirely necessary to even take the bus: you could walk, or go by another form of transport. But, effectively, this just swaps one dependency for another: if you walk, this might well take longer and use more energy, so you're just picking up Schedule Risk in another way.
- Events are a mitigation for Coordination Risk: a bus needn't necessarily *have* a fixed timetable. It could wait for each passenger until they turned up, and then go. (A bit like ride-sharing works). This would be a total disaster from a Coordination Risk perspective, as one person could cause everyone else to be really really late.

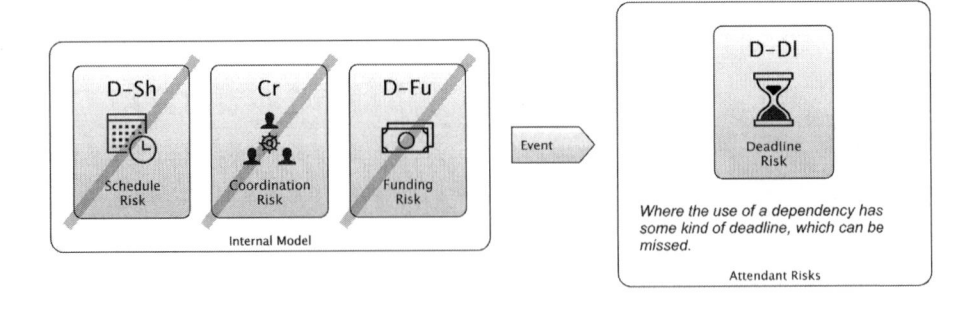

Figure 16.1: Action Diagram showing risks mitigated by having an **event**

- If you drive, you have a dependency on your car instead. So, there is often an *opportunity cost* with dependencies. Using the bus might be a cheaper way to travel, so you're picking up less Fuding Risk by using it.

16.2 But, Events Lead To Attendant Risk

By *deciding to use the bus* we've Taken Action. By agreeing a *time* and *place* for something to happen (creating an *event*, as shown in Figure 16.1), you're introducing Deadline Risk. Miss the deadline, and you miss the bus.

As discussed above, *schedules* (such as bus timetables) exist so that *two or more parties can coordinate*, and Deadline Risk is on *all* of the parties. While there's a risk I am late, there's also a risk the bus is late. I might miss the start of a concert, or the band might keep everyone waiting.

In software development, deadlines are set in order to *coordinate work between teams*. For example, having a product ready in production at the same time as the marketing campaign starts. Fixing on an agreed deadline mitigates inter-team Coordination Risk.

16.3 Slack

Each party can mitigate Deadline Risk with *slack*. That is, ensuring that the exact time of the event isn't critical to your plans:

- Don't build into your plans a *need* to start shopping at 9am.
- Arrive at the bus-stop *early*.

The amount of slack you build into the schedule is likely dependent on the level of risk you face: I tend to arrive a few minutes early for a bus, because the risk is *low* (there'll be another bus along soon). However, I try to arrive over an hour early for a flight, because I can't simply get on the next flight straight away and I've already paid for it, so the risk is *high*.

Deadline Risk becomes very hard to manage when you have to coordinate actions with lots of tightly-constrained events. So what else can give? We can reduce the number of *parties* involved in the event, which reduces risk, or, we can make sure all the parties are in the same *place* to begin with.

16.4 Focus

Often when running a software project you're given a team of people and told to get something delivered by a certain date, i.e. you have an artificially-imposed deadline on delivery.

What happens if you miss the deadline? It could be:

- The funding on the project runs out, and it gets cancelled.
- You have to go back to a budgeting committee to get more money.
- Members of the team get replaced because of lack of faith.

.. or something else. So Deadline Risk can be introduced by an authority in order to *sharpen focus*. This is how we arrive at tools like SMART Objectives[1] and KPI's (Key Performance Indicators)[2].

Deadlines change the way we evaluate goals and the solutions we choose because they force us to reckon with Deadline Risk. For example, in JFK's quote:

> "First, I believe that this nation should commit itself to achieving the goal, before this decade is out, of landing a man on the moon and returning him safely to the Earth." - John F. Kennedy, 1961

The 9-year timespan came from an authority figure (the president) and helped a huge team of people coordinate their efforts and arrive at a solution that would work within a given time-frame. The Deadline Risk allowed the team to focus on mitigating the risk of missing that deadline.

Compare with this quote:

---
[1] https://en.wikipedia.org/wiki/SMART_criteria
[2] https://en.wikipedia.org/wiki/Performance_indicator

> "I love deadlines. I love the whooshing noise they make as they go by."
>
> Douglas Adams[3]

As a successful author, Douglas Adams *didn't really care* about the deadlines his publisher's gave him. The Deadline Risk was minimal for him, because the publisher wouldn't be able to give his project to someone else to complete.

16.5 Deadline Risk and Schedule Risk

Schedule Risk and Deadline Risk are clearly related: they both refer to the risk of running out of time. However, the *risk profile* of each is very different:

- Schedule Risk is *continuous*, like money. i.e. you want to waste as little of it as possible. Every extra day you take compounds Schedule Risk additively. A day wasted at the start of the project is much the same as a day wasted at the end.
- Deadline Risk is *binary*. The impact of Deadline Risk is either zero (you make it in time) or one (you are late and miss the flight). You don't particularly get a reward for being early.

So, these are two separate concepts, both useful in software development and other fields. Next up, something more specific: Software Dependency Risk.

---

[3]https://en.wikipedia.org/wiki/Douglas_Adams

CHAPTER 17

Software Dependency Risk

In this chapter, we're going to look specifically at *Software* dependencies, although many of the concerns we'll raise here apply equally to all the other types of dependency we outlined in Dependency Risk.

17.1 Kolmogorov Complexity: Cheating

In the earlier chapter on Complexity Risk we tackled Kolmogorov Complexity, and the idea that your codebase had some kind of minimal level of complexity based on the output it was trying to create. This is a neat idea, but in a way, we cheated. Let's look at how.

We were trying to figure out the shortest (Javascript) program to generate this output:

abcdabcdabcdabcdabcdabcdabcdabcdabcd

And we came up with this:

```
const ABCD="ABCD";                       (11 symbols)

function out() {                         (7 symbols)
    return ABCD.repeat(10)               (7 symbols)
}                                        (1 symbol)
```

Which had **26** symbols in it.

Now, here's the cheat: the `repeat()` function was built into Javascript in 2015 in ECMAScript 6.0[1]. If we'd had to program it ourselves, we might have

---
[1] http://www.ecma-international.org/ecma-262/6.0/

137

added this:

```
function repeat(s,n) {          (10 symbols)
    var a=[];                   (7 symbols)
    while(a.length<n){          (9 symbols)
        a.push(s)               (6 symbols)
    }                           (1 symbol)
    return a.join('');          (10 symbols)
}                               (1 symbol)
```

... which would be an extra **44** symbols (in total **70**), and push us completely over the original string encoding of **53** symbols. So, *encoding language is important*.

Conversely, if ECMAScript 6.0 had introduced a function called abcdRepeater(n) we'd have been able to do this:

```
function out() {                (7 symbols)
    return abcdRepeater(10)     (6 symbols)
}                               (1 symbol)
```

.. and re-encode to **14** symbols. Now, clearly there are some problems with all this:

1. **Language Matters**: the Kolmogorov complexity is dependent on the language, and the features the language has built in.
2. **Exact Kolmogorov complexity is uncomputable anyway:** Since it's the *theoretical* minimum program length, it's a fairly abstract idea, so we shouldn't get too hung up on this. There is no function to be able to say, "What's the Kolmogorov complexity of string X?"
3. **What is this new library function we've created?** Is abcdRepeater going to be part of *every* Javascript? If so, then we've shifted Codebase Risk away from ourselves, but we've pushed Communication Risk and Dependency Risk onto every *other* user of Javascript. (Why these? Because abcdRepeater will be clogging up the JavaScript documentation for everyone, and other people will rely on it to function correctly.)
4. **Are there equivalent functions for every single other string?** If so, then compilation is no longer a tractable problem because now we have a massive library of different XXXRepeater functions to compile against. So, what we *lose* in Codebase Risk we gain in Dependency Risk.

5. **Language design, then, is about *ergonomics*:** After you have passed the relatively low bar of providing Turing Completeness[2], the key is to provide *useful* features that enable problems to be solved, without over-burdening the user with features they *don't* need. And in fact, all software is about this.

17.2 Ergonomics Examined

Have a look at some physical tools, like a hammer, or spanner. To look at them, they are probably *simple* objects, obvious, strong and dependable. Their entire behaviour is encapsulated in their form. Now, if you have a drill or sander to hand, look at the design of this too. If it's well-designed, then from the outside it is simple, perhaps with only one or two controls. Inside, it is complex and contains a motor, perhaps a transformer, and is maybe made of a hundred different components.

But outside, the form is simple, and designed for humans to use. This is *ergonomics*[3]:

> "Human factors and ergonomics (commonly referred to as Human Factors), is the application of psychological and physiological principles to the (engineering and) design of products, processes, and systems. The goal of human factors is to reduce human error, increase productivity, and enhance safety and comfort with a specific focus on the interaction between the human and the thing of interest."
> —Human Factors and Ergonomics, *Wikipedia*[4]

Protocols and Ergonomics

The *interface* of a tool is the part we touch and interact with, via its protocol. By striving for an ergonomic sweet spot, the protocol reduces Communication Risk. You can see this trade-off in Figure 17.1.

The interface of a system expands when you ask it to do a wide variety of things. An easy-to-use drill does one thing well: it turns drill-bits at useful levels of torque for drilling holes and sinking screws. But if you wanted it to also operate as a lathe, a sander or a strimmer (all basically mechanical things going round) you would have to sacrifice the conceptual integrity for

---
[2] https://en.wikipedia.org/wiki/Turing_completeness
[3] https://en.wikipedia.org/wiki/Human_factors_and_ergonomics
[4] https://en.wikipedia.org/wiki/Human_factors_and_ergonomics

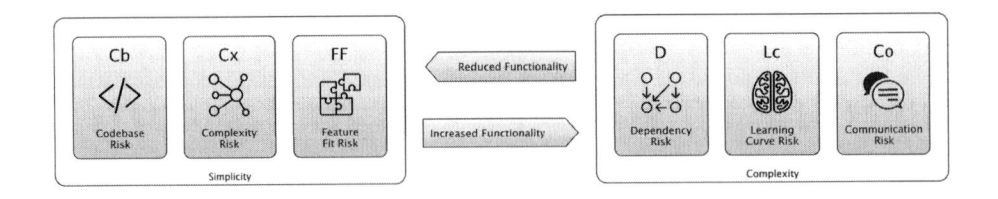

Figure 17.1: Software Dependency Ergonomics: finding the sweet spot between too many features and too few

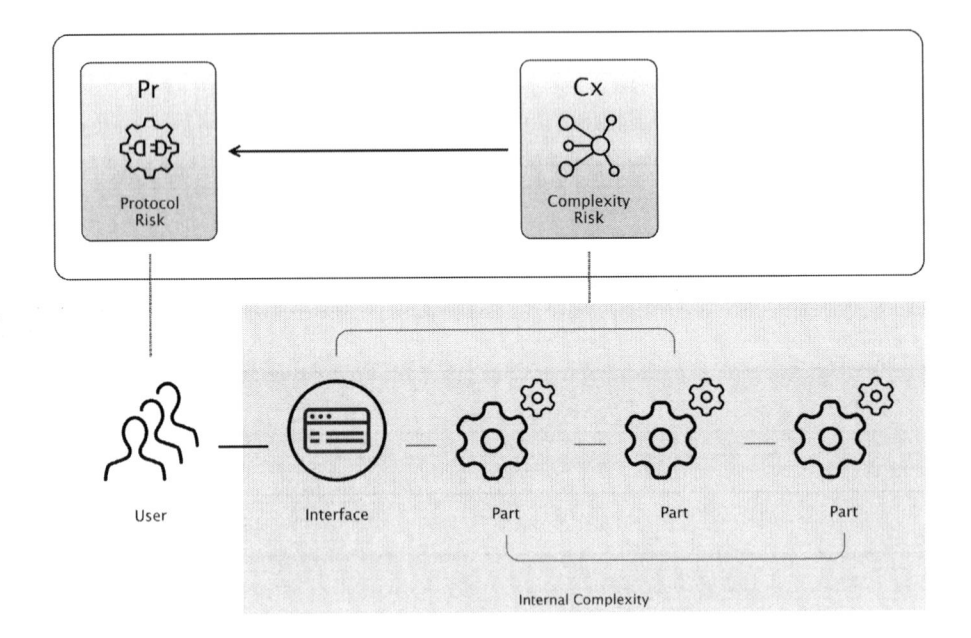

Figure 17.2: Types of Complexity For a Software Dependency

a more complex protocol, probably including adapters, extensions, handles and so on.

So, we now have split complexity into two:

- The inner complexity of the tool (how it works internally, its own internal complexity).
- The complexity of the instructions that we need to write to make the tool work, the protocol complexity, which will be a function of the complexity of the tool itself.

Software Tools

In the same way as with a hand-tool, the bulk of the complexity of a software tool is hidden behind its interface. But, the more complex the *purpose* of the tool, the more complex the interface will be.

Software is not constrained by *physical* ergonomics in the same way as a tool is. But ideally, it should have conceptual ergonomics: complexity is hidden away from the user behind the *User Interface*. This is the familiar concept of Abstraction we've already looked at. As we saw in Communication Risk, when we use a new protocol, we face Learning Curve Risk. To minimise this, we should apply the Principal Of Least Astonishment when designing protocols:

- **The abstractions should map easily to how the user expects the tool to work.** For example, I *expect* the trigger on a drill to start the drill turning.
- **The abstractions should leverage existing idioms and knowledge.** In a new car I *expect* to know what the symbols on the dashboard mean because I've driven other cars.
- **The abstractions provide me with only the functions I need.** Because everything else is confusing and gets in the way.

17.3 Types Of Software Dependencies

There are lots of ways you can depend on software. Here though, we're going to focus on just three main types:

1. **Code Your Own**: write some code ourselves to meet the dependency.
2. **Software Libraries**: importing code from the Internet, and using it in our project. Often, libraries are Open Source (this is what we'll consider here).
3. **Software-as-a-Service (SaaS)**: calling a service on the Internet, (probably via `http`) This is often known as SaaS, or Software as a Service[5].

All 3 approaches involve a different risk-profile. Let's look at each in turn, from the perspective of which risks get mitigated, and which risks are exacerbated.

---
[5] https://en.wikipedia.org/wiki/Software_as_a_service

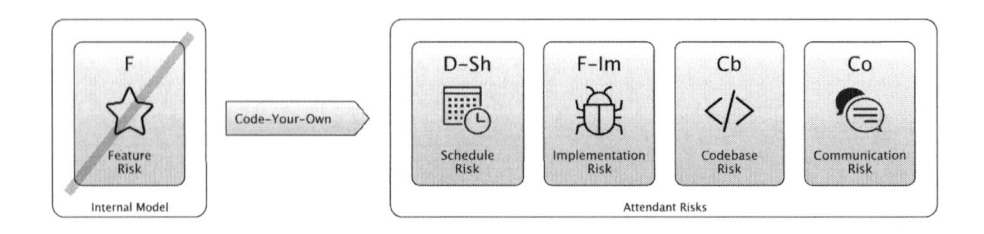

Figure 17.3: Code-Your-Own mitigates immediate feature risk, but at the expense of schedule risk, complexity risk and communication risk. There is also a hidden risk of features you don't yet know you need.

1. Code Your Own

Way before the Internet, this was the only game in town. Tool support was very thin-on-the-ground. Algorithms could be distributed as code snippets *in books and magazines* which could be transcribed and run, and added to your program. This spirit lives on somewhat in StackOverflow and JSFiddle, where you are expected to "adopt" others' code into your own project. Code-your-own is still the best option if you have highly bespoke requirements, or are dealing with unusual environmental contexts.

One of the hidden risks of embarking on a code-your-own approach is that the features you need are *not* apparent from the outset. What might appear to be a trivial implementation of some piece of functionality can often turn into its own industry as more and more hidden Feature Risk is uncovered. For example, as we discussed in our earlier treatment of Dead-End Risk, building log-in screens *seemed like a good idea*. However, this gets out-of-hand fast when you need:

- A password reset screen
- To email the reset links to the user
- An email verification screen
- A lost account screen
- Reminders to complete the sign up process
- ... and so on.

Unwritten Software

Sometimes you will pick up Dependency Risk from *unwritten software*. This commonly happens when work is divided amongst team members, or teams.

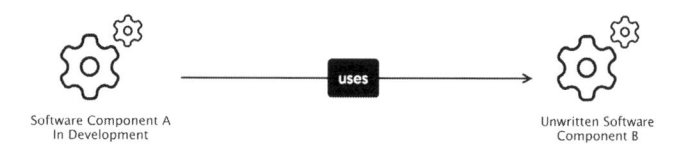

Figure 17.4: Sometimes, a module you're writing will depend on unwritten code

If a component **A** of our project *depends* on **B** for some kind of processing, you might not be able to complete **A** before writing **B**. This makes *scheduling* the project harder, and if component **A** is a risky part of the project, then the chances are you'll want to mitigate risk there first.

But it also hugely increases Communication Risk because now you're being asked to communicate with a dependency that doesn't really exist yet, *let alone* have any documentation.

There are a couple of ways of doing this:

- **Standards**: if component **B** is a database, a queue, mail gateway or something else with a standard interface, then you're in luck. Write **A** to those standards, and find a cheap, simple implementation to test with. This gives you time to sort out exactly what implementation of **B** you're going for. This is not a great long-term solution, because obviously, you're not using the *real* dependency- you might get surprised when the behaviour of the real component is subtly different. But it can reduce Schedule Risk in the short-term.

- **Coding To Interfaces**: if standards aren't an option, but the surface area of **B** that **A** uses is quite small and obvious, you can write a small interface for it, and work behind that, using a Mock[6] for **B** while you're waiting for finished component. Write the interface to cover only what **A** *needs*, rather than everything that **B** *does* in order to minimise the risk of Leaky Abstractions[7].

Conway's Law

Due to channel bandwidth limitations, if the dependency is being written by another person, another team or in another country, Communication

---

[6]https://en.wikipedia.org/wiki/Mock_object
[7]https://en.wikipedia.org/wiki/Leaky_abstraction

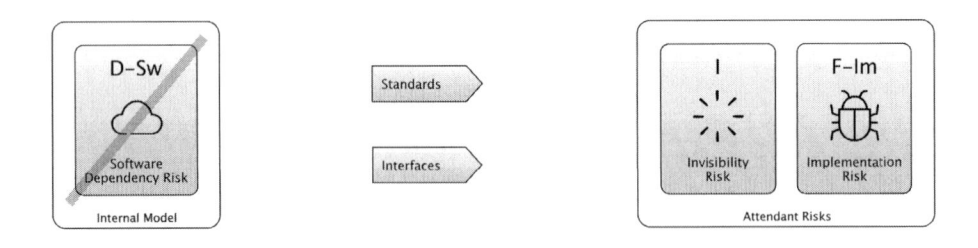

Figure 17.5: Coding to a standard on an interface breaks the dependency on unwritten software

Risk piles up. When this happens, you will want to minimise the interface complexity *as much as possible*, since the more complex the interface, the worse the Communication Risk will be. The tendency then is to make the interfaces between teams or people *as simple as possible*, modularising along these organisational boundaries.

In essence, this is Conway's Law:

> "organisations which design systems ... are constrained to produce designs which are copies of the communication structures of these organisations."
>
> —Melvin Conway, *Conway's Law*[8]

2. Software Libraries

By choosing a particular software library, we are making a move on the Risk Landscape in the hope of moving to a place with more favourable risks. Typically, using library code offers a Schedule Risk and Complexity Risk Silver Bullet - a high-speed route over the risk landscape to somewhere nearer where we want to be. But, in return we expect to pick up:

- **Communication Risk**: because we now have to learn how to communicate with this new dependency.
- **Boundary Risk**: - because now are limited to using the functionality provided by this dependency. We have chosen it over alternatives and changing to something else would be more work and therefore costly.

But, it's quite possible that we could wind up in a worse place than we started out, by using a library that's out-of-date, riddled with bugs or badly supported. i.e. full of new, hidden Feature Risk.

---

[8]https://en.wikipedia.org/wiki/Conways_law

It's *really easy* to make bad decisions about which tools to use because the tools don't (generally) advertise their deficiencies. After all, they don't generally know how *you* will want to use them.

Software Libraries - Attendant Risks

Currently, choosing software dependencies looks like a "bounded rationality"-type process:

> "Bounded rationality is the idea that when individuals make decisions, their rationality is limited by the tractability of the decision problem, the cognitive limitations of their minds, and the time available to make the decision."
> —Bounded Rationality, *Wikipedia*[9]

Unfortunately, we know that most decisions *don't* really get made this way. We have things like Confirmation Bias[10] (looking for evidence to support a decision you've already made) and Cognitive Inertia[11] (ignoring evidence that would require you to change your mind) to contend with.

But, leaving that aside, let's try to build a model of what this decision making process *should* involve. Luckily, other authors have already considered the problem of choosing good software libraries, so let's start there.

In Figure 17.6, I am summarising three different sources (linked at the end of the chapter), which give descriptions of which factors to look for when choosing open-source libraries. Here are some take-aways:

- **Feature Risk is a big concern**: How can you be sure that the project will do what you want it to do ahead of schedule? Will it contain bugs or missing features? By looking at factors like *release frequency* and *size of the community* you get a good feel for this which is difficult to fake.
- **Boundary Risk is also very important**: You are going to have to *live* with your choices for the duration of the project, so it's worth spending the effort to either ensure that you're not going to regret the decision, or that you can change direction later.
- **Third is Communication Risk**: how well does the project deal with its users? If a project is "famous", then it has communicated its usefulness to a wide, appreciative audience. Avoiding Communication Risk is also a good reason to pick *tools you are already familiar with*.

---

[9]https://en.wikipedia.org/wiki/Bounded_rationality
[10]https://en.wikipedia.org/wiki/Confirmation_bias
[11]https://en.wikipedia.org/wiki/Cognitive_inertia

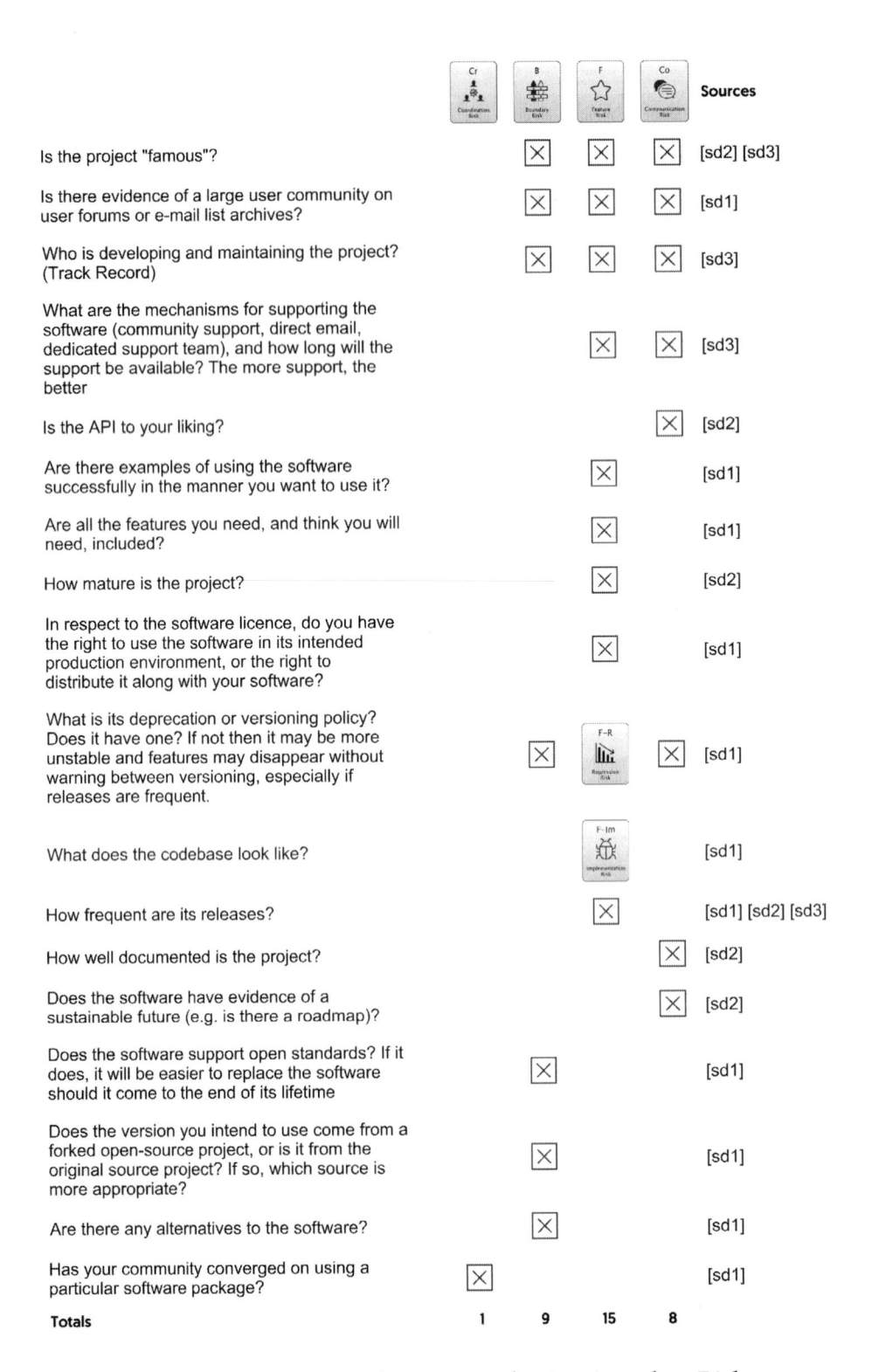

	Cr (Coordination Risk)	B (Boundary Risk)	F (Feature Risk)	Co (Communication Risk)	Sources
Is the project "famous"?		☒	☒	☒	[sd2] [sd3]
Is there evidence of a large user community on user forums or e-mail list archives?		☒	☒	☒	[sd1]
Who is developing and maintaining the project? (Track Record)		☒	☒	☒	[sd3]
What are the mechanisms for supporting the software (community support, direct email, dedicated support team), and how long will the support be available? The more support, the better		☒		☒	[sd3]
Is the API to your liking?				☒	[sd2]
Are there examples of using the software successfully in the manner you want to use it?			☒		[sd1]
Are all the features you need, and think you will need, included?			☒		[sd1]
How mature is the project?			☒		[sd2]
In respect to the software licence, do you have the right to use the software in its intended production environment, or the right to distribute it along with your software?			☒		[sd1]
What is its deprecation or versioning policy? Does it have one? If not then it may be more unstable and features may disappear without warning between versioning, especially if releases are frequent.		☒	F-R (Regression Risk)	☒	[sd1]
What does the codebase look like?			F-Im (Implementation Risk)		[sd1]
How frequent are its releases?			☒		[sd1] [sd2] [sd3]
How well documented is the project?				☒	[sd2]
Does the software have evidence of a sustainable future (e.g. is there a roadmap)?				☒	[sd2]
Does the software support open standards? If it does, it will be easier to replace the software should it come to the end of its lifetime		☒			[sd1]
Does the version you intend to use come from a forked open-source project, or is it from the original source project? If so, which source is more appropriate?		☒			[sd1]
Are there any alternatives to the software?		☒			[sd1]
Has your community converged on using a particular software package?	☒				[sd1]
Totals	1	9	15	8	

Figure 17.6: Software Library Dependencies, Attendant Risks

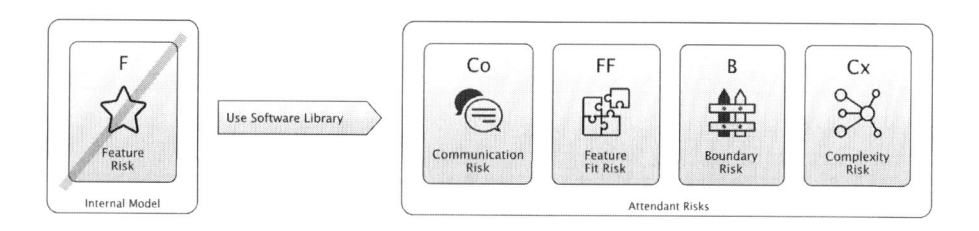

Figure 17.7: Software Libraries Risk Tradeoff

Sources

- sd1: Defending your code against dependency problems[12]
- sd2: How to choose an open source library[13]
- sd3: Open Source - To use or not to use[14]

Complexity Risk?

One thing that none of the sources in the table consider (at least from the outset) is the Complexity Risk of using a solution:

- Does it drag in lots of extra dependencies that seem unnecessary for the job in hand? If so, you could end up in Dependency Hell[15], with multiple, conflicting versions of libraries in the project.
- Do you already have a dependency providing this functionality? So many times, I've worked on projects that import a *new* dependency when some existing (perhaps transitive) dependency has *already brought in the functionality*. For example, there are plenty of libraries for JSON[16] marshalling, but if I'm also using a web framework the chances are it already has a dependency on one already.
- Does it contain lots of functionality that isn't relevant to the task you want it to accomplish? e.g. Using Java when a shell script would do (on a non-Java project)

Sometimes, the amount of complexity *goes up* when you use a dependency for *good reason*. For example, in Java you can use Java Database Connectivity

---

[12]https://www.software.ac.uk/resources/guides/defending-your-code-against-dependency-problems
[13]https://stackoverflow.com/questions/2960371/how-to-choose-an-open-source-library
[14]https://www.forbes.com/sites/forbestechcouncil/2017/07/20/open-source-to-use-or-not-to-use-and-how-to-choose
[15]https://en.wikipedia.org/wiki/Dependency_hell
[16]https://en.wikipedia.org/wiki/JSON

(JDBC)[17] to interface with various types of database. Spring Framework[18] (a popular Java library) provides a thing called a `JDBCTemplate`. This actually makes your code *more* complex, and can prove very difficult to debug. However, it prevents some security issues, handles resource disposal and makes database access more efficient. None of those are essential to interfacing with the database, but not having them is Operational Risk that can bite you later on.

3. Software-as-a-Service

Businesses opt for Software-as-a-Service (SaaS) because:

- It promises to vastly reduce the Complexity Risk they face in their organisations. e.g. managing the software or making changes to it.
- Payment is usually based on *usage*, mitigating Funding Risk. e.g. Instead of having to pay up-front for a license and hire in-house software administrators, they can leave this function to the experts.
- Potentially, you out-source the Operational Risk to a third party. e.g. ensuring availability, making sure data is secure and so on.

SaaS is now a very convenient way to provide *commercial* software. Popular examples of SaaS might be SalesForce[19], or GMail[20]. Both of which follow the commonly-used Freemium[21] model, where the basic service is provided free but upgrading to a paid account gives extra benefits.

Figure 17.8 summarises the risks raised in some of the available literature (sources below). Some take-aways:

- Clearly, Operational Risk is now a big concern. By depending on a third-party organisation you are tying yourself to its success or failure in a much bigger way than just by using a piece of open-source software. What happens to data security, both in the data centre and over the Internet? Although you might choose a SaaS solution to mitigate *internal* Operational Risk, you might just be "throwing it over the wall" to a third party, who might do a worse job.
- With Feature Risk you now have to contend with the fact that the software will be upgraded *outside your control*, and you may have limited control over which features get added or changed.

---

[17] https://en.wikipedia.org/wiki/Java_Database_Connectivity
[18] https://en.wikipedia.org/wiki/Spring_Framework
[19] https://en.wikipedia.org/wiki/Salesforce.com
[20] https://en.wikipedia.org/wiki/Gmail
[21] https://en.wikipedia.org/wiki/Freemium

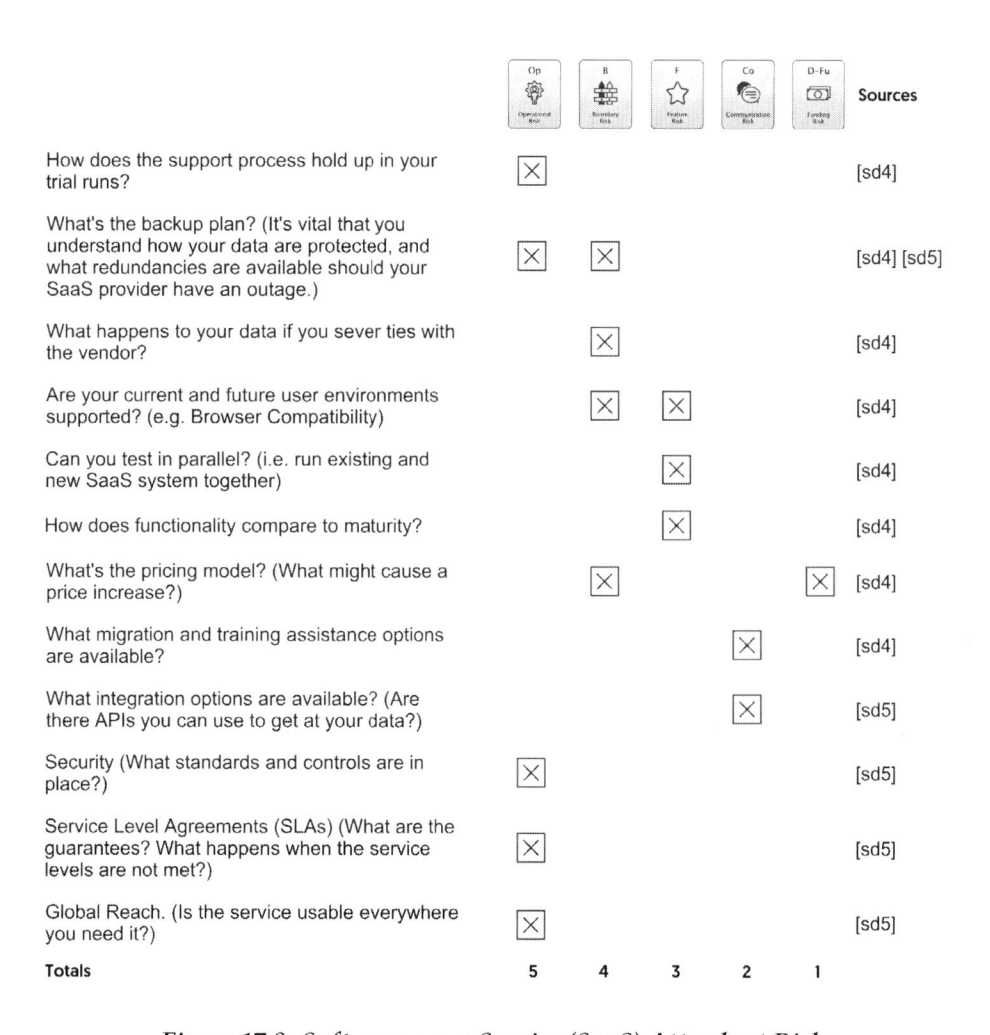

	Op	B	F	Co	D-Fu	Sources
How does the support process hold up in your trial runs?	☒					[sd4]
What's the backup plan? (It's vital that you understand how your data are protected, and what redundancies are available should your SaaS provider have an outage.)	☒	☒				[sd4] [sd5]
What happens to your data if you sever ties with the vendor?		☒				[sd4]
Are your current and future user environments supported? (e.g. Browser Compatibility)		☒	☒			[sd4]
Can you test in parallel? (i.e. run existing and new SaaS system together)			☒			[sd4]
How does functionality compare to maturity?			☒			[sd4]
What's the pricing model? (What might cause a price increase?)		☒			☒	[sd4]
What migration and training assistance options are available?				☒		[sd4]
What integration options are available? (Are there APIs you can use to get at your data?)				☒		[sd5]
Security (What standards and controls are in place?)	☒					[sd5]
Service Level Agreements (SLAs) (What are the guarantees? What happens when the service levels are not met?)	☒					[sd5]
Global Reach. (Is the service usable everywhere you need it?)	☒					[sd5]
Totals	5	4	3	2	1	

Figure 17.8: Software-as-a-Service (SaaS) Attendant Risks

- Boundary Risk is also a different proposition: you are tied to the software provider by *a contract*. If the service changes in the future, or isn't to your liking, you can't simply fork the code (like you could with an open source project).

Sources

- sd4: SaaS Checklist - Nine Factors to Consider[22]
- sd5: How to Evaluate SaaS Vendors.[23]

---

[22] https://www.zdnet.com/article/saas-checklist-nine-factors-to-consider-when-selecting-a-vendor
[23] http://sandhill.com/article/how-to-evaluate-saas-vendors-five-key-considerations

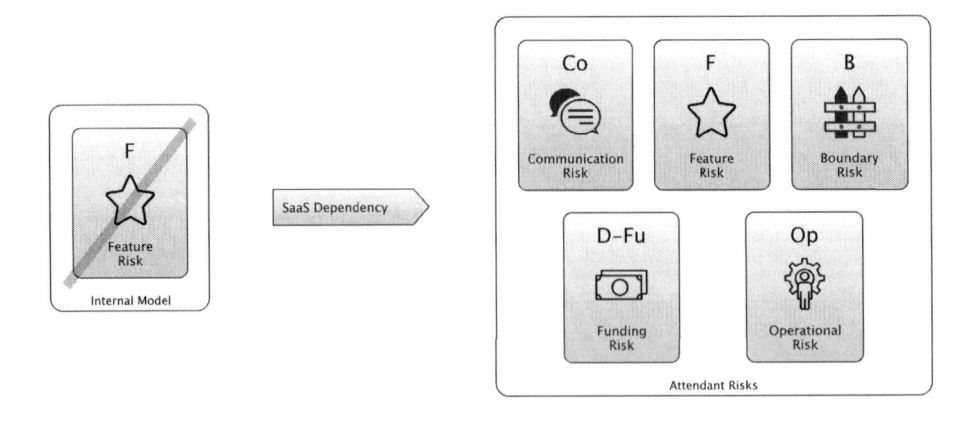

Figure 17.9: Risk Tradeoff From Using Software as a Service (SaaS)

17.4 A Matrix of Options

We've looked at just 3 different ways of providing a software dependency: Code-Your-Own, Libraries and SaaS.

But these are not the only ways to do it, and there's clearly no one *right* way. Although here we have looked just at "Commercial SaaS" and "Free Open Source", in reality, these are just points in a two-dimensional space involving *Pricing* and *Hosting*.

Let's expand this view slightly and look at where different pieces of software sit on these axes:

- Where there is value in **the Network Effect**[24] it's often a sign that the software will be free, or open source: programming languages and Linux are the obvious examples of this. Bugs are easier to find when there are lots of eyes looking, and learning the skill to use the software has less Boundary Risk if you know you'll be able to use it at any point in the future.
- At the other end of the spectrum, clients will happily pay for software if it clearly **reduces Operational Risk**. Take Amazon Web Services (AWS)[25]. The essential trade here is that you substitute the complexity of hosting and maintaining various pieces of hardware, in exchange for metered payments (Funding Risk for you). Since the AWS *interfaces* are specific to Amazon, there is significant Boundary Risk in choosing this option.

---

[24] https://en.wikipedia.org/wiki/Network_effect
[25] https://en.wikipedia.org/wiki/Amazon_Web_Services

Pricing	On Premises 3rd Party	In Cloud / Browser 3rd Party	Risk Profile
Free	**OSS Libraries** • Tools • Java • Firefox • Linux • Programming Languages	**Freemium** • Splunk • Spotify • GitHub	• Low Boundary Risk Drives Adoption • Value In Network Effect
Advertising Supported	**Commercial Software** • Phone Apps • e.g. Angry Birds	**Commercial SaaS** • Google Search • GMail • Twitter	• Low Boundary Risk • High Availability Of Substitutes
Monthly / Metered Subscription	**Commercial Software** • Oracle Database • Windows • Office	**Commercial SaaS** • Office 365 • Amazon Web Services • SalesForce	Easy arguments for reduced: • Complexity Risk • Communication Risk • Coordination Risk Higher Boundary Risk

Figure 17.10: Software Dependencies, Pricing, Delivery Matrix Risk Profiles

- In the middle there are lots of **substitute options** and therefore high competition. Because of this prices are pushed towards zero and therefore often advertising is used to monetise the product. Angry Birds[26] is a classic example: initially, it had demo and paid versions, however Rovio[27] discovered there was much more money to be made through advertising than from the paid-for app[28].

17.5 Software Dependencies as Features

So far we've looked at different *approaches* to software dependencies and the risk profiles they present. But the category is less important than the specifics: we are choosing *specific tools for specific tasks*. Software Dependencies allows us to construct dependency networks to give us all kinds of features and mitigate all kinds of risk. That is, the features we are looking for in a dependency *are to mitigate some kind of risk*.

For example, I might start using WhatsApp[29] because I want to be able to send my friends photos and text messages. However, it's likely that those same features allow us to mitigate Coordination Risk when we're next trying to meet up.

Let's look at some more examples:

Risk	Software Mitigating That Risk
Coordination Risk	Calendar tools, Bug Tracking, Distributed Databases
Schedule-Risk	Planning Software, Project Management Software
Communication-Risk	Email, Chat tools, CRM tools like SalesForce, Forums, Twitter, Protocols
Process-Risk	Reporting tools, online forms, process tracking tools
Agency-Risk	Auditing tools, transaction logs, Time-Sheet software, HR Software
Operational-Risk	Support tools like ZenDesk, Grafana, InfluxDB, Geneos, Security Tools
Feature-Risk	Every piece of software you use!

---

[26] https://en.wikipedia.org/wiki/Angry_Birds
[27] https://en.wikipedia.org/wiki/Rovio_Entertainment
[28] https://www.deconstructoroffun.com/blog/2017/6/11/how-angry-birds-2-multiplied-quadrupled-revenue-in-a-year
[29] https://en.wikipedia.org/wiki/WhatsApp

17.6 Choice

Choosing dependencies can be extremely difficult. As we discussed above, the usefulness of any tool depends on its fit for purpose, its *ergonomics within a given context*. It's all too easy to pick a good tool for the wrong job:

> "I suppose it is tempting, if the only tool you have is a hammer, to treat everything as if it were a nail."
> —Abraham Maslow, *Toward a Psychology of Being*[30]

Having chosen a dependency, whether or not you end up in a more favourable position risk-wise is going to depend heavily on the quality of the execution and the skill of the implementor. With software dependencies we often have to live with the decisions we make for a long time: *choosing* the software dependency is far easier than *changing it later*.

Let's take a closer look at this problem in the chapter on Boundary Risk. But first, lets looks at processes.

---

[30] https://en.wiktionary.org/wiki/if_all_you_have_is_a_hammer,_everything_looks_like_a_nail

CHAPTER 18

Process Risk

Process Risk is the risk you take on whenever you embark on completing a *process*.

> "**Process**: a process is a set of activities that interact to achieve a result."
>
> —Process, *Wikipedia*[1]

Processes commonly involve *forms*: if you're filling out a form (whether on paper or on a computer) then you're involved in a process of some sort, whether an "Account Registration" process, "Loan Application" process or "Consumer Satisfaction Survey" process. Sometimes, they involve events occurring: a build process[2] might start after you commit some code, for example. The *code we write* is usually describing some kind of process we want performed.

18.1 The Purpose Of Process

As Figure 18.1 shows, process exists to mitigate other kinds of risk. For example:

- **Coordination Risk**: you can often use process to help people coordinate. For example, a Production Line[3] is a process where work being done by one person is pushed to the next person when it's done. A room booking process is designed to efficiently allocate meeting rooms.

---

[1]https://en.wikipedia.org/wiki/Process
[2]https://en.wikipedia.org/wiki/Software_build
[3]https://en.wikipedia.org/wiki/Production_line

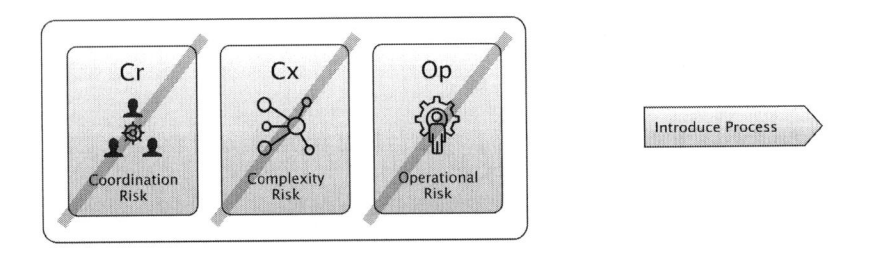

Figure 18.1: Introducing process can mitigate many risks

- **Operational Risk**: this encompasses the risk of people *not doing their job properly*. But, by having a process, (and asking, did this person follow the process?) you can draw a distinction between a process failure and a personnel failure. For example, accepting funds from a money launderer *could* be a failure of a bank employee. But, if they followed the *process*, it's a failure of the Process itself.
- **Complexity Risk**: working *within a process* can reduce the amount of Complexity you have to think about. We accept that processes are going to slow us down, but we appreciate the reduction in risk this brings. Clearly, the complexity hasn't gone away, but it's hidden within design of the process. For example, McDonalds[4] tries to design its operation so that preparing each food item is a simple process to follow, reducing complexity (and training time) for the staff.

These are all examples of Risk Mitigation for the *owners* of the process. But often the *consumers* of the process end up picking up Process Risks as a result:

- **Invisibility Risk**: it's often not possible to see how far along a process is to completion. Sometimes, you can do this to an extent. For example, when I send a package for delivery, I can see roughly how far it's got on the tracking website. But this is still less-than-complete information and is a representation of reality.
- **Dead-End Risk**: even if you have the right process, initiating a process has no guarantee that your efforts won't be wasted and you'll be back where you started from. The chances of this happening increase as you get further from the standard use-case for the process, and the sunk cost increases with the length of time the process takes to complete.

---

[4] https://en.wikipedia.org/wiki/McDonald's

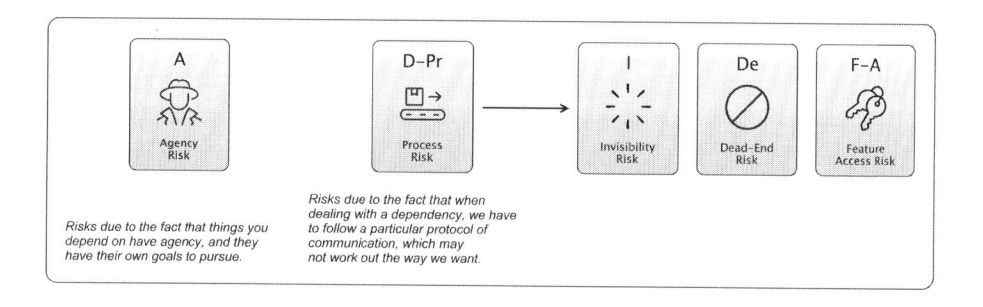

Figure 18.2: Process Risk, and its consequences, compared with Agency Risk

- **Feature Access Risk**: processes generally handle the common stuff, but ignore the edge cases. For example, a form on a website might not be designed to be accessible to disabled people, or might only cater to some common subset of use-cases.

When we talk about "Process Risk" we are really referring to these types of risks, arising from "following a set of instructions." Compare this with Agency Risk (which we will review in a forthcoming chapter), which is risks due to *not* following the instructions, as shown in Figure 18.2 . Let's look at two examples, how Process Risk can lead to Invisibility Risks and Agency Risk.

Processes And Invisibility Risk

Processes tend to work well for the common cases because *practice makes perfect*, but they are really tested when unusual situations occur. Expanding processes to deal with edge-cases incurs Complexity Risk, so often it's better to try and have clear boundaries of what is "in" and "out" of the process' domain.

Sometimes, processes are *not* used commonly. How can we rely on them anyway? Usually, the answer is to build in extra feedback loops:

- Testing that backups work, even when no backup is needed.
- Running through a disaster recovery scenario at the weekend.
- Increasing the release cadence, so that we practice the release process more.

The feedback loops allow us to perform Retrospectives and Reviews to improve our processes.

Processes, Sign-Offs and Agency Risk

Often, Processes will include sign-off steps. The Sign-Off is an interesting mechanism:

- By signing off on something for the business, people are usually in some part staking their reputation on something being right.
- Therefore, you would expect that sign-off involves a lot of Agency Risk: people don't want to expose themselves in career-limiting ways.
- Therefore, the bigger the risk they are being asked to swallow, the more cumbersome and protracted the sign-off process.

Often, Sign-Offs boil down to a balance of risk for the signer: on the one hand, *personal, career risk* from signing off, on the other, the risk of upsetting the rest of the staff waiting for the sign-off, and the Dead End Risk of all the effort gone into getting the sign-off if they don't.

This is a nasty situation, but there are a couple of ways to de-risk this:

- Break Sign-Offs down into bite-size chunks of risk that are acceptable to those doing the signing-off.
- Agree far-in-advance the sign-off criteria. As discussed in Risk Theory, people have a habit of heavily discounting future risk, and it's much easier to get agreement on the *criteria* than it is to get the sign-off.

18.2 Evolution Of Process

Writing software and designing processes are often overlapping activities. Often we build processes when we are writing software. Since designing a process is an activity like any other on a project, you can expect that the Risk-First explanation for why we do this is *risk management*.

Processes arise because of a desire to mitigate risk. When whole organisations follow that desire independently, they end up following an evolutionary or gradient-descent approach to risk reduction (as we will see below).

Here, we are going to look at how a Business Process[5] might mature within an organisation.

> "**Business Process** or **Business Method** is a collection of related, structured activities or tasks that in a specific sequence

---
[5]https://en.wikipedia.org/wiki/Business_process

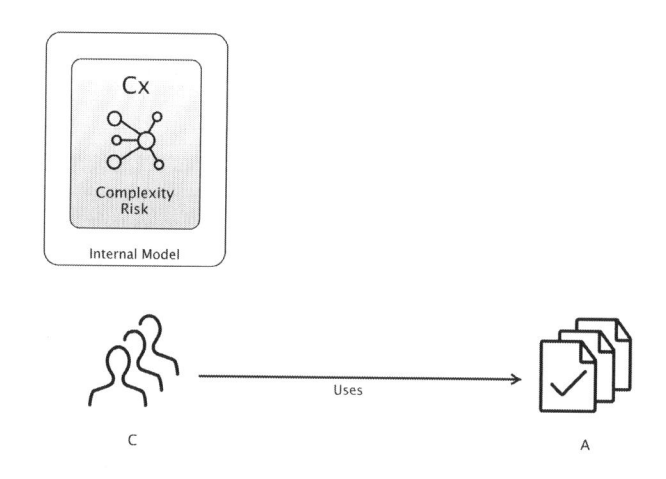

Figure 18.3: Step 1: clients C need A to do their jobs, incurring Complexity Risk.

produces a service or product (serves a particular business goal) for a particular customer or customers."
—Business Process, *Wikipedia*[6]

Let's look at an example of how that can happen in a step-wise way.

1. As Figure 18.3 shows, there exists a group of people inside a company C, which need a certain something A in order to get their jobs done. Because they are organising, providing and creating A to do their jobs, they are responsible for all the Complexity Risk of A.

2. Because A is risky, a new team (B) is spun up to deal with the Complexity Risk, which might let C get on with their "proper" jobs. As shown in Figure 18.4, this is really useful: C's is job much easier (reduced Complexity Risk) as they have an easier path to A than before. But the risk for A hasn't really gone - they're now just dependent on B instead. When members of B fail to deliver, this is Staff Risk for C.

3. Problems are likely to occur eventually in the B/C relationship. Perhaps some members of the B team give better service than others, or deal

---
[6]https://en.wikipedia.org/wiki/Business_process

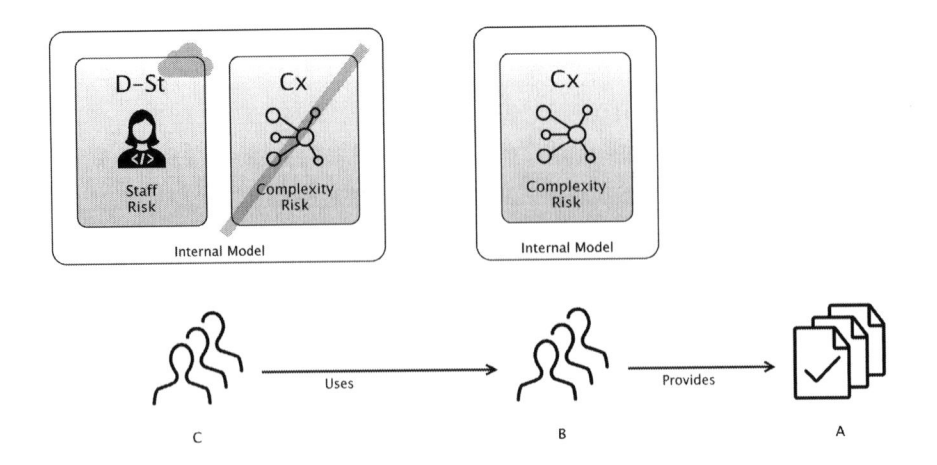

Figure 18.4: Step 2: team B doing A for clients C. Complexity Risk is transferred to B, but C pick up Staff Risk.

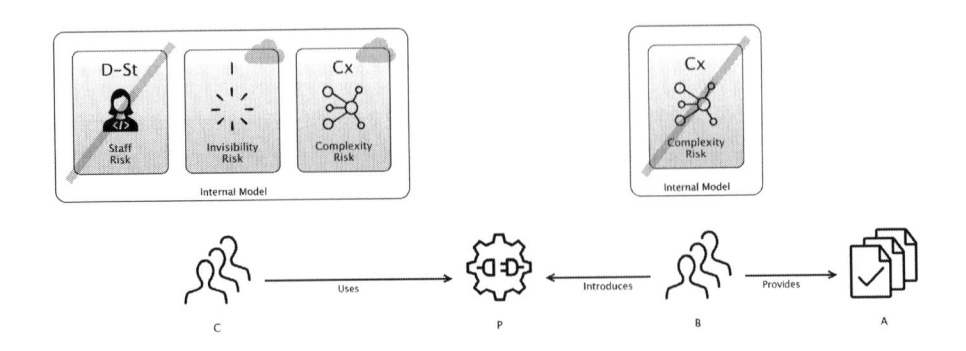

Figure 18.5: Step 3: team B formalises the dependency with a Process

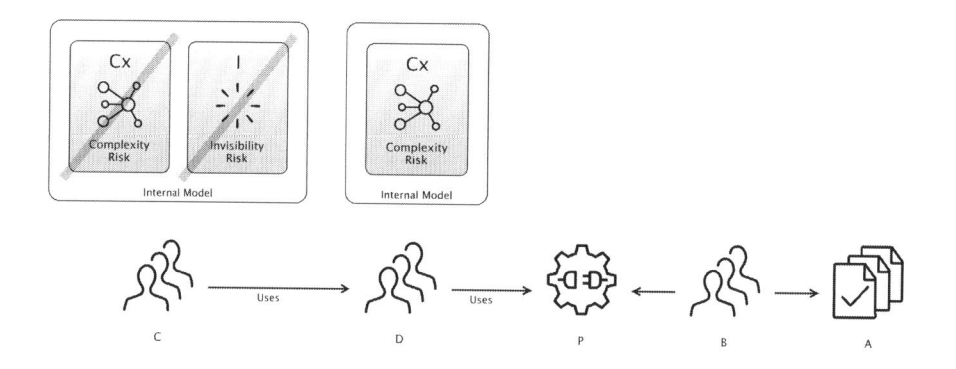

Figure 18.6: Person D acts as a middleman for customers needing some variant of A, transferring Complexity Risk

with more variety in requests? In order to standardise the response from B and also to reduce scope-creep in requests from C, B organises bureaucratically so that there is a controlled process (P) by which A can be accessed. Members of teams B and C now interact via some request mechanism like forms (or another protocol).

- As shown in Figure 18.5, because of P, B can now process requests on a first-come-first-served basis and deal with them all in the same way: the more unusual requests from C might not fit the model. These Process Risks are now the problem of the form-filler in C.
- Since this is Abstraction, C now has Invisibility Risk since it can't access team B and see how it works.
- Team B may also use P to introduce other bureaucracy like authorisation and sign-off steps or payment barriers. All of this increases Process Risk for team C.

4. Teams like B can sometimes end up in "Monopoly" positions within a business. This means that clients like C are forced to deal with whatever process B wishes to enforce. Although they are unable to affect process P, C still have risks they want to transfer.

- In Figure 18.6, Person D, who has experience working with team B acts as a middleman for some of C, requiring some variant of A . They are able to help navigate the bureaucracy (handle with Process Risk).

- The cycle potentially starts again: will D end up becoming a new team, with a new process?

In this example, you can see how the organisation evolves process to mitigate risk around the use (and misuse) of A. This is an example of *Process following Strategy*:

> In this conception, you can see how the structure of an organisation (the teams and processes within it, the hierarchy of control) will 'evolve' from the resources of the organisation and the strategy it pursues. Processes evolve to meet the needs of the organisation."
>
> —Henry Minzberg, *Strategy Safari*[7]

Two key take-aways from this:

- **The System Gets More Complex**: with different teams working to mitigate different risks in different ways, we end up with a more complex situation than when we started. Although we've *evolved* in this direction by mitigating risks, it's not necessarily the case that the end result is *more efficient*. In fact, as we will see in Map-And-Territory Risk, this evolution can lead to some very inadequate (but nonetheless stable) systems.
- **Organisational process evolves to mitigate risk**: just as we've shown that actions are about mitigating risk, we've now seen that these actions get taken in an evolutionary way. That is, there is "pressure" on our internal processes to reduce risk. The people maintaining these processes feel the risk, and modify their processes in response. Let's look at a real-life example:

18.3 An Example - Release Processes

Over the years I have worked in the Finance Industry it's given me time to observe how, across an entire industry, process can evolve both in response to regulatory pressure, organisational maturity and mitigating risk:

1. Initially, I could release software by logging onto the production accounts with a shared password that everyone knew, and deploy software or change data in the database.

---

[7]http://www.mintzberg.org/books/strategy-safari

2. The first issue with this is Agency Risk from bad actors: how could you know that the numbers weren't being altered in the databases? *Production Auditing* was introduced so that at least you could tell what was being changed and when, in order to point the blame later.
3. But there was still plenty of scope for deliberate or accidental Dead-End Risk damage. Next, passwords were taken out of the hands of developers and you needed approval to "break glass" to get onto production.
4. The increasing complexity (and therefore Complexity Risk) in production environments meant that sometimes changes collided with each other, or were performed at inopportune times. Change Requests were introduced. This is an approval process which asks you to describe what you want to change in production, and why you want to change it.
5. The change request software is generally awful, making the job of raising change requests tedious and time-consuming. Therefore, developers would *automate* the processes for release, sometimes including the process to write the change request. This allowed them to improve release cadence at the expense of owning more code.
6. Auditors didn't like the fact that this automation existed, because effectively, that meant that developers could get access to production with the press of a button, taking you back to step 1...

18.4 Bureaucracy

Where we've talked about process evolution above, the actors involved have been acting in good faith: they are working to mitigate risk in the organisation. The Process Risk that accretes along the way is an *unintended consequence*: There is no guarantee that the process that arises will be humane and intuitive. Many organisational processes end up being baroque or Kafka-esque, forcing unintuitive behaviour on their users. This is partly because process design is *hard* and it's difficult to anticipate all the various ways a process will be used ahead-of-time.

But Parkinson's Law[8] takes this one step further: the human actors shaping the organisation will abuse their positions of power in order to further their own careers (this is Agency Risk, which we will come to in a future chapter):

> "Parkinson's law is the adage that "work expands so as to fill the time available for its completion". It is sometimes applied to

---
[8] https://en.wikipedia.org/wiki/Parkinsons_law

the growth of bureaucracy in an organisation... He explains this growth by two forces: (1) 'An official wants to multiply subordinates, not rivals' and (2) 'Officials make work for each other.'"

—Parkinson's Law, *Wikipedia*[9]

This implies that there is a tendency for organisations to end up with *needless levels of Process Risk*.

To fix this, design needs to happen at a higher level. In our code, we would Refactor these processes to remove the unwanted complexity. In a business, it requires re-organisation at a higher level to redefine the boundaries and responsibilities between the teams.

Next in the tour of Dependency Risks, it's time to look at Boundary Risk.

---

[9]https://en.wikipedia.org/wiki/Parkinsons_law

CHAPTER 19

Boundary Risk

In the previous chapters on Dependency Risk we've touched on Boundary Risk several times, but now it's time to tackle it head-on and discuss this important type of risk.

As shown in Figure 19.1, Boundary Risk is the risk we face due to *commitments* around dependencies and the limitations they place on our ability to change. To illustrate, lets consider two examples:

- Although I eat cereals for breakfast, I don't have Boundary Risk on them. If the supermarket runs out of cereals when I go, I can just buy some other food and eat that.
- However the hot water system in my house uses gas. If that's not available I can't just switch to using oil or solar without cost. There is Boundary Risk, but it's low because the supply of gas is plentiful and seems like it will stay that way.

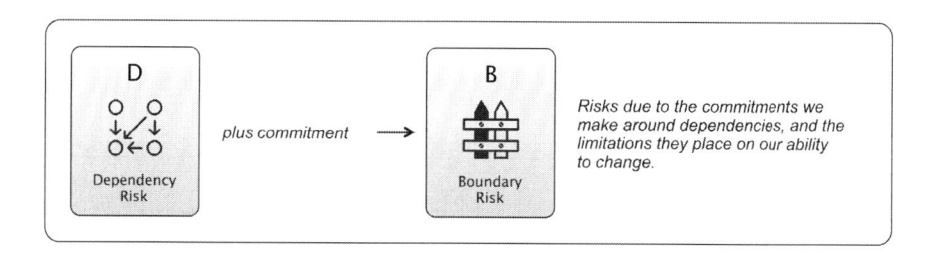

Figure 19.1: Boundary Risk is due to Dependency Risk and commitment

165

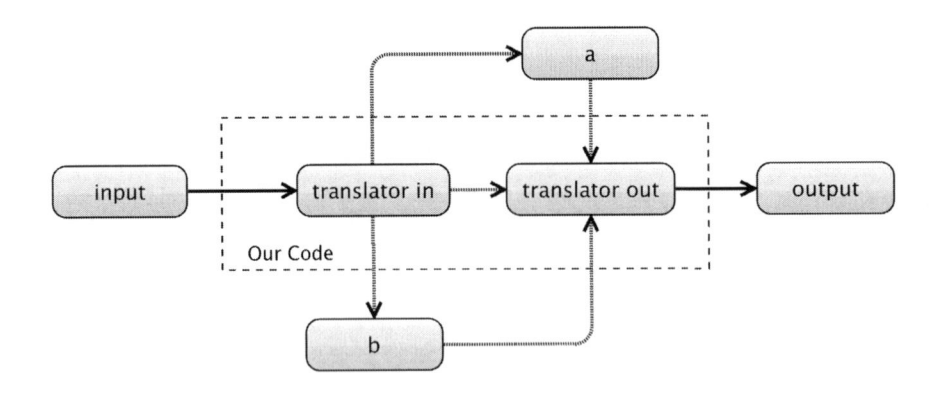

*Figure 19.2: Our System receives data from the **input**, translates it and sends it to the **output**. But which dependency should we use for the translation, if any?*

In terms of the Risk Landscape, Boundary Risk is exactly as it says: a *boundary, wall* or other kind of obstacle in your way to making a move you want to make. This changes the nature of the Risk Landscape, and introduces a maze-like component to it. It also means that we have to make *commitments* about which way to go, knowing that our future paths are constrained by the decisions we make.

As we discussed in Complexity Risk, there is always the chance we end up at a Dead End, having done work that we need to throw away. In this case, we'll have to head back and make a different decision.

19.1 In Software Development

In software development, although we might face Boundary Risk choosing staff or offices, most of the everyday dependency commitments we have to make are around *abstractions*.

As discussed in Software Dependency Risk, if we are going to use a software tool as a dependency, we have to accept the complexity of its protocols. You have to use its protocol: it won't come to you.

Let's take a look at a hypothetical system structure, in Figure 19.2. In this design, we are transforming data from the **input** to the **output**. But how should we do it?

- We could transform via library 'a', using the Protocols of 'a', and having a dependency on 'a'.
- We could use library 'b', using the Protocols of 'b', and having a dependency on 'b'.
- We could use neither, and avoid the dependency, but potentially pick up lots more Codebase Risk and Schedule Risk because we have to code our own alternative to 'a' and 'b'.

The choice of approach presents us with Boundary Risk because we don't know that we'll necessarily be successful with any of these options until we *go down the path* of committing to one:

- Maybe 'a' has some undocumented drawbacks that are going to hold us up.
- Maybe 'b' works on some streaming API basis, that is incompatible with the input protocol.
- Maybe 'a' runs on Windows, whereas our code runs on Linux

... and so on.

This is a toy example, but in real life this dilemma occurs when we choose between database vendors, cloud hosting platforms, operating systems, software libraries etc. and it was a big factor in our analysis of Software Dependency Risk.

19.2 Factors In Boundary Risk

The degree of Boundary Risk is dependent on a number of factors:

- **The Sunk Cost** of the Learning Curve we've overcome to integrate the dependency, which may fail to live up to expectations (*cf.* Feature Fit Risks). We can avoid accreting this by choosing the *simplest* and *fewest* dependencies for any task, and trying to Meet Reality quickly.
- **Life Expectancy**: libraries and products come and go. A choice that was popular when it was made may be superseded in the future by something better. (*cf.* Market Risk). This may not be a problem until you try to renew a support contract, or try to do an operating system update. Although no-one can predict how long a technology will last, The Lindy Effect[1] suggests that *future life expectancy is proportional to*

---
[1] https://en.wikipedia.org/wiki/Lindy_effect

current age. So, you might expect a technology that has been around for ten years to be around for a further ten.
- **The level of Lock In**, where the cost of switching to a new dependency in the future is some function of the level of commitment to the current dependency. As an example, consider the level of commitment you have to your mother tongue. If you have spent your entire life committed to learning and communicating in English, there is a massive level of lock-in. Overcoming this to become fluent in Chinese may be an overwhelming task.
- **Future needs**: will the dependency satisfy your expanding requirements going forward? (*cf.* Feature Drift Risk)
- **Ownership changes:** Microsoft buys GitHub[2]. What will happen to the ecosystem around GitHub now?
- **Licensing changes:** (e.g. Oracle[3] buys Tangosol who make Coherence[4] for example). Having done this, they increase the licensing costs of Coherence to huge levels, milking the Cash Cow[5] of the installed user-base, but ensuring no-one else is likely to commit to it in the future.

19.3 Ecosystems and Lock-In

Sometimes, one choice leads to another, and you're forced to "double down" on your original choice, and head further down the path of commitment.

On the face of it, WordPress[6] and Drupal[7] *should* be very similar:

- They are both Content Management Systems[8].
- They both use a LAMP (Linux, Apache, MySql, PHP) Stack[9].
- They were both started around the same time (2001 for Drupal, 2003 for WordPress).
- They are both Open-Source, and have a wide variety of *plugins*[10], that is, ways for other programmers to extend the functionality in new directions.

But crucially, the underlying abstractions of WordPress and Drupal are different, so the plugins available for each are different. The quality and choice

---
[2]https://en.wikipedia.org/wiki/GitHub
[3]http://oracle.com
[4]https://en.wikipedia.org/wiki/Oracle_Coherence
[5]https://en.wikipedia.org/wiki/Cash_cow
[6]https://en.wikipedia.org/wiki/WordPress
[7]https://en.wikipedia.org/wiki/Drupal
[8]https://en.wikipedia.org/wiki/Content_management_system
[9]https://en.wikipedia.org/wiki/LAMP_(software_bundle)
[10]https://en.wikipedia.org/wiki/Plug-in_(computing)

of plugins for a given platform, along with factors such as community and online documentation, is often called its *ecosystem*:

> "... a set of businesses functioning as a unit and interacting with a shared market for software and services, together with relationships among them. These relationships are frequently underpinned by a common technological platform and operate through the exchange of information, resources, and artifacts."
> —Software Ecosystem, *Wikipedia*[11]

You can think of the ecosystem as being like the footprint of a town or a city, consisting of the buildings, transport network and the people that live there. Within the city, and because of the transport network and the amenities available, it's easy to make rapid, useful moves on the Risk Landscape. In a software ecosystem it's the same: the ecosystem has gathered together to provide a way to mitigate various different Feature Risks in a common way.

Ecosystem size is one key determinant of Boundary Risk:

- **A large ecosystem** has a large boundary circumference. Boundary Risk is lower in a large ecosystem because your moves on the Risk Landscape are unlikely to collide with it. The boundary *got large* because other developers before you hit the boundary and did the work building the software equivalents of bridges and roads and pushing it back so that the boundary didn't get in their way.
- In **a small ecosystem**, you are much more likely to come into contact with the edges of the boundary. *You* will have to be the developer that pushes back the frontier and builds the roads for the others. This is hard work.

Big Ecosystems Get Bigger

In the real world, there is a tendency for *big cities to get bigger*. The more people that live there, the more services they provide and need, and therefore, the more immigrants they attract. It's the same in the software world too. In both cases, this is due to the *Network Effect*:

> "... the positive effect described in economics and business that an additional user of a good or service has on the value of that product to others. When a network effect is present, the

---
[11] https://en.wikipedia.org/wiki/Software_ecosystem

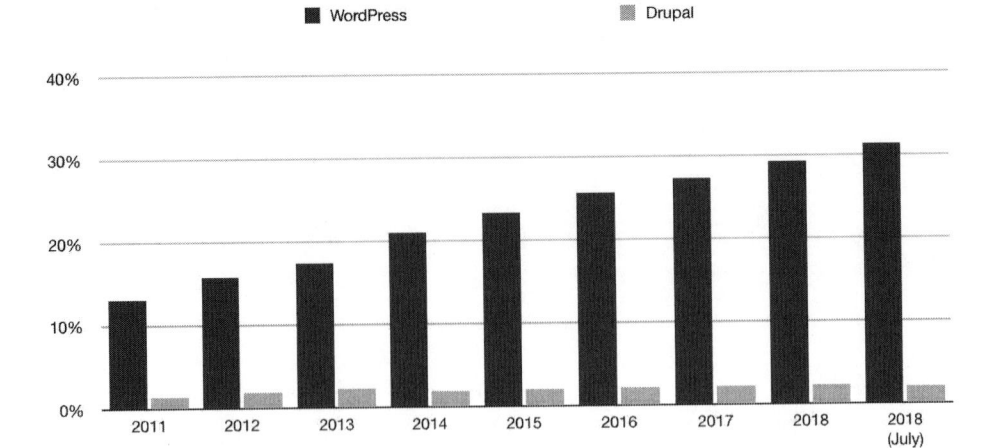

Figure 19.3: WordPress vs Drupal adoption over 8 years, according to w3techs.com[13]

value of a product or service increases according to the number of others using it."

—Network Effect, *Wikipedia*[12]

You can see the same effect in the software ecosystems with the adoption rates of WordPress and Drupal, shown in Figure 19.3. Note: this is over *all sites on the internet*, so Drupal accounts for hundreds of thousands of sites. In 2018, WordPress is approximately 32% of all web-sites. For Drupal it's 2%.

Did WordPress gain this march because it was always *better* than Drupal? That's arguable. Certainly, they're not different enough that WordPress is 16x better. That it's this way round could be *entirely accidental*, and a result of Network Effect.

But, by now, if they *are* to be compared side-by-side, WordPress *might be better* due to the sheer number of people in this ecosystem who are...

- Creating web sites.
- Using those sites.
- Submitting bug requests.
- Fixing bugs.
- Writing documentation.
- Building plugins.

---

[12]https://en.wikipedia.org/wiki/Network_effect

- Creating features.
- Improving the core platform.

But is bigger always better? Perhaps not.

Big Ecosystems Are More Complex

When a tool or platform is popular, it is under pressure to increase in complexity. This is because people are attracted to something useful and want to extend it to new purposes. This is known as *The Peter Principle*:

> "The Peter principle is a concept in management developed by Laurence J. Peter, which observes that people in a hierarchy tend to rise to their 'level of incompetence'."
> —The Peter Principle, *Wikipedia*[14]

Although designed for *people*, it can just as easily be applied to any other dependency you can think of. This means when things get popular, there is a tendency towards Conceptual Integrity Risk and Complexity Risk.

Figure 19.4 is an example of this: look at how the number of public classes in Java (a good proxy for the boundary) has increased with each release.

Backward Compatibility

As we saw in Software Dependency Risk, The art of good design is to afford the greatest increase in functionality with the smallest increase in complexity possible, and this usually means Refactoring[15]. But, this is at odds with Backward Compatibility.

Each new version has a greater functional scope than the one before (pushing back Boundary Risk), making the platform more attractive to build solutions in. But this increases the Complexity Risk as there is more functionality to deal with.

You can see in Figure 19.5 the Peter Principle at play: as more responsibility is given to a dependency, the more complex it gets and the greater the learning curve to work with it. Large ecosystems like Java react to Learning Curve Risk by having copious amounts of literature to read or buy to help, but it is still off-putting.

---

[14]https://en.wikipedia.org/wiki/Peter_principle
[15]https://en.wikipedia.org/wiki/Refactoring

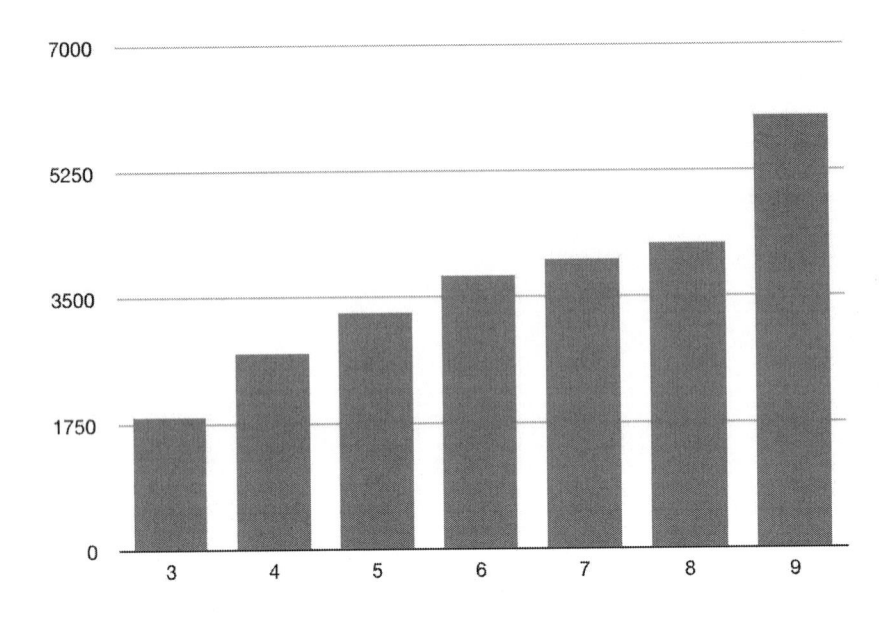

Figure 19.4: Java Public Classes By Version (3-9)

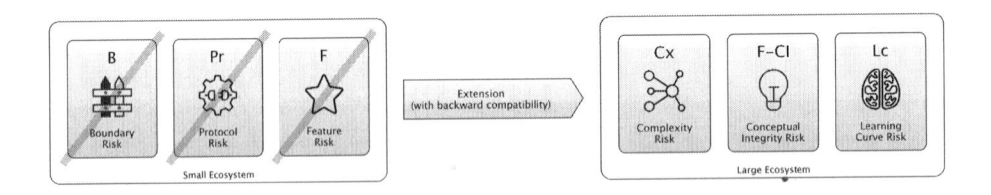

Figure 19.5: Tradeoff between large and small ecosystems

Because Complexity is Mass, large ecosystems can't respond quickly to Feature Drift. This means that when the world changes, new ecosystems are likely to appear to fill gaps, rather than old ones moving in.

19.4 Managing Boundary Risk

Let's look at two ways in which we can manage Boundary Risk: *bridges* and *standards*.

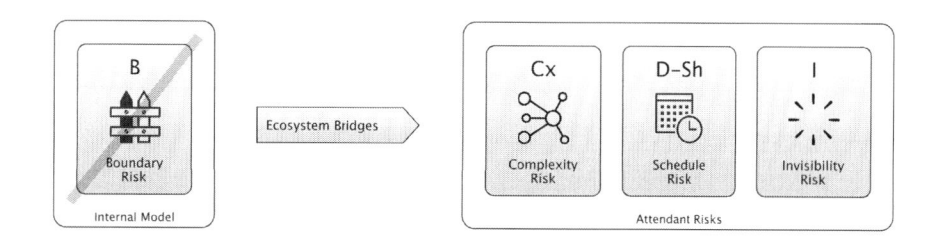

Figure 19.6: Boundary Risk is mitigated when a bridge is built between ecosystems

Ecosystem Bridges

Sometimes, technology comes along that allows us to cross boundaries, like a *bridge* or a *road*. This has the effect of making it easy to to go from one self-contained ecosystem to another. Going back to WordPress, a simple example might be the Analytics Dashboard[16] which provides Google Analytics[17] functionality inside WordPress.

I find, a lot of code I write is of this nature: trying to write the *glue code* to join together two different *ecosystems*.

As shown in Figure 19.6, mitigating Boundary Risk involves taking on complexity. The more Protocol Complexity there is on either side of the two ecosystems, the more complex the bridge will necessarily be. The below table shows some examples of this.

Protocol Risk From A	Protocol Risk From B	Resulting Bridge Complexity	Example
Low	Low	Simple	Changing from one date format to another.
High	Low	Moderate	Status Dashboard.
High	High	Complex	Object-Relational Mapping (ORM) Tools.

---

[16]https://en-gb.wordpress.org/plugins/google-analytics-dashboard-for-wp/
[17]https://en.wikipedia.org/wiki/Google_Marketing_Platform

From examining the Protocol Risk at each end of the bridge you are creating, you can get a rough idea of how complex the endeavour will be:

- If it's low-risk at both ends, you're probably going to be able to knock it out easily. Like translating a date, or converting one file format to another.
- Where one of the protocols is *evolving*, you're definitely going to need to keep releasing new versions. The functionality of a `Calculator` app on my phone remains the same, but new versions have to be released as the phone APIs change, screens change resolution and so on.

Standards

Standards mitigate Boundary Risk in one of two ways:

1. **Abstract over the ecosystems.** Provide a *standard* protocol (a *lingua franca*) which can be converted down into the protocol of any of a number of competing ecosystems.

    - The C[18] programming language provided a way to get the same programs compiled against different CPU instruction sets, therefore providing some *portability* to code.

    - Java[19] took what C did and went one step further, providing interoperability at the library level. Java code could run anywhere where Java was installed.

2. **Force adoption.** All of the ecosystems start using the standard for fear of being left out in the cold. Sometimes, a standards body is involved, but other times a "de facto" standard emerges that everyone adopts.

    - ASCII[20]: fixed the different-character-sets Boundary Risk by being a standard that others could adopt. Before everyone agreed on ASCII, copying data from one computer system to another was a massive pain, and would involve some kind of translation. Unicode[21] continues this work.

---

[18]https://en.wikipedia.org/wiki/C_(programming_language)
[19]https://en.wikipedia.org/wiki/Java_(programming_language)
[20]https://en.wikipedia.org/wiki/ASCII
[21]https://en.wikipedia.org/wiki/Unicode

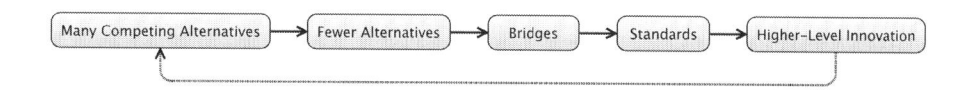

Figure 19.7: Boundary Risk Decreases With Bridges and Standards

- Internet Protocol. As we saw in Communication Risk, the Internet Protocol (IP) is the *lingua franca* of the modern Internet. However, at one period of time, there were many competing standards. IP was the ecosystem that "won", and was subsequently standardised by the IETF[22]. This is actually an example of *both* approaches: as we saw in Communication Risk, Internet Protocol is also an abstraction over lower-level protocols.

19.5 Boundary Risk Cycle

Boundary Risk seems to progress in cycles. As a piece of technology becomes more mature, there are more standards and bridges, and Boundary Risk is lower. Once Boundary Risk is low and a particular approach is proven, there will be innovation upon this, giving rise to new opportunities for Boundary Risk (see Figure 19.7). Here are some examples:

- **Processor Chips.** By providing features (instructions) on their processors that other vendors didn't have, manufacturers made their processors more attractive to system integrators. However, since the instructions were different on different chips, this created Boundary Risk for the integrators. Intel and Microsoft were able to use this fact to build a big ecosystem around Windows running on Intel chips (so called, WinTel). The Intel instruction set is nowadays a *de-facto* standard for PCs.

- **Browsers.** In the late 1990s, faced with the emergence of the nascent World Wide Web, and the Netscape Navigator[23] browser, Microsoft[24] adopted a strategy known as Embrace and Extend[25]. The idea of this was to subvert the HTML standard to their own ends by *embracing* the standard and creating their own browser Internet Explorer and then *extending* it with as much functionality as possible, which would then

---
[22]https://en.wikipedia.org/wiki/Internet_Engineering_Task_Force
[23]https://en.wikipedia.org/wiki/Netscape_Navigator
[24]https://en.wikipedia.org/wiki/Microsoft
[25]https://en.wikipedia.org/wiki/Embrace_and_extend

not work in Netscape Navigator. They then embarked on a campaign to try and get everyone to "upgrade" to Internet Explorer. In this way, they hoped to "own" the Internet, or at least, the software of the browser, which they saw as analogous to being the "operating system" of the Internet, and therefore a threat to their own operating system, Windows[26].

- **Mobile Operating Systems.** We currently have just two main *mobile* ecosystems (although there used to be many more): Apple's iOS[27] and Google's Android[28], which are both *very* different and complex ecosystems with large, complex boundaries. They are both innovating as fast as possible to keep users happy with their features. Bridging tools like Xamarin[29] exist which allow you to build applications sharing code over both platforms.

- **Cloud Computing.** Amazon Web Services (AWS) are competing with Microsoft Azure[30] and Google Cloud Platform[31] over building tools for Platform as a Service (PaaS)[32] (running software in the cloud). They are both racing to build new functionality, but it's hard to move from one vendor to another as there is no standardisation on the tools.

19.6 Everyday Boundary Risks

Although ecosystems are one very pernicious type of boundary in software development, it's worth pointing out that Boundary Risk occurs all the time. Let's look at some ways:

- **Configuration**. When software has to be deployed onto a server, there has to be configuration (usually on the command line, or via configuration property files) in order to bridge the boundary between the *environment it's running in* and the *software being run*. Often this is setting up file locations, security keys and passwords, and telling it where to find other files and services.

- **Integration Testing**. Building a unit test is easy. You are generally testing some code you have written, aided with a testing framework.

---

[26] https://en.wikipedia.org/wiki/Microsoft_Windows
[27] https://en.wikipedia.org/wiki/IOS
[28] https://en.wikipedia.org/wiki/Android_(operating_system)
[29] https://en.wikipedia.org/wiki/Xamarin
[30] https://en.wikipedia.org/wiki/Microsoft_Azure
[31] https://en.wikipedia.org/wiki/Google_Cloud_Platform
[32] https://en.wikipedia.org/wiki/Platform_as_a_service

Your code and the framework are both written in the same language, which means low Boundary Risk. But to *integration test* you need to step outside this boundary and so it becomes much harder. This is true whether you are integrating with other systems (providing or supplying them with data) or parts of your own system (say testing the client-side and server parts together).

- **User Interface Testing**. The interface with the user is a complex, under-specified risky protocol. Although tools exist to automate UI testing (such as Selenium[33], these rarely satisfactorily mitigate this protocol risk: can you be sure that the screen hasn't got strange glitches, that the mouse moves correctly, that the proportions on the screen are correct on all browsers?

- **Jobs**. When you pick a new technology to learn and add to your CV, it's worth keeping in mind how useful this will be to you in the future. It's career-limiting to be stuck in a dying ecosystem with the need to retrain.

- **Teams**. if you're asked to build a new tool for an existing team, are you creating Boundary Risk by using tools that the team aren't familiar with?

- **Organisations**. Getting teams or departments to work with each other often involves breaking down Boundary Risk. Often the departments use different tool-sets or processes, and have different goals making the translation harder.

19.7 Patterns In Boundary Risk

In Feature Risk, we saw that the features people need change over time. Let's get more specific about this:

- **Human need is Fractal**[34]: this means that over time, software products have evolved to more closely map human needs. Software that would have delighted us ten years ago lacks the sophistication we expect today.

- **Software and hardware are both improving with time**: due to evolution and the ability to support greater and greater levels of complexity.

---

[33]https://en.wikipedia.org/wiki/Selenium_(software)
[34]https://en.wikipedia.org/wiki/Fractal

- **Abstractions accrete too**: as we saw in Process Risk, we *encapsulate* earlier abstractions in order to build later ones.

The only thing we can expect in the future is that the lifespan of any ecosystem will follow the arc shown in Figure 19.7, through creation, adoption, growth, use and finally either be abstracted over or abandoned.

Although our discipline is a young one, we should probably expect to see "Software Archaeology" in the same way as we see it for biological organisms. Already we can see the dead-ends in the software evolutionary tree: COBOL and BASIC languages, CASE systems. Languages like FORTH live on in PostScript, SQL is still embedded in everything

Let's move on now to the last Dependency Risk chapter, and look at Agency Risk.

CHAPTER 20

Agency Risk

Coordinating a team is difficult enough when everyone on the team has a single Goal. But people have their own goals too. Sometimes their goals harmlessly co-exist with the team's goal, other times they don't.

This is Agency Risk. This term comes from finance and refers to the situation where you (the "principal") entrust your money to someone (the "agent") in order to invest it, but they don't necessarily have your best interests at heart. They may instead elect to invest the money in ways that help them, or outright steal it.

> "This dilemma exists in circumstances where agents are motivated to act in their own best interests, which are contrary to those of their principals, and is an example of moral hazard."
> —Principal-Agent Problem, *Wikipedia*[1]

The less visibility you have of the agent's activities, the bigger the risk. However, the *whole point* of giving the money to the agent was that you would have to spend less time and effort managing it, hence the dilemma. In software development, we're not lending each other money, but we *are* being paid by the project sponsor, so they are assuming Agency Risk by employing us.

As we saw in the previous chapter on Process Risk, Agency Risk doesn't just apply to people: it can apply to *running software* or *whole teams* - anything which has agency over its actions.

---

[1] https://en.wikipedia.org/wiki/Principal–agent_problem

> "Agency is the capacity of an actor to act in a given environment... Agency may either be classified as unconscious, involuntary behaviour, or purposeful, goal directed activity (intentional action)."
>
> —Agency, *Wikipedia*[2])

Agency Risk clearly includes the behaviour of Bad Actors[3] but is not limited to them: there are various "shades of grey" involved. So first, we will look at some examples of Agency Risk, in order to sketch out where the domain of this risk lies, before looking at three common ways to mitigate it: monitoring, security and goal alignment.

Personal Lives

We shouldn't expect people on a project to sacrifice their personal lives for the success of the project, right? Except that "Crunch Time"[4] is exactly how some software companies work:

> "Game development... requires long working hours and dedication... Some video game developers (such as Electronic Arts) have been accused of the excessive invocation of 'crunch time'. 'Crunch time' is the point at which the team is thought to be failing to achieve milestones needed to launch a game on schedule."
>
> —Crunch Time, *Wikipedia*[5]

People taking time off, going to funerals, looking after sick relatives and so on are all acceptable forms of Agency Risk. They are the Attendant Risk of having *staff* rather than *slaves*.

The Hero

> "The one who stays later than the others is a hero."
>
> —Hero Culture, *Ward's Wiki*[6]

Heroes put in more hours and try to rescue projects single-handedly, often cutting corners like team communication and process in order to get there.

---

[2] https://en.wikipedia.org/wiki/Agency_(philosophy)
[3] https://en.wiktionary.org/wiki/bad_actor
[4] https://en.wikipedia.org/wiki/Video_game_developer#%22Crunch_time%22
[5] https://en.wikipedia.org/wiki/Video_game_developer#"Crunch_time"
[6] http://wiki.c2.com/?HeroCulture

Sometimes projects don't get done without heroes. But other times, the hero has an alternative agenda to just getting the project done:

- A need for control and for their own vision.
- A preference to work alone.
- A desire for recognition and acclaim from colleagues.
- For the job security of being a Key Person[7].

A team *can* make use of heroism but it's a double-edged sword. The hero can become a bottleneck to work getting done and because they want to solve all the problems themselves, they under-communicate.

CV Building

CV Building is when someone decides that the project needs a dose of "Some Technology X", but in actual fact, this is either completely unhelpful to the project (incurring large amounts of Complexity Risk), or merely a poor alternative to something else.

It's very easy to spot CV building: look for choices of technology that are incongruently complex compared to the problem they solve and then challenge by suggesting a simpler alternative.

Devil Makes Work

Heroes can be useful, but *underused* project members are a nightmare. The problem is, people who are not fully occupied begin to worry that actually the team would be better off without them, and then wonder if their jobs are at risk.

Even if they don't worry about their jobs, sometimes they need ways to stave off *boredom*. The solution to this is "busy-work": finding tasks that, at first sight, look useful, and then delivering them in an over-elaborate way that'll keep them occupied. This is also known as *Gold Plating*. This will leave you with more Complexity Risk than you had in the first place.

Pet Projects

> "A project, activity or goal pursued as a personal favourite, rather than because it is generally accepted as necessary or important."
>
> —Pet Project, *Wiktionary*[8]

---

[7]https://en.wikipedia.org/wiki/Key_person_insurance
[8]https://en.wiktionary.org/wiki/pet_project

Sometimes budget-holders have projects they value more than others without reference to the value placed on them by the business. Perhaps the project has a goal that aligns closely with the budget holder's passions, or it's related to work they were previously responsible for.

Working on a pet project usually means you get lots of attention (and more than enough budget), but it can fall apart very quickly under scrutiny.

Morale Risk

> "Morale, also known as Esprit de Corps, is the capacity of a group's members to retain belief in an institution or goal, particularly in the face of opposition or hardship"
>
> —Morale, *Wikipedia*[9]

Sometimes the morale of the team or individuals within it dips, leading to lack of motivation. Morale Risk is a kind of Agency Risk because it really means that a team member or the whole team isn't committed to the Goal and may decide their efforts are best spent elsewhere. Morale Risk might be caused by:

- **External Factors**: perhaps the employee's dog has died, or they're simply tired of the industry, or are not feeling challenged.
- **The goal feels unachievable**: in this case people won't commit their full effort to it. This might be due to a difference in the evaluation of the risks on the project between the team members and the leader. In military science, a second meaning of morale is how well supplied and equipped a unit is. This would also seem like a useful reference point for IT projects. If teams are under-staffed or under-equipped, it will impact on motivation too.
- **The goal isn't sufficiently worthy**, or the team doesn't feel sufficiently valued.

Software Processes

There is significant Agency Risk in running software *at all*. Since computer systems follow rules we set for them, we shouldn't be surprised when those rules have exceptions that lead to disaster. For example:

- A process continually writing log files until the disks fill up, crashing the system.

---

[9]https://en.wikipedia.org/wiki/Morale

- Bugs causing data to get corrupted, causing financial loss.
- Malware exploiting weaknesses in a system, exposing sensitive data.

Teams

Agency Risk applies to *whole teams* too. It's perfectly possible that a team within an organisation develops Goals that don't align with those of the overall organisation. For example:

- A team introduces excessive Bureaucracy in order to avoid work it doesn't like.
- A team gets obsessed with a particular technology, or their own internal process improvement, at the expense of delivering business value.
- A marginalised team forces their services on other teams in the name of "consistency". (This can happen a lot with "Architecture", "Branding" and "Testing" teams, sometimes for the better, sometimes for the worse.)

When you work with an external consultancy, there is *always* more Agency Risk than with a direct employee. This is because as well as your goals and the employee's goals, there is also the consultancy's goals.

This is a good argument for avoiding consultancies, but sometimes the technical expertise they bring can outweigh this risk.

20.1 Mitigating Agency Risk

Let's look at three common ways to mitigate Agency Risk: Monitoring, Security. and Goal Alignment. Let's start with Monitoring.

Monitoring

A the core of the Principal-Agent Problem is the issue that we *want* our agents to do work for us so we don't have the responsibility of doing it ourselves. However, we pick up the second-order responsibility of managing the agents instead.

As a result (and as shown in Figure 20.1), we need to *Monitor* the agents. The price of mitigating Agency Risk this way is that we have to spend time doing the monitoring (Schedule Risk) and we have to understand what the agents are doing (Complexity Risk).

Monitoring of *software process* agents is an important part of designing reliable systems and it makes perfect sense that this would also apply to *human* agents

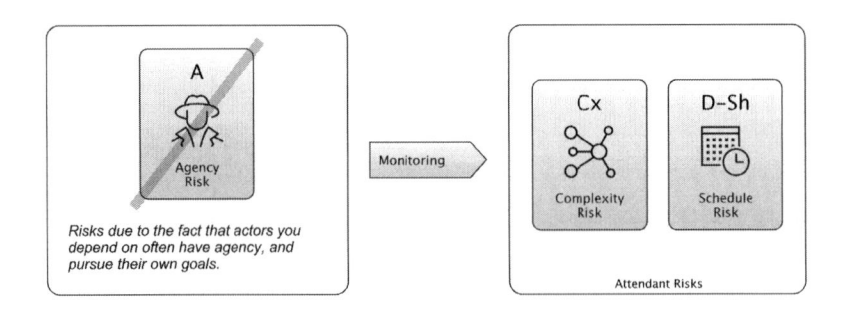

Figure 20.1: Mitigating Agency Risk Through Monitoring

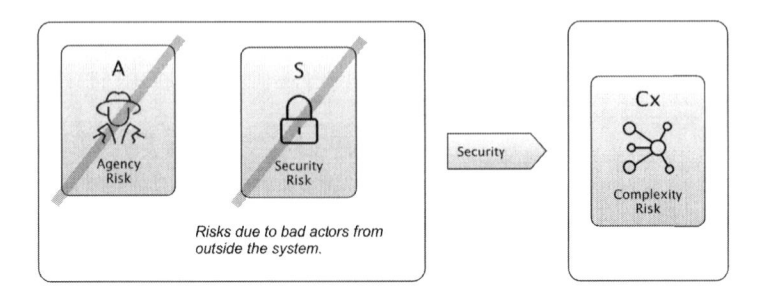

Figure 20.2: Security as a mitigation for Agency Risk

too. But for people, the *knowledge of being monitored* can instil corrective behaviour. This is known as the Hawthorne Effect:

> "The Hawthorne effect (also referred to as the observer effect) is a type of reactivity in which individuals modify an aspect of their behaviour in response to their awareness of being observed."
>
> —Hawthorne Effect, *Wikipedia*[10]

Security

Security is all about *setting limits* on agency - both within and outside a system.

Within a system we may wish to prevent our agents from causing accidental (or deliberate) harm but we also have Agency Risk from unwanted agents *outside* the system. So security is also about ensuring that the environment

---
[10]https://en.wikipedia.org/wiki/Hawthorne_effect

we work in is *safe* for the good actors to operate in while keeping out the bad actors.

Interestingly, security is handled in very similar ways in all kinds of systems, whether biological, human or institutional:

- **Walls**: defences *around* the system, to protect its parts from the external environment.
- **Doors**: ways to get *in* and *out* of the system, possibly with *locks*.
- **Guards**: to make sure only the right things go in and out. (i.e. to try and keep out *bad actors*).
- **Police**: to defend from *within* the system against internal Agency Risk.

- **Subterfuge**: hiding, camouflage, disguises, pretending to be something else.

These work at various levels in **our own bodies**: our *cells* have *cell walls* around them, and *cell membranes* that act as the guards to allow things in and out. Our *bodies* have *skin* to keep the world out, and we have *mouths*, *eyes*, *pores* and so on to allow things in and out. We have an *immune system* to act as the police.

Our societies work in similar ways: in medieval times, a city would have walls, guards and gates to keep out intruders. Nowadays, we have customs control, borders and passports.

We're waking up to the realisation that our software systems need to work the same way: we have Firewalls[11] and we lock down *ports* on servers to ensure there are the minimum number of *doors* to guard, we *police* the servers with monitoring tools, and we *guard* access using passwords and other identification approaches.

Agency Risk and Security Risk thrive on complexity: the more complex the systems we create, the more opportunities there are for bad actors to insert themselves and extract their own value. The dilemma is, *increasing security* also means increasing Complexity Risk, because secure systems are necessarily more complex than insecure ones.

Goal Alignment

As we stated at the beginning, Agency Risk at any level comes down to differences of Goals between the different agents, whether they are *people*, *teams* or *software*.

---

[11]https://en.wikipedia.org/wiki/Firewall_(computing)

So, if you can *align the goals* of the agents involved, you can mitigate Agency Risk. Nassim Nicholas Taleb calls this "skin in the game": that is, the agent is exposed to the same risks as the principal.

> "Which brings us to the largest fragilizer of society, and greatest generator of crises, absence of 'skin in the game.' Some become antifragile at the expense of others by getting the upside (or gains) from volatility, variations, and disorder and exposing others to the downside risks of losses or harm."
> —Nassim Nicholas Taleb, *Antifragile*[12]

This kind of financial exposure isn't very common on software projects. Fixed Price Contracts and Employee Stock Options[13] are two exceptions. But David McClelland's Needs Theory suggests that there are other kinds of skin-in-the-game: the intrinsic interest in the work being done, or extrinsic factors such as the recognition, achievement, or personal growth derived from it.

> "Need theory... proposed by psychologist David McClelland, is a motivational model that attempts to explain how the needs for achievement, power, and affiliation affect the actions of people from a managerial context... McClelland stated that we all have these three types of motivation regardless of age, sex, race, or culture. The type of motivation by which each individual is driven derives from their life experiences and the opinions of their culture."
> —Need Theory, *Wikipedia*[14]

So one mitigation for Agency Risk is therefore to employ these extrinsic factors. For example, by making individuals responsible and rewarded for the success or failure of projects, we can align their personal motivations with those of the project.

> "One key to success in a mission is establishing clear lines of blame."
> —Henshaw's Law, *Akin's Laws Of Spacecraft Design*[15]

---

[12] http://a.co/d/07LfBTI
[13] https://en.wikipedia.org/wiki/Employee_stock_option
[14] https://en.wikipedia.org/wiki/Need_theory
[15] https://spacecraft.ssl.umd.edu/akins_laws.html

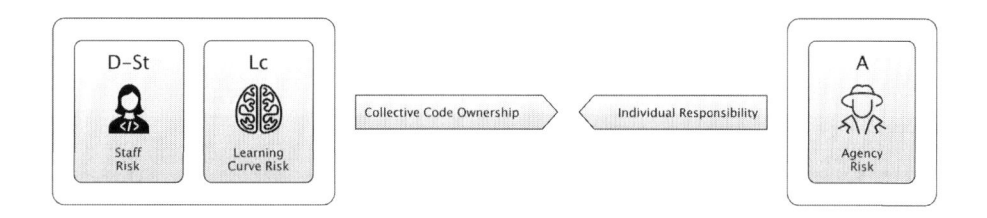

Figure 20.3: Collective Code Ownership, Individual Responsibility

But *extrinsic motivation* is a complex, difficult-to-apply tool. In Map And Territory Risk we will come back to this and look at the various ways in which it can go awry.

Tools like Pair Programming and Collective Code Ownership[16] are about mitigating Staff Risks like Key Person Risk and Learning Curve Risk, but these push in the opposite direction to *individual responsibility*.

This is an important consideration: in adopting *those* tools, you are necessarily setting aside certain tools to manage Agency Risk as a result.

We've looked at various different shades of Agency Risk and three different mitigations for it. Agency Risk is a concern at the level of *individual agents*, whether they are processes, people, systems or teams.

So having looked at agents *individually*, it's time to look more closely at Goals, and the Attendant Risks when aligning them amongst multiple agents.

On to Coordination Risk...

---

[16] https://en.wikipedia.org/wiki/Collective_ownership

CHAPTER 21

Coordination Risk

As in Agency Risk, we are going to use the term *agent*, which refers to anything with agency in a system to make decisions: that is, an agent has an Internal Model and can take actions based on it. Here, we work on the assumption that the agents *are* working towards a common Goal, even though in reality it's not always the case, as we saw in the chapter on Agency Risk.

Coordination Risk is the risk that agents can fail to coordinate to meet their common goal and end up making things worse. Coordination Risk is embodied in the phrase "Too Many Cooks Spoil The Broth": more people, opinions or *agents* often make results worse.

In this chapter, we'll first build up a model of Coordination Risk, describing exactly coordination means and why we do it. Then, we'll look at some classic problems of coordination. Then, we're going to consider agency at several different levels (because of Scale Invariance) . We'll look at:

- Team Decision Making,
- Living Organisms,
- Larger Organisations and the staff within them,
- and Software Processes.

... and we'll consider how Coordination Risk is a problem at each of these scales.

But for now, let's crack on and examine where Coordination Risk comes from.

21.1 A Model Of Coordination Risk

Earlier, in Dependency Risk, we looked at various resources (time, money, people, events etc) and showed how we could depend on them taking on

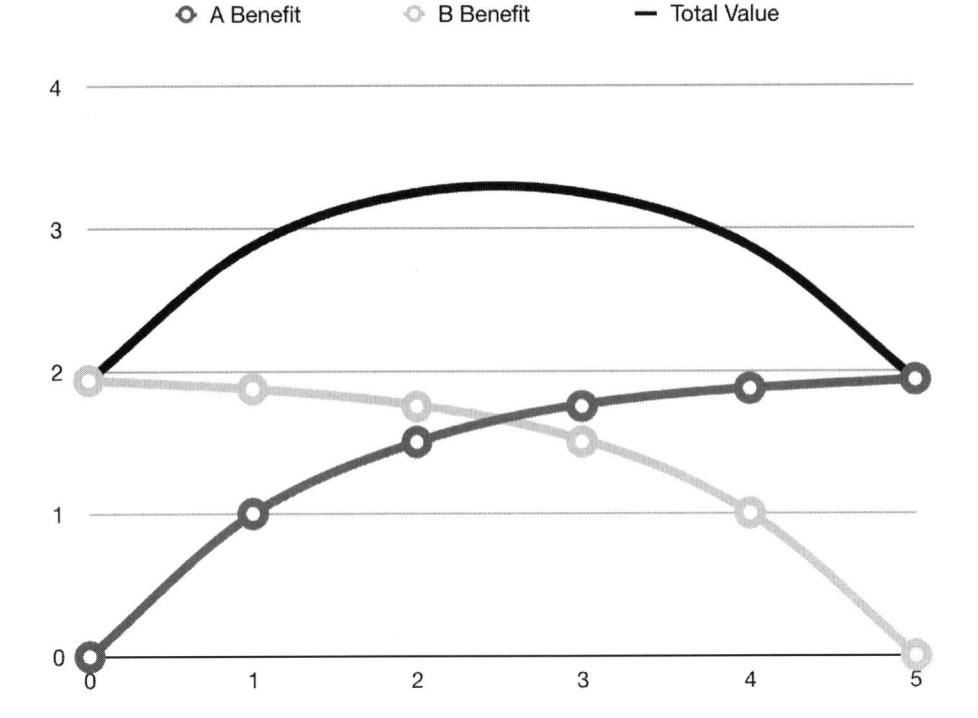

Figure 21.1: Sharing Resources. 5 units are available, and the X axis shows A's consumption of the resource. B gets whatever remains. Total benefit is maximised somewhere in the middle

risk. Here, let's consider the situation where there is *competition for those dependencies* due to Scarcity Risk: other agents want to use them in a different way.

Law Of Diminishing Returns

One argument for coordination could come from Diminishing Returns[1], which says that the earlier units of a resource (say, chocolate bars) give you more benefit than later ones.

We can see this in Figure 21.1. Let's say A and B compete over a resource, of which there are 5 units available. For every extra A takes, B loses one. The X axis shows A's consumption of the resource. While the biggest benefit to A is in taking *all* of the resources, the greatest *increase* in benefit comes from the consumption of the first unit.

---

[1] https://en.wikipedia.org/wiki/Diminishing_returns

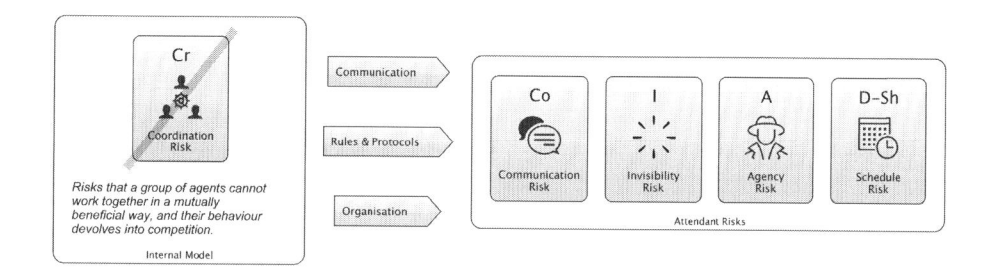

Figure 21.2: Coordination Risk - Mitigated by Communication

As you can see, by *sharing*, it's possible that the *total benefit* is greater than it can be for either individual. But sharing requires coordination. Further, the more competitors involved, the *worse* a winner-take-all outcome is for total benefit.

Just two things are needed for competition to occur:

- Multiple, Individual agents, trying to achieve Goals.
- Scarce Resources, which the agents want to use as Dependencies.

Coordination via Communication

The only way that the agents can move away from competition towards coordination is via Communication, and this is where their coordination problems begin.

Coordination Risk commonly occurs where people have different ideas about how to achieve a goal, and they have different ideas because they have different Internal Models. As we saw in the chapter on Communication Risk, we can only hope to synchronise Internal Models if there are high-bandwidth Channels available for communication.

You might think, therefore, that this is just another type of Communication Risk problem, and that's often a part of it, but even with synchronized Internal Models, coordination risk can occur. Imagine the example of people all trying to madly leave a burning building. They all have the same information (the building is on fire). If they coordinate, and leave in an orderly fashion, they might all get out. If they don't, and there's a scramble for the door, more people might die.

21.2 Problems Of Coordination

Let's unpack this idea, and review some classic problems of coordination, none of which can be addressed without good communication. Here are some examples:

1. **Merging Data**: if you are familiar with the source code control system, Git, you will know that this is a *distributed* version control system. That means that two or more people can propose changes to the same files without knowing about each other. This means that at some later time, Git then has to merge (or reconcile) these changes together. Git is very good at doing this automatically, but sometimes different people can independently change the same lines of code and these will have to be merged manually. In this case, a human arbitrator "resolves" the difference, either by combining the two changes or picking a winner.

2. **Consensus**: making group decisions (as in elections) is often decided by votes. But having a vote is a coordination issue and requires that everyone has been told the rules:

   - Where will the vote be held?
   - How long do you provide for the vote?
   - What do you do about absentees?
   - What if people change their minds in the light of new information?
   - How do you ensure everyone has enough information to make a good decision?

3. **Factions**: sometimes, it's hard to coordinate large groups at the same time and "factions" can occur. That the world isn't a single big country is probably partly a testament to this: countries are frequently separated by geographic features that prevent the easy flow of communication (and force). We can also see this in distributed systems, with the "split brain" problem. This is where subset of the total system becomes disconnected (usually due to a network failure) and you end up with two, smaller networks with different knowledge. We'll address in more depth later.

4. **Resource Allocation**[2]: ensuring that the right people are doing the right work, or the right resources are given to the right people is a coordination issue. On a grand scale we have Logistics and Economic

---
[2] https://en.wikipedia.org/wiki/Resource_allocation

Systems[3]. On a small scale the office's *room booking system* solves the coordination issue of who gets a meeting room using a first-come-first-served booking algorithm.

5. **Deadlock** refers to a situation where, in an environment where multiple parallel processes are running, the processing stops and no-one can make progress because the resources each process needs are being reserved by another process. This is a specific issue in Resource Allocation, but it's one we're familiar with in the computer science industry. Compare with Gridlock[4], where traffic can't move because other traffic is occupying the space it wants to move to already.

6. **Race Conditions** are where we can't be sure of the result of a calculation, because it is dependent on the ordering of events within a system. For example, two separate threads writing the same memory at the same time (one ignoring and over-writing the work of the other) is a race.

7. **Contention**: where there is Scarcity Risk for a dependency, we might want to make sure that everyone gets fair use of it, by taking turns, booking, queueing and so on. As we saw in Scarcity Risk, sometimes this is handled for us by the Dependency itself. However if it isn't, it's the *users* of the dependency who'll need to coordinate to use the resource fairly, again, by communicating with each other.

21.3 Decision Making

Within a team, Coordination Risk is at its core about resolving Internal Model conflicts in order that everyone can agree on a Goal In Mind and cooperate on getting it done. Therefore, Coordination Risk is worse on projects with more members, and worse in organisations with more staff.

As an individual, do you suffer from Coordination Risk at all? Maybe: sometimes, you can feel "conflicted" about the best way to solve a problem. And weirdly, usually *not thinking about it* helps. Sleeping too. (Rich Hickey calls this "Hammock Driven Development[5]"). This is probably because, unbeknownst to you, your subconscious is furiously communicating internally, trying to resolve these conflicts itself, and will let you know when it has come to a resolution.

---

[3] https://en.wikipedia.org/wiki/Economic_system
[4] https://en.wikipedia.org/wiki/Gridlock
[5] https://www.youtube.com/watch?v=f84n5oFoZBc

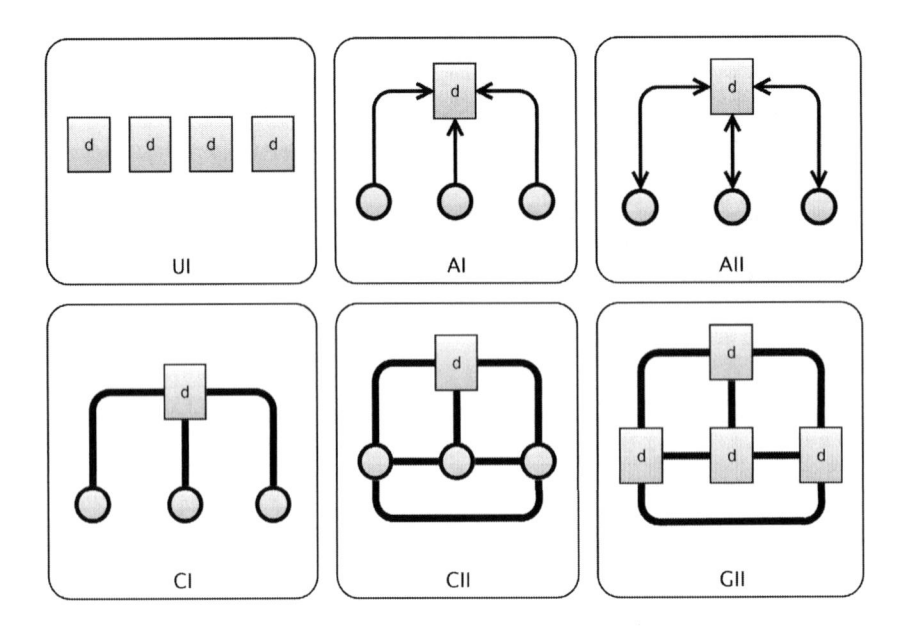

*Figure 21.3: Vroom And Yetton Decision Making Styles. "d" indicates authority in making a decision, circles are subordinates. Thin lines with arrow-heads show information flow, whilst thick lines show **opinions** being passed around.*

Vroom and Yetton[6] introduced a model of group decision making which delineated five different styles of decision making within a team. These are summarised in the table below (**AI, AII, CI, CII, GII**). To this, I have added a sixth (**UI**), which is the *uncoordinated* option, where everyone competes. Figure 21.3 illustrates these, with the following conventions:

- Thin lines with arrow-heads show a flow of *information*, either one-way or two-way.
- Thick lines show a flow of *opinion*.
- "d" boxes are *decision makers*, whereas circles don't have a part in the decision.

Type	Description	Decision Makers	Opinions	Channels	Risk
UI	Uncoordinated	1	1	0	Competition

[6]https://en.wikipedia.org/wiki/Vroom-Yetton_decision_model

194

Type	Description	Decision Makers	Opinions	Channels	Risk
AI	Autocratic (with upward information flow)	1	1	s	Maximum Coordination Risk
AII	Autocratic (up and down information flow)	1	1	s	
CI	Consultative (Individual)	1	1 + s	2s	
CII	Consultative (Group)	1	1 + s	s^2	
GII	Group Consultation and Voting	1 + s	1 + s	s^2	Maximum Communication Risk, Schedule Risk

s = subordinate

At the top, you have the *least* consultative styles, and at the bottom, the *most*. At the top, decisions are made with just the leader's Internal Model, but moving down, the Internal Models of the *subordinates* are increasingly brought into play.

The decisions at the top are faster, but don't do much for mitigating Coordination Risk. The ones below take longer (incurring Schedule Risk) but mitigate more Coordination Risk. Group decision-making inevitably involves everyone *learning* and improving their Internal Models.

The trick is to be able to tell which approach is suitable at which time. Everyone is expected to make decisions *within their realm of expertise*: you can't have developers continually calling meetings to discuss whether they should be using an Abstract Factory[7] or a Factory Method[8]: it would waste time. The critical question is therefore, "what's the biggest risk?"

- Is the Coordination Risk greater? Are we going to suffer Dead End Risk if the decision is made wrongly? What if people don't agree with it? Poor leadership has an impact on Morale too.

[7] https://en.wikipedia.org/wiki/Abstract_factory_pattern
[8] https://en.wikipedia.org/wiki/Factory_method_pattern

- Is the Schedule Risk greater? If you have a 1-hour meeting with eight people to decide a decision, that's *one person day* gone right there: group decision making is *expensive*.

So *organisation* can reduce Coordination Risk but to make this work we need more *communication*, and this has attendant complexity and time costs.

Staff As Agents

Staff in a team have a dual nature: they are **Agents** and **Resources** at the same time. The team depends on staff for their resource of *labour*, but they're also part of the decision making process of the team, because they have *agency* over their own actions.

Part of Coordination Risk is about trying to mitigate differences in Internal Models. So it's worth considering how varied people's models can be:

- Different skill levels
- Different experiences
- Expertise in different areas
- Preferences
- Personalities

The job of harmonising this on a project would seem to fall to the team leader, but actually people are self-organising to some extent. This process is called Team Development[9]:

> "The forming–storming–norming–performing model of group development was first proposed by Bruce Tuckman in 1965, who said that these phases are all necessary and inevitable in order for the team to grow, face up to challenges, tackle problems, find solutions, plan work, and deliver results."
> —Tuckman's Stages Of Group Development, *Wikipedia*[10]

Specifically this describes a process whereby a new group will form and then be required to work together. In the process, they will have many *disputes*. Ideally, the group will resolve these disputes internally and emerge as a team, with a common Goal In Mind.

---

[9]https://en.wikipedia.org/wiki/Tuckmans_stages_of_group_development
[10]https://en.wikipedia.org/wiki/Tuckmans_stages_of_group_development

Since Coordination is about Resource Allocation the skills of staff can potentially be looked at as resources to allocate. This means handling Coordination Risk issues like:

- People leaving, taking their Internal Models and expertise with them (Key Person Risk).
- People requiring external training, to understand new tools and techniques (Learning Curve Risk).
- People being protective about their knowledge in order to protect their jobs (Agency Risk).

> "As a rough rule, three programmers organised into a team can do only twice the work of a single programmer of the same ability - because of time spent on coordination problems."
>
> —Gerald Wienberg, *The Psychology of Computer Programming*[11]

21.4 In Living Organisms

Vroom and Yetton's organisational model isn't relevant to just teams of people. We can see it in the natural world too. Although *the majority* of cellular life on earth (by weight) is single celled organisms[12], the existence of *humans* (to pick a single example) demonstrates that sometimes it's better for cells to try to mitigate Coordination Risk and work as a team, accepting the Complexity Risk and Communication Risk this entails. For example, in the human body, we have:

- **Various systems**[13]: such as the Respiratory System[14] or the Digestive System[15]. Each of these systems contains...
- **Organs**, such as the heart or lungs, which contain..
- **Tissues**, which contain...
- **Cells** of different types. (Even cells are complex systems containing multiple different, communicating sub-systems.)

There is huge attendant Coordination Risk to running a complex multi-cellular system like the human body, but given the success of humanity

---

[11] https://en.wikipedia.org/wiki/Gerald_Weinberg
[12] http://www.stephenjaygould.org/library/gould_bacteria.html
[13] https://en.wikipedia.org/wiki/List_of_systems_of_the_human_body
[14] https://en.wikipedia.org/wiki/Respiratory_system
[15] https://en.wikipedia.org/wiki/Human_digestive_system

as a species, you must conclude that these steps on the *evolutionary* Risk Landscape have benefited us in our ecological niche.

Decision Making

The key observation from looking at biology is this: most of the cells in the human body *don't get a vote*. Muscles in the motor system have an **AI** or **AII** relationship with the brain - they do what they are told, but there are often nerves to report pain back. The only place where **CII** or **GII** *could* occur is in our brains, when we try to make a decision and weigh up the pros and cons.

This means that there is a deal: *most* of the cells in our body accede control of their destiny to "the system". Living within the system of the human body is a better option than going it alone as a single-celled organism. Occasionally, due to mutation, we can end up with Cancer[16], which is where one cell genetically "forgets" its purpose in the whole system and goes back to selfish individual self-replication (**UI**). We have White Blood Cells[17] in the body to shut down this kind of behaviour and try to kill the rogue cells. In the same way, societies have police forces to stop undesirable behaviour amongst their citizens.

21.5 Large Organisations

Working in a large organisation often feels like being a cell in a larger organism. Cells live and die and the organism goes on. Workers come and go from a large company but the organisation goes on. By working in an organisation, we give up self-control and competition and accept **AI** and **AII** power structures above us, but we trust that there is symbiotic value creation on both sides of the employment deal.

Less consultative decision making styles are more appropriate then when we don't have the luxury of high-bandwidth channels for discussion. When the number of parties rises above a room-full of people it's not possible to hear everyone's voice. As you can see from Figure 21.3, for **CII** and **GII** decision-making styles, the amount of communication increases non-linearly with the number of participants, so we need something simpler.

As we saw in the Complexity Risk chapter, hierarchies are an excellent way of economising on number of different communication channels, and we use these frequently when there are lots of parties to coordinate.

---

[16]https://en.wikipedia.org/wiki/Cancer
[17]https://en.wikipedia.org/wiki/White_blood_cell

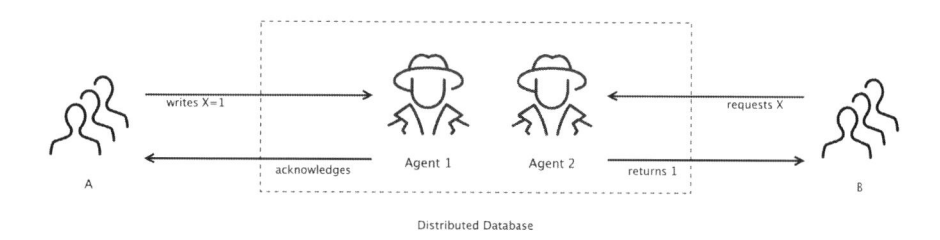

Figure 21.4: User A and User B are both using a distributed database, managed by Agents 1 and 2, whom each have their own Internal Model

In large organisations, teams are created and leaders chosen for those teams precisely to mitigate this Communication Risk. We're all familiar with this: control of the team is ceded to the leader, who takes on the role of 'handing down' direction from above, but also 'reporting up' issues that cannot be resolved within the team. In Vroom and Yetton's model, this is moving from a **GII** or **CII** to an **AI** or **AII** style of leadership.

Clearly, this is just a *model*, it's not set in stone and decision making styles usually change from day-to-day and decision-to-decision. The same is not true in our software - *rules are rules*.

21.6 In Software Processes

It should be pretty clear that we are applying our Scale Invariance rule to Coordination Risk: all of the problems we've described as affecting teams and organisations also affect software, although the scale and terrain are different. Software processes have limited *agency* - in most cases they follow fixed rules set down by the programmers, rather than self-organising like people can (so far).

As before, in order to face Coordination Risk in software, we need multiple agents all working together. Coordination Risks (such as race conditions or deadlock) only really occur where *more than one agent working at the same time*. This means we are considering *at least* multi-threaded software, and anything above that (multiple CPUs, servers, data-centres and so on).

CAP Theorem

Imagine talking to a distributed database, where your request (*read* or *write*) can be handled by one of many agents.

Figure 21.5: In an AP system, the User B may get back a stale value for X

In Figure 21.4, we have just two agents 1 and 2, in order to keep things simple. User A *writes something* to the database, then User B *reads it back* afterwards.

According to the CAP Theorem[18], there are three properties we could desire in such a system:

- **Consistency (C)**: Every read receives the most recent value from the last write.
- **Availability (A)**: Every request receives a response.
- **Partition tolerance (P)**: The system can operate despite the isolation (lack of communication with) some of its agents.

The CAP Theorem states that this is a Trilemma[19]. That is, you can only have two out of the three properties.

There are plenty of resources on the Internet that discuss this in depth, but let's just illustrate with some diagrams to show how this plays out. In Figure 21.4, we can see a 2-agent distributed database. Either agent can receive a read or write. So this might be a **GII** decision making system, because all the agents are going to need to coordinate to figure out what the right value is to return for a read, and what the last value written was.

In Figure 21.4, you can already see that there is a *race condition*: if A and B both make their requests at the same time, what will B get back? The original value of X, or the new value?

With an AP System

Here, we are going to consider what happens when communication breaks down between Agents 1 and 2. That is, they are *isolated* from communicating

---
[18]https://en.wikipedia.org/wiki/CAP_theorem
[19]https://en.wikipedia.org/wiki/Trilemma

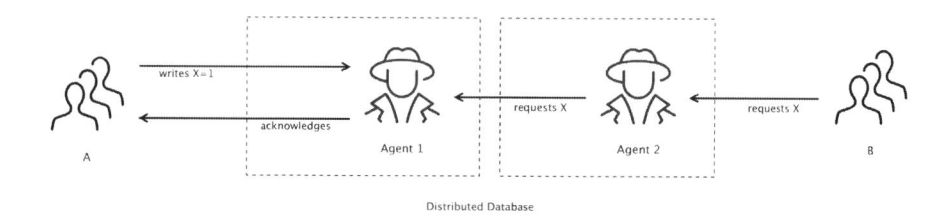

Figure 21.6: In an CP system, the User B won't get anything back for X, because Agent 2 can't be sure it has the latest value

with each other. As shown in Figure 21.5, in an `AP` system, we have a database that is able to survive partitioning, and always returns a response, but may not be consistent. The value `B` will get back will depend on whether they talk with Agent 1 or Agent 2.

With an CP System

To be consistent, Agent 2 needs to check with Agent 1 to make sure it has the latest value for X. Where Agent 2 is left waiting for Agent 1 to re-appear, we are *blocked*. So CP systems will block when partitioned.

With an CA System

Finally, if we have a CA system, we are essentially saying that *only one agent is doing the work*. (You can't partition a single agent, after all). But this leads to Resource Allocation and **Contention** around use of the scarce resource of `Agent 2`'s attention. (Both Coordination Risk issues we met earlier.)

Some Real-Life Examples

This sets a lower bound on Coordination Risk: we *can't* get rid of it completely in a software system, -or- a system on any other scale. Fundamentally, coordination problems are inescapable at some level. The best we can do is mitigate it by agreeing on protocols and doing lots of communication.

Let's look at some real-life examples of how this manifests in software.

ZooKeeper

First, ZooKeeper[20] is an Open-Source datastore, which is used in building distributed systems (like the one above) and ensuring things like configuration

---
[20]https://zookeeper.apache.org

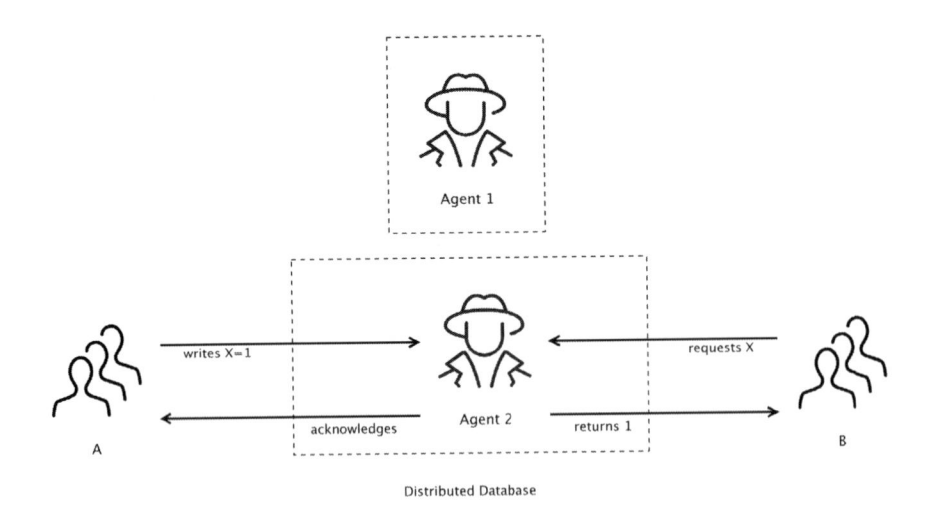

Figure 21.7: In an CA system, we can't have partition tolerance, so in order to be consistent a single Agent has to do all the work

information are consistent across all agents.

This *seems* trivial, but it quickly gets out-of-hand: what happens if only some of the agents receive the new information? What happens if a datacentre gets disconnected while the update is happening? There are lots of edge-cases.

ZooKeeper handles this by communicating inter-agent with its own protocol. It elects a **master agent** (via **GII**-style voting), turning it into an **AI**-style team. If the master is lost for some reason, a new leader is elected. *Writes* are then coordinated via the **master agent** who makes sure that a *majority of agents* have received and stored the configuration change before telling the user that the transaction is complete. Therefore, ZooKeeper is a CP system.

Git

Second, Git is a (mainly) write-only ledger of source changes. However, as we already discussed above, where different agents make incompatible changes, someone has to decide how to resolve the conflicts so that we have a single source of truth.

The Coordination Risk just *doesn't go away*.

Since multiple users can make all the changes they like locally, and merge them later, Git is an AP system where everyone's opinion counts (**GII**): indi-

202

vidual users may have *wildly* different ideas about what the source looks like until the merge is complete.

Bitcoin

Finally, Bitcoin (BTC)[21] is a write-only distributed ledger[22], where agents *compete* to mine BTC (a **UI** style organisation), but also at the same time record transactions on the ledger. BTC is also `AP`, in a similar way to Git. But new changes can only be appended if you have the latest version of the ledger. If you append to an out-of-date ledger, your work will be lost.

Because it's based on outright competition, if someone beats you to completing a mining task, then your work is wasted. So, there is *huge* Coordination Risk.

For this reason, BTC agents coordinate into mining consortia[23], so they can avoid working on the same tasks at the same time, turning it into a **CI**-type organisation.

This in itself is a problem because the whole *point* of BTC is that it's competitive and no one entity has control. So, mining pools tend to stop growing before they reach 50% of the BTC network's processing power. Taking control would be politically disastrous[24] and confidence in the currency (such as there is) would likely be lost.

21.7 Communication Is For Coordination

CAP theory gives us a fundamental limit on how much Coordination Risk we can mitigate. We've looked at different organisational structures used to manage Coordination Risk within teams of people, organisations or living organisms, so it's the case in software.

At the start of this chapter, we questioned whether Coordination Risk was just another type of Communication Risk. However, it should be clear after looking at the examples of competition, cellular life and Vroom and Yetton's Model that this is exactly *backwards*.

- Most single-celled life has no need for communication: it simply competes for the available resources. If it lacks anything it needs, it dies.

---

[21]https://en.wikipedia.org/wiki/Bitcoin
[22]https://en.wikipedia.org/wiki/Distributed_ledger
[23]https://en.bitcoin.it/wiki/Comparison_of_mining_pools
[24]https://www.reddit.com/r/Bitcoin/comments/5fe9vz/in_the_last_24hrs_three_mining_pools_have_control/

- There are *no* lines of communication on the **UI** decision-type. It's only when we want to avoid competition, by sharing resources and working towards common goals that we need to communicate.
- Therefore, the whole point of communication *is for coordination*.

In the next chapter, Map And Territory Risk, we're going to look at some new ways in which systems can fail, despite their attempts to coordinate.

CHAPTER 22

Map And Territory Risk

As we discussed in the Communication Risk chapter, our understanding of the world is informed by abstractions we create and the names we give them.

For example, Risk-First is about naming *risks* within software development, so we can discuss and understand them better.

Our Internal Models of the world are constructed from these abstractions and their relationships.

As Figure 22.1 shows, there is a translation going on here: observations about the arrangement of *atoms* in the world are *communicated* to our Internal Models and stored as patterns of *information* (measured in bits and bytes).

The Map
(Bits / Information)

Communication

Territory
(Atoms etc.)

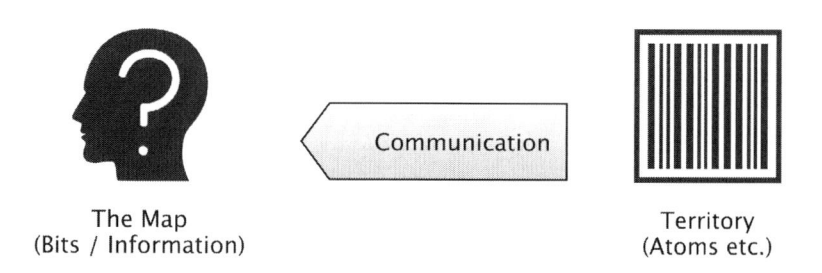

Figure 22.1: Maps and Territories, and Communication happening between them

205

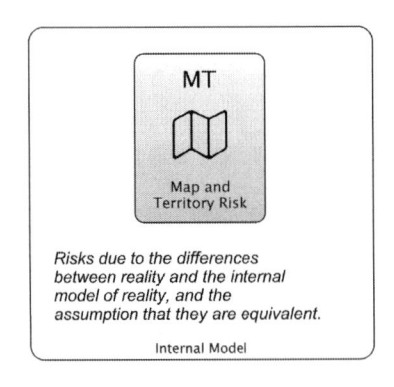

Figure 22.2: Map And Territory Risk defined

We face Map And Territory Risk because we base our behaviour on our Internal Models rather than reality itself. It comes from the expression "Confusing the Map for the Territory", attributed to Alfred Korzybski:

> "Polish-American scientist and philosopher Alfred Korzybski remarked that"the map is not the territory" and that "the word is not the thing", encapsulating his view that an abstraction derived from something, or a reaction to it, is not the thing itself. Korzybski held that many people *do* confuse maps with territories, that is, confuse models of reality with reality itself."
>
> —Map-Territory Relation, *Wikipedia*[1]

As Figure 22.2 shows, there are two parts to this risk, which we are going to examine in this chapter:

- **The internal model may be insufficient.** This leads to issues along the same axes we introduced in Feature Risk (that is Fitness, Audience and Evolution). We'll look at the examples of SatNavs, Software Metrics and Hype-Cycles along the way to illustrate this.
- **The assumption that the model is right.** We're going to look at Map and Territory Risk within the contexts of **machines, people, hierarchies** and **markets**.

---

[1] https://en.wikipedia.org/wiki/MapâÄŞterritory_relation

A van got stuck on a narrow footpath when the driver took a wrong turn while blindly following his sat-nav. Photo: MEN

Figure 22.3: Sat Nav Blunder Sends Asda Van Crashing Narrow Footpath - Telegraph Newspaper

22.1 Fitness

In the Feature Risk chapter we looked at ways in which our software project might have risks due to having *inappropriate* features (Feature Fit Risk), *broken* features (Feature Implementation Risk) or *too many of the wrong* features (Conceptual Integrity Risk). Let's see how these same categories also apply to Internal Models.

Example: The SatNav

In Figure 22.3, taken from the Telegraph newspaper[2], the driver *trusted* the SatNav to such an extent that he didn't pay attention to the road-signs around him and ended up getting stuck.

This wasn't borne of stupidity, but experience: SatNavs are pretty reliable. *So many times* the SatNav had been right, that the driver stopped *questioning its fallibility*.

---

[2] https://www.telegraph.co.uk/news/newstopics/howaboutthat/6413887/Asda-van-crashes-after-sat-nav-sends-driver-to-narrow-footpath.html

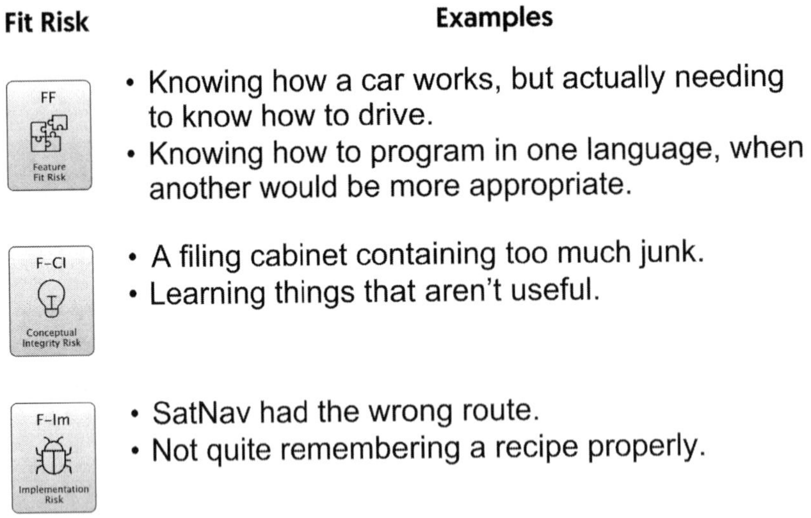

Fit Risk	Examples
FF (Feature Fit Risk)	• Knowing how a car works, but actually needing to know how to drive. • Knowing how to program in one language, when another would be more appropriate.
F-CI (Conceptual Integrity Risk)	• A filing cabinet containing too much junk. • Learning things that aren't useful.
F-Im (Implementation Risk)	• SatNav had the wrong route. • Not quite remembering a recipe properly.

Figure 22.4: Some examples of Feature Fit Risks, as manifested in the Internal Model

There are two Map and Territory Risks here:

- The Internal Model of the *SatNav* contained information that was wrong: the track had been marked up as a road, rather than a path.
- The Internal Model of the *driver* was wrong: his abstraction of "the SatNav is always right" turned out to be only *mostly* accurate.

You could argue that both the SatNav and the Driver's *Internal Model* had bugs in them. That is, they both suffer the Feature Implementation Risk we saw in the Feature Risk chapter. If a SatNav has too much of this, you'd end up not trusting it, and getting a new one. With your *personal* Internal Model, you can't buy a new one, but you may learn to *trust your assumptions less*.

Figure 22.4 shows how types of Feature Fit Risk can manifest in the Internal Model.

22.2 Audience

Communication allows us to *share* information between Internal Models of a whole audience of people. The Communication Risk and Coordination Risk chapters covered the difficulties inherent in aligning Internal Models so that they cooperate.

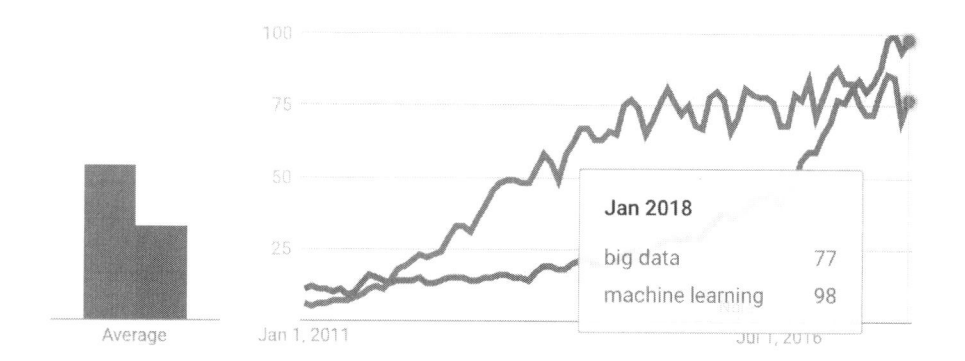

Figure 22.5: Relative popularity of "Machine Learning" and "Big Data" as search terms on Google Trends[3], 2011-2018

But how does Map and Territory Risk apply across a population of Internal Models? Can we track the rise-and-fall of *ideas* like we track stock prices? In effect, this is what Google Trends[4] does. In Figure 22.5, we can see the relative popularity of two search terms over time. This is probably as good an indicator as any of the changing popularity of an abstraction within an audience.

Example: Map And Territory Risk Drives The Hype Cycle

Most ideas (and most products) have a slow, hard climb to wide-scale adoption. But some ideas seem to disperse much more rapidly and are picked up quickly because they are exciting, having greater "memetic potential" within a population. One way this evolution manifests itself in the world is though the Hype Cycle[5]:

> "The hype cycle is a branded graphical presentation developed and used by the American research, advisory and information technology firm Gartner, for representing the maturity, adoption and social application of specific technologies. The hype cycle provides a graphical and conceptual presentation of the maturity of emerging technologies through five phases."
> —Hype Cycle, *Wikipedia*[6]

---

[4]https://trends.google.com
[5]https://en.wikipedia.org/wiki/Hype_cycle
[6]https://en.wikipedia.org/wiki/Hype_cycle

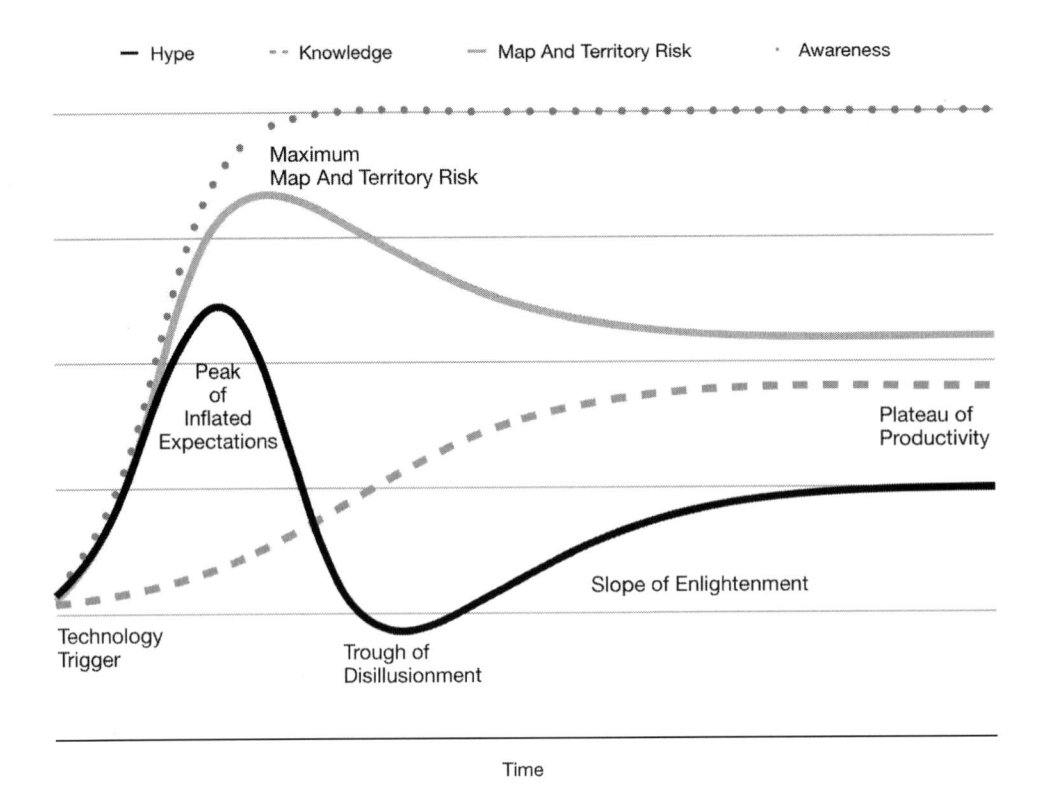

Figure 22.6: Hype Cycle, along with Map & Territory Risk

The five phases (and the "Hype" itself as the thick black line) are shown in Figure 22.6. We start off at the "Technology Trigger", moving to the "Peak of Inflated Expectations", then to the "Trough of Disillusionment" and finally up the "Slope of Enlightenment" to the "Plateau of Productivity".

The concept of Map and Territory Risk actually helps explain why this curve has the shape it does. To see why, let's consider each line in turn:

- The **Awareness** (or enthusiasm for) the idea within the population is the dotted line.

- The **Knowledge** (or *understanding*) of the idea within the audience (a Learning Curve, if you will) is the dashed line. Both of these are modelled with Cumulative Distribution[7] functions which are often used for modelling the spread of a phenomena (disease, product uptake, idea) within a population. As you would expect, **Knowledge** increases less rapidly than **Awareness**.

---

[7]https://en.wikipedia.org/wiki/Cumulative_distribution_function#Use_in_statistical_analysis

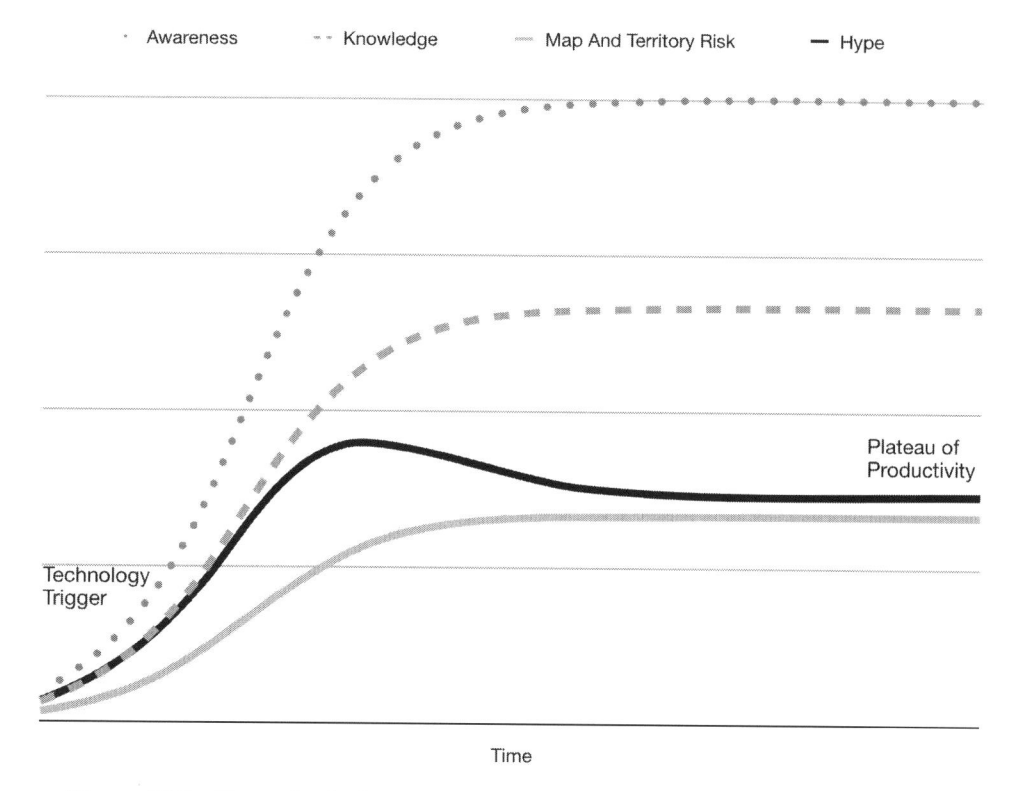

Figure 22.7: Hype Cycle 2: more even growth of Awareness and Knowledge means no "Trough of Disillusionment"

- **Map And Territory Risk** is the difference between **Awareness** and **Knowledge**. It's highest point is where the **Awareness** of the idea is farthest from the **Knowledge** of it.

- **Hype** is calculated here as being the **Awareness** line, subtracting **Map and Territory Risk** from a point lagging behind the current time (since it takes time to appreciate this risk). As the population appreciates more Map and Territory Risk, **Hype** decreases.

At the point where the effect of Map and Territory Risk is at its greatest we end up in the "Trough of Disillusionment". Eventually, we escape the trough as **Knowledge** and understanding of the idea increases, reducing Map and Territory Risk.

As you might expect, the "Trough of Disillusionment" exists because the **Awareness** of the idea and the **Knowledge** about it increase at different rates.

Audience Risk	Examples
F-A Feature Access Risk	• Memes, echo-chambers. • Ideas going "out of fashion".
F-Ma Market Risk	• Demand for courses, skills and experts in a field. • Popularity of a given technology. • Hype Cycles: .com boom, blockchain everywhere.

Figure 22.8: Audience Feature Risks, as manifested in the Internal Model

Where the **Awareness** and **Knowledge** grow more evenly together, there is no spike in Map and Territory Risk and we don't see the corresponding "Trough of Disillusionment" at all, as shown in Figure 22.7.

Figure 22.8 shows how Audience-type Feature Risks can manifest in the Internal Model. (The Hype Cycle model is available in **Numbers** format here[8].)

22.3 Evolution

So concepts and abstractions spread through an audience. But what happens next?

- People will use and abuse new ideas up to the point when they start breaking down. (We also discussed this as the **Peter Principle** in Boundary Risk.)
- At the same time, reality itself *evolves* in response to the idea: the new idea displaces old ones, behaviour changes, and the idea itself can change.

Example: Metrics

Let's dive into a specific example now: someone finds a useful new metric that helps in evaluating performance.

---

[8]https://github.com/risk-first/website/blob/master/RiskMatrix.numbers

It might be:

- **Source Lines Of Code (SLOC)**: i.e. the number of lines of code each developer writes per day/week whatever.
- **Function Points**: the number of function points a person on the team completes, each sprint.
- **Code Coverage**: the number of lines of code exercised by unit tests.
- **Response Time**: the time it takes to respond to an emergency call, say, or to go from a feature request to production.
- **Release Cadence**: number of releases a team performs, per month, say.

With some skill, they may be able to *correlate* this metric against some other more abstract measure of success. For example:

- "quality is correlated with more releases"
- "user-satisfaction is correlated with SLOC"
- "revenue is correlated with response time"

Because the *thing on the right* is easier to measure than *the thing on the left*, it becomes used as a proxy (or, Map) for the thing they are really interested in (the Territory). At this point, it's *easy* to communicate this idea with the rest of the team, and *the market value of the idea is high*: it is a useful representation of reality, which is shown to be accurate at a particular point in time.

But *correlation* doesn't imply *causation*. The *cause* might be different:

- Quality and number of releases might both be down to the simplicity of the product.
- User satisfaction and SLOC might both be down to the calibre of the developers.
- Response time and revenue might both be down to clever team planning.

Metrics are seductive because they simplify reality and are easily communicated. But they *inherently* contain Map and Territory Risk: by relying *only* on the metrics, you're not really *seeing* the reality.

The devil is in the detail.

Reality Evolves

In the same way that markets evolve to demand more features, our behaviour evolves to incorporate new ideas. The more popular an idea is, the more people will modify their behaviour as a result of it, and the more the world will change.

In the case of metrics this is where they start being used for more than just indicators but as measures of performance or targets:

- If a team is *told* to do lots of releases, they will perform lots of releases *at the expense of something else*.
- If team members are promoted according to SLOC, they will make sure their code takes up as many lines as possible.
- In the UK, ambulances were asked to wait before admitting patients to Emergency wards, in order that hospitals could meet their targets[9].

> "Any observed statistical regularity will tend to collapse once pressure is placed upon it for control purposes."
> —Goodhart's Law, *Wikipedia*[10]

Some of this seems obvious: *Of course* SLOC is a terrible measure performance! We're not that stupid anymore. The problem is, it's not so much the *choice* of metric, but the fact that *all* metrics merely approximate reality with a few numbers. The map is *always* simpler than the territory, therefore there can be no perfect metrics.

Will the idea still be useful as the world adapts? Although the Hype Cycle model doesn't cover it, ideas and products all eventually have their day and decline in usefulness.

Bad Ideas

There are plenty of ideas which *seem a really good idea at the time* but then end up being terrible. It's only as we *improve our internal model* and realize the hidden risks that we stop using them. While SLOC is a minor offender, CFCs[11] or Leaded Petrol[12] are more significant examples.

Figure 22.9 shows an initially promising idea that turns out to be terrible. That is, the **Knowledge** value of it ends up being significantly less than the

---

[9] https://en.wikipedia.org/wiki/NHS_targets
[10] https://en.wikipedia.org/wiki/Goodharts_law
[11] https://en.wikipedia.org/wiki/Chlorofluorocarbon
[12] https://en.wikipedia.org/wiki/Tetraethyllead

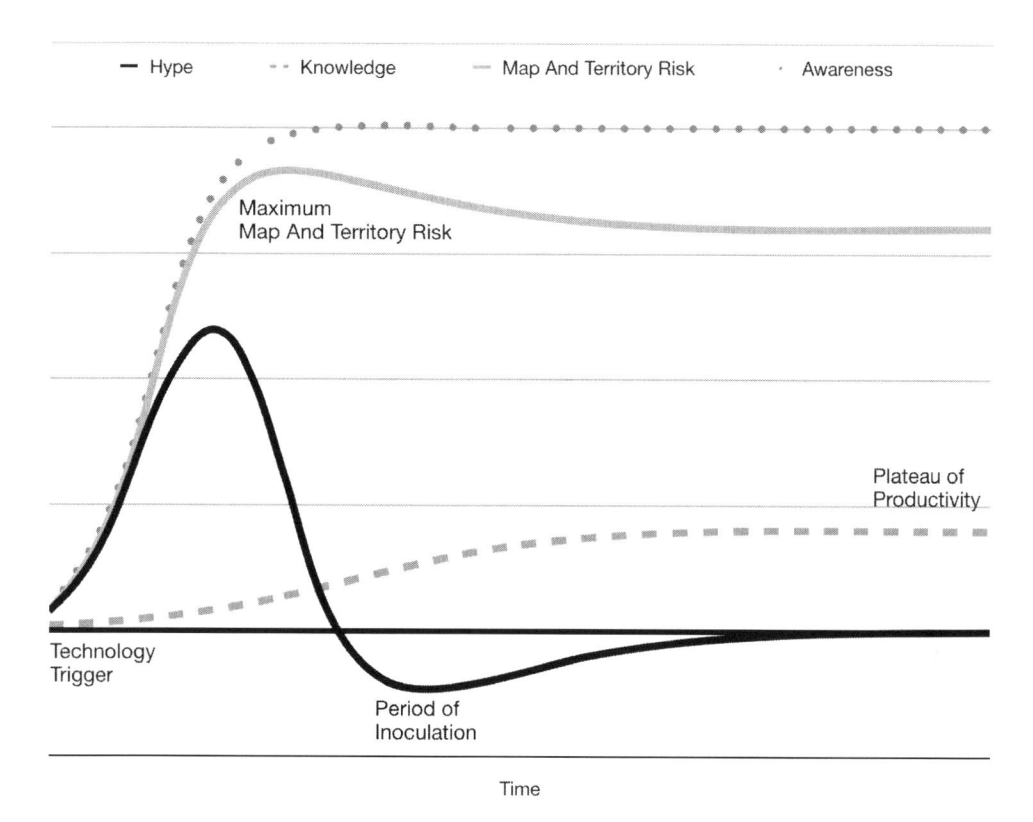

*Figure 22.9: Hype Cycle for something that turns out to be a **bad** idea*

Map and Territory Risk of using it. Hence, there is a "Period of Inoculation" where the population realise their mistake - there is "negative hype" as they work to phase out the offending idea until it's forgotten.

SLOC is not on its own a *bad idea*, but using it as a metric for developer productivity *is*.

> "Measuring programming progress by lines of code is like measuring aircraft building progress by weight."
>
> Bill Gates[13]

Figure 22.10 shows how Evolution-type Feature Risks can manifest in the Internal Model.

---

[13] https://www.goodreads.com/quotes/536587

Evolution Risk	Examples
F–R Regression Risk	• Stories and ideas that evolve over time, such as religions or urban legends.
F–D Feature Drift Risk	• Banning harmful products, such as CFCs. • Gaming metrics. • Goodhart's Law.

Figure 22.10: Evolution Feature Risks, as manifested in the Internal Model

22.4 Humans and Machines

In the example of the SatNav, we saw how the *quality* of Map and Territory Risk is different for *people* and *machines*. Whereas people *should* be expected show skepticism for new (unlikely) information our databases accept it unquestioningly. *Forgetting* is an everyday, usually benign part of our human Internal Model, but for software systems it is a production crisis involving 3am calls and backups.

For Humans, Map and Territory Risk is exacerbated by cognitive biases[14]:

> "Cognitive biases are systematic patterns of deviation from norm or rationality in judgement, and are often studied in psychology and behavioural economics."
>
> —Cognitive Bias, *Wikipedia*[15]

There are *lots* of cognitive biases. But let's just mention some that are relevant to Map and Territory Risk:

- **Availability Heuristic**: people overestimate the importance of knowledge they have been exposed to.
- **The Ostrich Effect**: which is where dangerous information is ignored or avoided because of the emotions it will evoke.
- **Bandwagon Effect**: people like to believe things that other people believe. (Could this be a factor in the existence of the Hype Cycle?)

---
[14]https://en.wikipedia.org/wiki/List_of_cognitive_biases
[15]https://en.wikipedia.org/wiki/List_of_cognitive_biases

22.5 Hierarchical Organisations

Map And Territory Risk "trickles down" through an organisation. The higher levels have an out-sized ability to pervert the incentives at lower levels because once an organisation begins to pursue a "bullshit objective" the whole company can align to this.

The Huffington Post[16] paints a brilliant picture of how Volkswagen managed to get caught faking their emissions tests. As they point out:

> "The leadership culture of VW probably amplified the problem by disconnecting itself from the values and trajectory of society, by entrenching in what another executive in the auto industry once called a "bullshit-castle"... No engineer wakes up in the morning and thinks, OK, today I want to build devices that deceive our customers and destroy our planet. Yet it happened. Why? Because of hubris at the top."
> —Otto Scharmer, *Huffington Post*[17].

This article identifies the following process:

- **De-sensing**: VW Executives ignored *The Territory* of society around them (such as the green movement), ensuring their maps were out of date. The top-down culture made it hard for reality to propagate back up the hierarchy.
- **Hubris/Absencing**: they pursued their own metrics of *volume* and *cost*, rather than seeking out others (a la the Availability Heuristic Bias). That is, focusing on their own *Map*, which is *easier* than checking the *Territory*.
- **Deception**: backed into a corner, engineers had no choice but to find "creative" ways to meet the metrics.
- **Destruction**: eventually, the truth comes out, to the detriment of the company, the environment and the shareholders. As the article's title summarizes "A fish rots from the head down".

22.6 Markets

We've considered Map and Territory Risk for individuals, teams and organisations. Inadequate Equilibria[18] by Eleizer Yudkovsky, looks at how perverse

---
[16] https://www.huffingtonpost.com/otto-scharmer/the-fish-rots-from-the-he_b_8208652.html
[17] https://www.huffingtonpost.com/otto-scharmer/the-fish-rots-from-the-he_b_8208652.html
[18] https://equilibriabook.com

incentive mechanisms break not just departments, but entire societal systems. He highlights one example involving *academics* and *grantmakers* in academia:

- It's not very apparent which academics are more worthy of funding.
- One proxy is what they've published (scientific papers) and where they've published (journals).
- Universities want to attract research grants, and the best way to do this is to have the best academics.
- Because "best" isn't measurable, they use the publications proxy.
- Therefore immense power rests in the hands of the journals, since they can control this metric.
- Therefore journals are able to charge large amounts of money to universities for subscriptions.

> "Now consider the system of scientific journals... Some journals are prestigious. So university hiring committees pay the most attention to publications in that journal. So people with the best, most interesting-looking publications try to send them to that journal. So if a university hiring committee paid an equal amount of attention to publications in lower-prestige journals, they'd end up granting tenure to less prestigious people. Thus, the whole system is a stable equilibrium that nobody can unilaterally defy except at cost to themselves."
> —Inadequate Equilibria, *Eleizer Yudkovsky*[19]

As the book points out, while everyone *persists* in using an inadequate abstraction, the system is broken. However, Coordination would be required for everyone to *stop* doing it this way, which is hard work. (Maps are easier to fix in a top-down hierarchy.)

Scientific journals are a single example taken from a closely argued book investigating lots of cases of this kind. It's worth taking the time to read a couple of the chapters on this interesting topic. (Like Risk-First it is available to read online).

As usual, this chapter forms a grab-bag of examples in a complex topic. But it's time to move on as there is one last stop we have to make on the Risk Landscape, and that is to look at Operational Risk.

---

[19]https://equilibriabook.com/molochs-toolbox/

CHAPTER 23

Operational Risk

> "The risk of loss resulting from inadequate or failed internal processes, people and systems or from external events."
> —Operational Risk, *Wikipedia*[1]

In this chapter we're going to start considering the realities of running software systems in the real world.

There is a lot to this subject, so this chapter is just a taster: we're going to set the scene by looking at what constitutes an Operational Risk, and then look at the related discipline of Operations Management. Following this background, we'll apply the Risk-First model and have a high-level look at the various mitigations for Operational Risk.

23.1 Operational Risks

When building software, it's tempting to take a very narrow view of the dependencies of a system, but Operational Risks are often caused by dependencies we *don't* consider - i.e. the **Operational Context** within which the system is operating. Here are some examples:

- **Staff Risks**:
    - Freak weather conditions affecting ability of staff to get to work, interrupting the development and support teams.
    - Reputational damage caused when staff are rude to the customers.
- **Reliability Risks**:

---
[1] https://en.wikipedia.org/wiki/Operational_risk#Definition

- A data-centre going off-line, causing your customers to lose access.
- A power cut causing backups to fail.
- Not having enough desks for everyone to sit at.

- **Process Risks**:
  - Regulatory change, which means you have to adapt your business model.
  - Insufficient controls which means you don't notice when some transactions are failing, leaving you out-of-pocket.
  - Data loss because of bugs introduced during an untested release.

- **Software Dependency Risk**:
  - Hackers exploit weaknesses in a piece of 3rd party software, bringing your service down.

- **Agency Risk**:
  - Workers going on strike.
  - Employees trying to steal from the company (bad actors).
  - Other crime, such as hackers stealing data.

This is a long laundry-list of everything that can go wrong due to operating in "The Real World". Although we've spent a lot of time looking at the varieties of Dependency Risk on a software project, with Operational Risk we have to consider that these dependencies will fail in any number of unusual ways, and we can't be ready for all of them. Preparing for this comes under the umbrella of Operations Management.

23.2 Operations Management

If we are designing a software system to "live" in the real world we have to be mindful of the **Operational Context** we're working in and craft our software and processes accordingly. This view of the "wider" system is the discipline of Operations Management.

> "Operations management is an area of management concerned with designing and controlling the process of production and re-designing business operations in the production of goods or services. It involves the responsibility of ensuring that business operations are efficient in terms of using as few resources as needed and effective in terms of meeting customer requirements."
>
> —Operations Management, *Wikipedia*[2]

[2]https://en.wikipedia.org/wiki/Operations_management

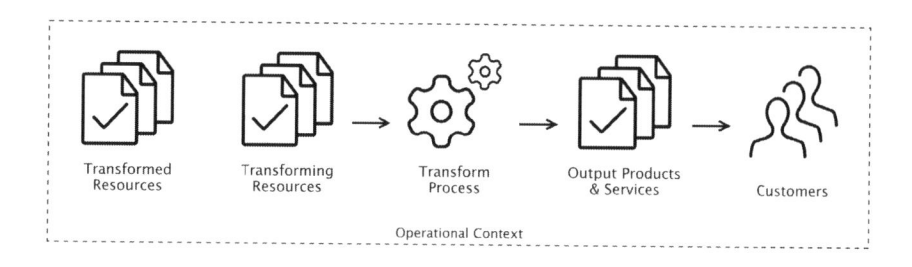

Figure 23.1: Model of Operations Management, adapted from Slack et al.

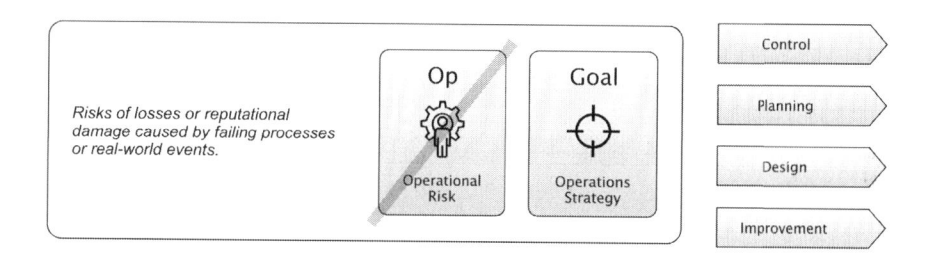

Figure 23.2: Risk-First Operations Management: Taking Action, inspired by the work of Slack et al.

Figure 23.1 is a Risk-First interpretation of Slack *et al*'s model of Operations Management[3]. This model breaks down some of the key abstractions of the discipline:

- **A Transform Process** (the **Operation** itself), which tries to achieve an...
- **Operational Strategy** (the objectives of the operation) and is embedded in the wider...
- **Operational Context**, which supplies the **Transform Process** with three key dependencies. These are...
- **Resources**: whether *transformed* resources (like electricity or information, say) or *transforming* resources (like staff or equipment).
- **Customers**: which supply it with money in return for goods and services.

---

[3] http://amzn.eu/d/b6ZjuMu

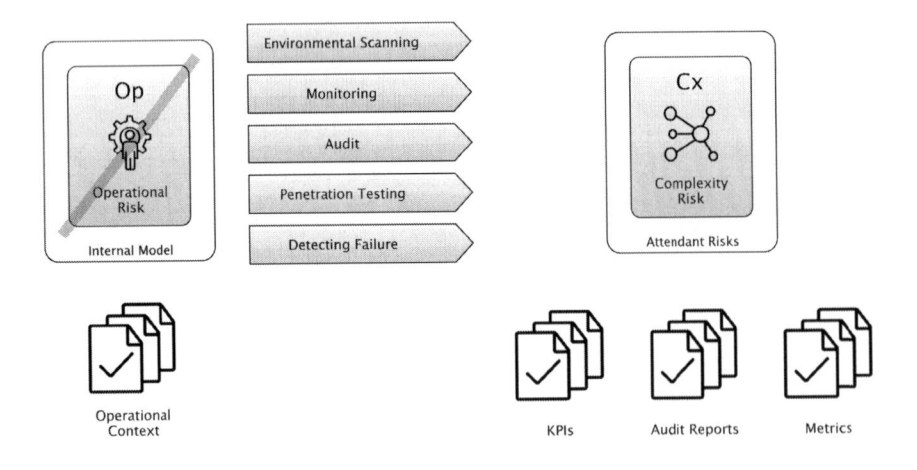

Figure 23.3: Control, Monitoring And Detection

The healthy functioning of the **Transform Process** is the domain of Operations Management. As Figure 23.2 shows (again, modified from Slack *et al.*) this involves the following types of actions.

- **Control**: ensuring that the Transform Process is working according to its targets. This includes day-to-day quality control and monitoring .
- **Planning**: this covers aspects such as capacity planning, forecasting and project planning. This is about making sure the transform process has targets to meet and the resources to meet them.
- **Design**: ensuring that the design of the product and the transform process itself fulfils an Operational Strategy.
- **Improvement**: improving the operation in response to changes in the **Environment** and the Operational Strategy, detecting failure and recovering from it.

Let's look at each of these actions in turn.

23.3 Control

Since humans and machines have different areas of expertise, and because Operational Risks are often novel, it's often not optimal to try and automate everything. A good operation will consist of a mix of human and machine actors, each playing to their strengths (see the table below).

The aim is to build a human-machine operational system that is *Homeostatic*[4]. This is the property of living things to try and maintain an equilibrium (for example, body temperature or blood glucose levels), but also applies to systems at any scale. The key to homeostasis is to build systems with feedback loops, even though this leads to more complex systems overall. Figure 23.3 shows some of the actions involved in these kind of feedback loops within IT operations.

Humans Are...	Machines Are...
Good at novel situations	Good at repetitive situations
Good at adaptation	Good at consistency
Expensive at scale	Cheap at scale
Reacting and Anticipating	Recording

As we saw in Map and Territory Risk, it's very easy to fool yourself, especially around Key Performance Indicators (KPIs) and metrics. Large organisations have Audit[5] functions precisely to guard against their own internal failing processes and Agency Risk. Audits could be around software tools, processes, practices, quality and so on. Practices such as Continuous Improvement[6] and Total Quality Management[7] also figure here.

Scanning The Operational Context

There are plenty of Hidden Risks within the operation's environment. These change all the time in response to economic, legal or political change. In order to manage a risk, you have to uncover it, so part of Operations Management is to look for trouble.

- **Environmental Scanning** is all about trying to determine which changes in the environment are going to impact your operation. Here we are trying to determine the level of Dependency Risk we face for external dependencies, such as suppliers, customers, markets and regulation. Tools like PEST[8] are relevant, as is
- **Penetration Testing**[9]: looking for security weaknesses within the operation. See OWASP[10] for examples.

---

[4] https://en.wikipedia.org/wiki/Homeostasis
[5] https://en.wikipedia.org/wiki/Audit
[6] https://en.wikipedia.org/wiki/Continual_improvement_process
[7] https://en.wikipedia.org/wiki/Total_quality_management
[8] https://en.wikipedia.org/wiki/PEST_analysis
[9] https://en.wikipedia.org/wiki/Penetration_test
[10] https://en.wikipedia.org/wiki/OWASP

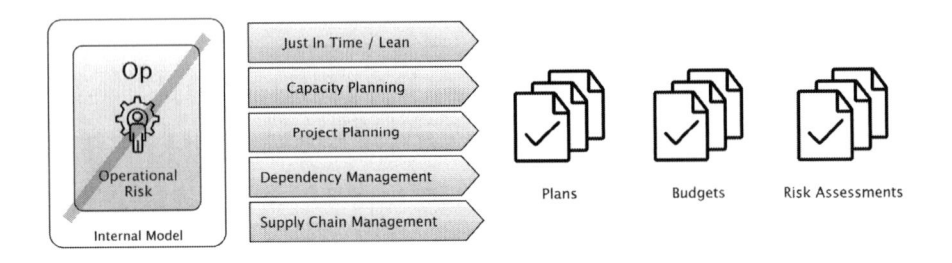

Figure 23.4: Forecasting and Planning Actions

- **Vulnerability Management**[11] is about keeping up-to-date with vulnerabilities in Software Dependencies.

23.4 Planning

In order to *control* an operation, we need targets and plans to *control against*. For a system to run well, it needs to carefully manage unreliable dependencies, and ensure their safety and availability. In the example of the humans, say, it's the difference between Hunter-Gathering[12] (picking up food where we find it) and Agriculture[13] (controlling the environment and the resources to grown crops).

As Figure 23.4 shows, we can bring Planning to bear on dependency management, and this usually falls to the more human end of the operation.

23.5 Design

Since our operation exists in a world of risks like Red Queen Risk and Feature Drift Risk, we would expect that the output of our Planning actions would result in changes to our operation.

While *planning* is a day-to-day operational feedback loop, *design* is a longer feedback loop changing not just the parameters of the operation, but the operation itself.

You might think that for an IT operation, tasks like Design belong within a separate "Development" function within an organisation. Traditionally, this might have been the case. However separating Development from Operations implies Boundary Risk between these two functions. For example,

---

[11] https://en.wikipedia.org/wiki/Vulnerability_management
[12] https://en.wikipedia.org/wiki/Hunter-gatherer
[13] https://en.wikipedia.org/wiki/Agriculture

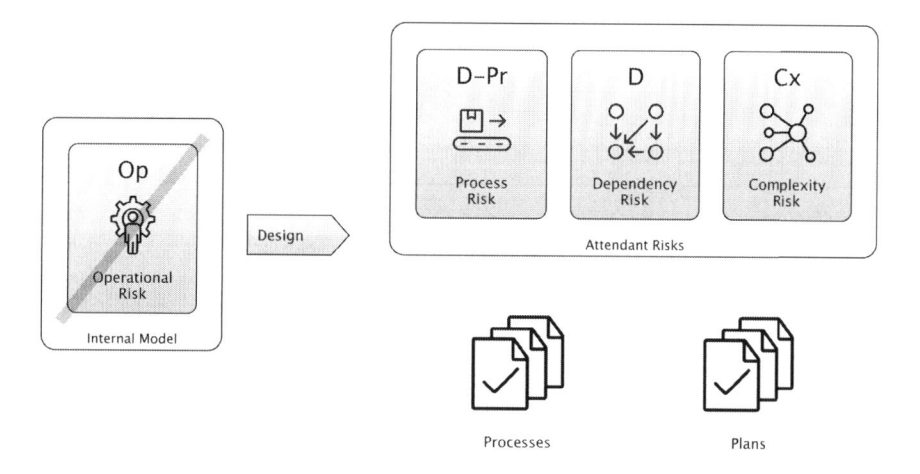

Figure 23.5: Design and Change Activities

the developers might employ different tools, equipment and processes to the Operations team resulting in a mismatch when software is delivered.

In recent years the DevOps movement has brought this Boundary Risk into sharper focus. This specifically means:

- Using code to automate previously manual Operations functions, like monitoring and releasing.
- Involving Operations in the planning and design, so that the delivered software is optimised for the environment it runs in.

23.6 Improvement

No system can be perfect, and after it meets the real world, we will want to improve it over time. But Operational Risk includes an element of Trust & Belief Risk: we have a *reputation* and the good will of our customers to consider when we make improvements. Because this is very hard to rebuild, we should consider this before releasing software that might not live up to expectations.

So there is a tension between "you only get one chance to make a first impression" and "gilding the lily" (perfectionism). In the past I've seen this stated as *pressure to ship vs pressure to improve*.

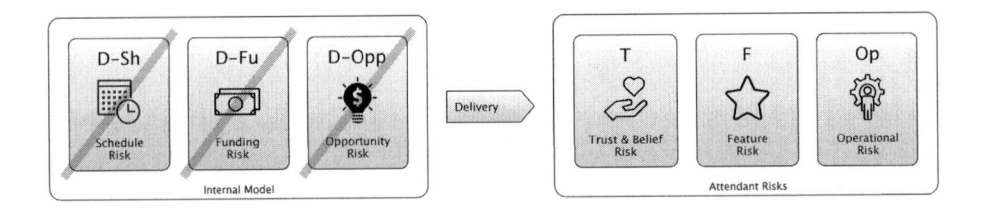

Figure 23.6: Balance of Risks from Delivering Software

A Risk-First re-framing of this (as shown in Figure 23.6) might be the balance between:

- The perceived Scarcity Risks (such as funding, time available, etc) of staying in development (pressure to ship).
- The perceived Trust & Belief Risk, Feature Risk and Operational Risk of going to production (pressure to improve).

The "should we ship?" decision is therefore a complex one. In Meeting Reality, we discussed that it's better to do this "sooner, more frequently, in smaller chunks and with feedback". We can meet Operational Risk *on our own terms* by doing so:

Meet Reality...	Techniques
Sooner	Beta Testing, Soft Launches, Business Continuity Testing
More Frequently	Continuous Delivery, Sprints
In Smaller Chunks	Modular Releases, Microservices, Feature Toggles, Trial Populations
With Feedback	User Communities, Support Groups, Monitoring, Logging, Analytics

23.7 The End Of The Road

In a way, actions like **Design** and **Improvement** bring us right back to where we started from: identifying Dependency Risks, Feature Risks and Complexity Risks that hinder our operation, and mitigating them through actions like *software development*.

Our safari of risk is finally complete: it's time to reflect on what we've seen in the next chapter, Staging and Classifying.

CHAPTER 24

Staging and Classifying

Our tour is complete.

But if we are good collectors, then before we finish we should *Stage*[1] our specimens and do some work in classifying what we've seen.

---

[1]https://en.wikipedia.org/wiki/Entomological_equipment_for_mounting_and_storage

Figure 24.1: Staged and Classified Beetle Collection, (Credit: Fir0002, Wikipedia)

24.1 Towards A "Periodic Table" Of Risks

As we said at the start, Risk-First is all about developing *A Pattern Language*. We can use the terms like "Feature Risk" or "Learning Curve Risk" to explain phenomena we see on software projects. If we want to De-Risk our work, we need this power of explanation so we can talk about how to go about it.

Figure 24.2 compiles all of the risks we've seen so far on our tour across the Risk Landscape. Just like a periodic table, there are perhaps others left to discover. *Unlike* a periodic table, these risks are not completely distinct: they mix like paint and blend into one another.

If you've been reading closely, you'll notice that a number of themes come up again and again within the different chapters. It's time to look at the *patterns within the patterns*.

24.2 The Power Of Abstractions

Abstraction appears as a concept continually: in Communication Risk, Complexity Metrics, Map and Territory Risk or how it causes Boundary Risk. We've looked at some complicated examples of abstractions, such as network protocols, dependencies on technology or Business Processes.

Let's now *generalize* what is happening with abstraction. To do this, we'll consider the simplest example of abstraction: *naming a pattern* of behaviour we see in the real world, such as "Binge Watching" or "Remote Working", or naming a category of insects as "Beetles".

Using A Known Abstraction

As shown in Figure 24.3, *using an abstraction you already know* means:

- **Mitigating Feature Risk**: because the abstraction is providing you with something *useful*. For example, using the word "London" allows you to refer to a whole (but slightly non-specific) geographic area.
- **Accepting Communication Risk**: because if you are using the abstraction in conversation the people you are using it with *need to understand it too*.
- **Accepting Map and Territory Risk**: because the abstraction is a simplification and not the actual thing itself.
- **Living with Dependency Risks**: we depend on a word in our language (or a function in our library, or a service on the Internet). But words are unreliable. Language *changes* and *evolves*, and the words you are using

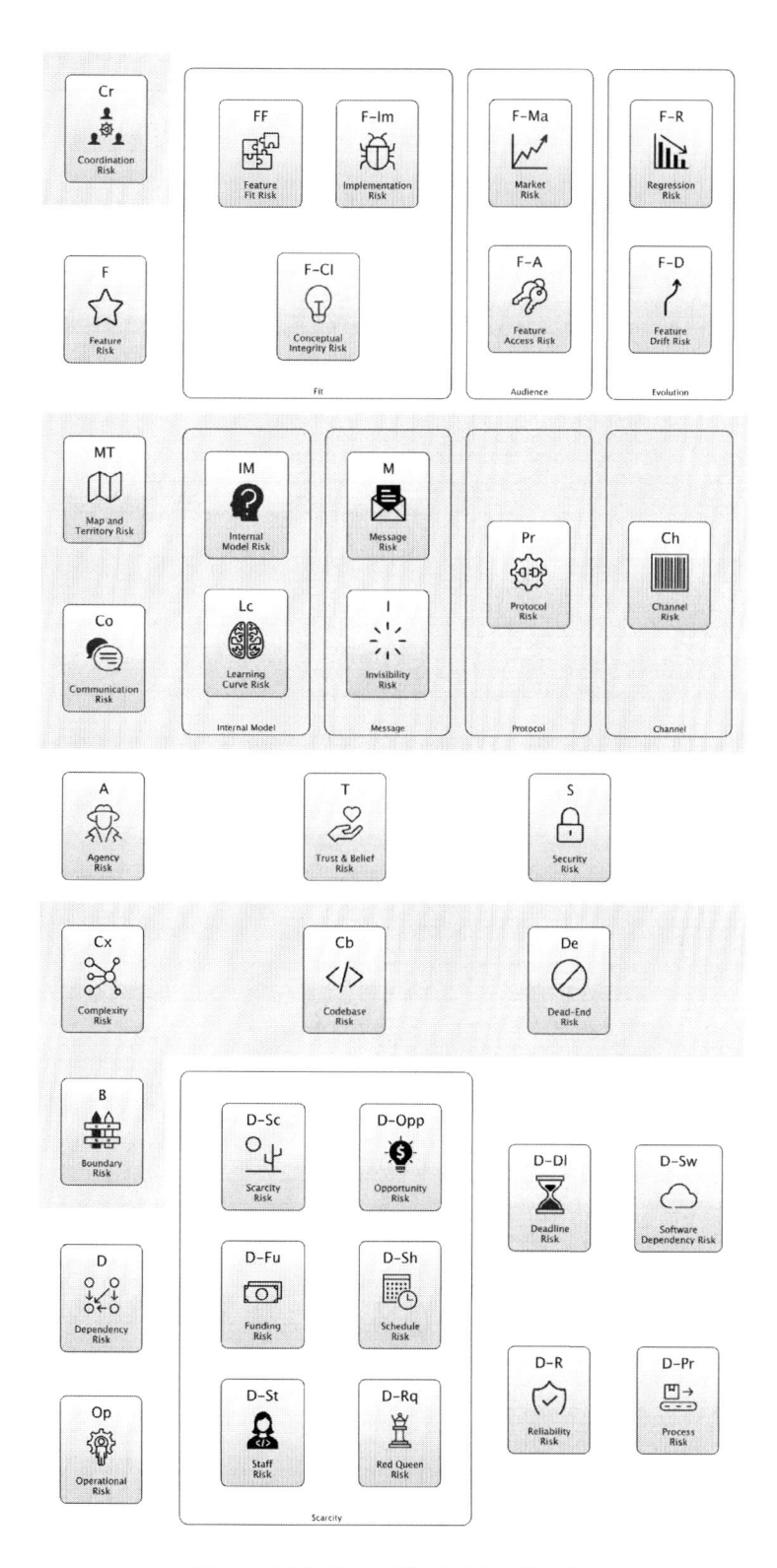

Figure 24.2: Periodic Table of Risks

231

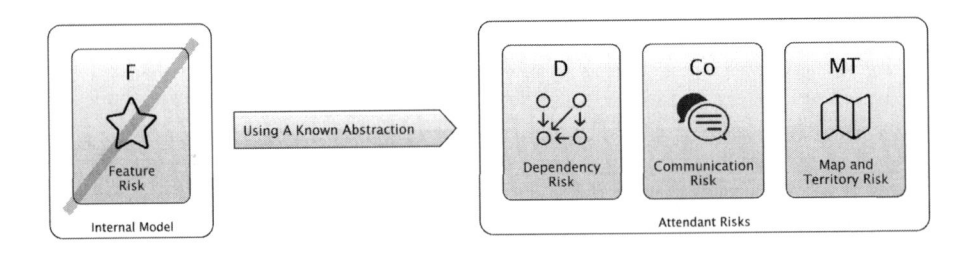

Figure 24.3: Using A Known Abstraction

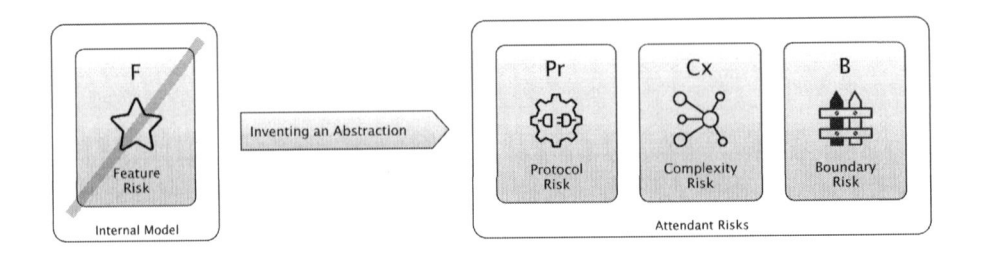

Figure 24.4: Inventing A New Abstraction

now might not always mean what you want them to mean. (Software too changes and evolves: We've seen this in Red Queen Risk and Feature Drift Risk.)

Inventing A New Abstraction

As shown in Figure 24.4, *inventing a new abstraction* means:

- **Mitigating Feature Risk.** By *giving a name to something* (or building a new product, or a way of working) you are offering up something that someone else can use. This should mitigate Feature Risk in the sense that other people can choose to use your it, if it fits their requirements.

- **Creating a Protocol.** Introducing *new words to a language* creates Protocol Risk as most people won't know what it means.
- **Increasing Complexity Risk.** Because, the more words we have, the more complex the language is.
- **Creating the opportunity for Boundary Risk.** By naming something, you *implicitly* create a boundary, because the world is now divided into "things which *are* X" and "things which *are not* X". *Boundary Risk arises from abstractions.*

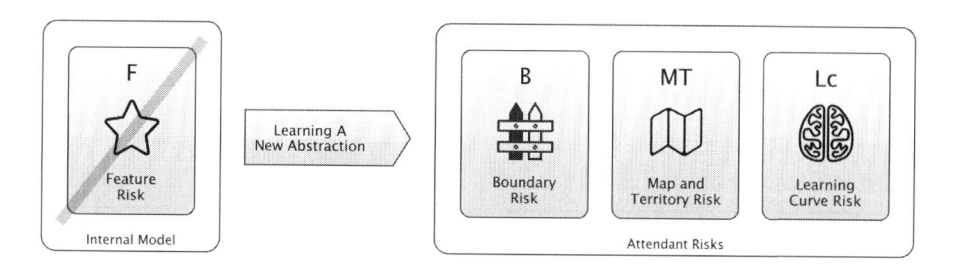

Figure 24.5: Learning a New Abstraction

Learning A New Abstraction

As shown in Figure 24.5, *learning a new abstraction* means:

- **Overcoming a Learning Curve**: because you have to *learn* a name in order to use it (whether it is the name of a function, a dog, or someone at a party).
- **Accepting Boundary Risks.** Commitment to one abstraction over another means that you have the opportunity cost of the other abstractions that you could have used.
- **Accepting Map And Territory Risk.** Because the word refers to the *concept* of the thing, and *not the thing itself*.

Abstraction is everywhere and seems to be at the heart of what our brains do. But clearly, like taking any other action there is always trade-off in terms of risk.

24.3 Your Feature Risk is Someone Else's Dependency Risk

In the Feature Risk chapter, we looked at the problems of *supplying something for a client to use as a dependency*: you've got to satisfy a demand (Market Risk) and service a segment of the user community (Feature Access Risk).

However over the rest of the Dependency Risk chapters we looked at this from the point of view of *being a client of someone else*: you want to find trustworthy, reliable dependencies that don't give up when you least want them to.

So Feature Risk and Dependency Risk are *two sides of the same coin*, they capture the risks in *demand* and *supply*.

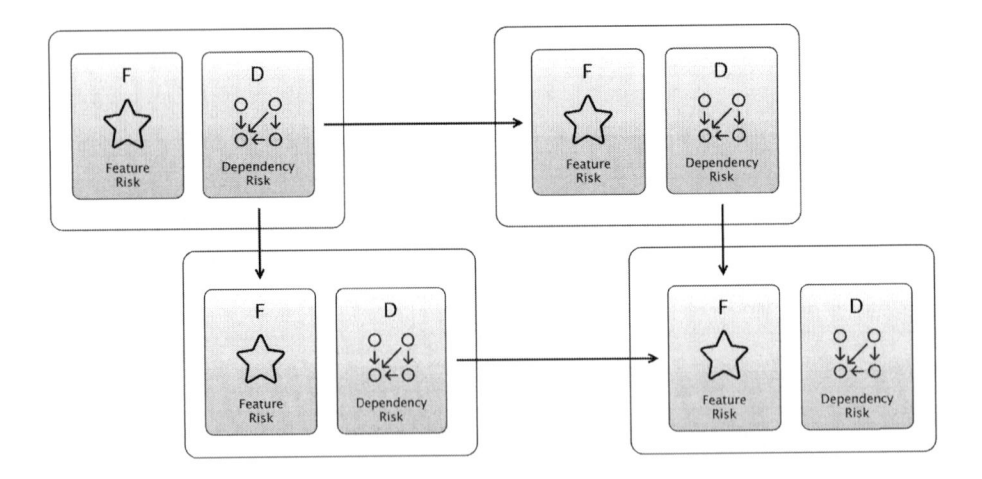

Figure 24.6: Features And Dependencies

As shown in Figure 24.6, relationships of features/dependencies are the basis of Supply Chains and the world-wide network of goods and services that forms the modern economy. The incredible complexity of this network mean incredible Complexity Risk, too. Humans are masters at coordinating and managing our dependencies.

24.4 The Work Continues

On this journey around the Risk Landscape we've collected a (hopefully) good, representative sample of Risks and where to find them. But there are more out there. How many of these have you seen on your projects? What is missing? What is wrong?

Please help by reporting back what you find.

Part III

Tools & Practices

CHAPTER 25

Coming Next

This is nearly the end of *Risk-First: The Menagerie*. But, it's not the full picture. We've had Part 1 (The Introduction) and Part 2 (The Risk Landscape), but you're yet to read parts 3 & 4. These are to be published together in the next book, *Risk-First: Tools and Techniques*, but are also available at `https://riskfirst.org`.

But it feels a shame to end with Part 2, which is just a long list of all the troubles you'll face on a software project. So in order to improve the tone somewhat, here we have a single chapter from Part 3 .

As an encore, if you will.

CHAPTER 26

Estimates

In this chapter, we're going to put a Risk-First spin on the process of Estimating. But in order to get there, we first need to start with understanding *why* we estimate. We're going to look at some "Old Saws" of software estimation and what we can learn from them. Finally, we'll bring our Risk-First menagerie to bear on de-risking the estimation process.

26.1 The Purpose Of Estimating

Why bother estimating at all? There are two reasons why estimates are useful:

1. **To allow for the creation of** *events.* As we saw in Deadline Risk, if we can put a date on something, we can mitigate lots of Coordination Risk. Having a *release date* for a product allows whole teams of people to coordinate their activities in ways that hugely reduce the need for Communication. "Attack at dawn" allows disparate army units to avoid the Coordination Risk inherent in "attack on my signal". This is a *good reason for estimating* because by using events you are mitigating Coordination Risk. This is often called a *hard deadline*.

2. **To allow for the estimation of the Payoff of an action.** This is a *bad reason for estimating* as we will discuss in detail below. But briefly the main issue is that Payoff isn't just about figuring out Schedule Risk - you should be looking at all the other Attendant Risks of the action too.

26.2 How Estimates Fail

Estimates are a huge source of contention in the software world:

> "Typically, effort estimates are over-optimistic and there is a strong over-confidence in their accuracy. The mean effort overrun seems to be about 30% and not decreasing over time."
> —Software Development Effort Estimation, *Wikipedia*[1].

In their research "Anchoring and Adjustment in Software Estimation", Aranda and Easterbrook[2] asked developers split into three groups (A, B and Control) to give individual estimates on how long a piece of software would take to build. They were each given the same specification. However:

- Group A was given the hint: "I admit I have no experience with software, but I guess it will take about two months to finish".
- Group B were given the same hint, except with *20* months.

How long would members of each group estimate the work to take? The results were startling. On average,

- Group A estimated 5.1 months.
- The Control Group estimated 7.8 months.
- Group B estimated 15.4 months.

The anchor mattered more than experience, how formal the estimation method, or anything else. *We can't estimate time at all.*

26.3 Is Risk To Blame?

Why is it so bad? The problem with a developer answering a question such as:

> "How long will it take to deliver X?"

Seems to be the following:

---

[1] https://en.m.wikipedia.org/wiki/Software_development_effort_estimation
[2] http://www.cs.toronto.edu/%7Esme/papers/2005/ESEC-FSE-05-Aranda.pdf

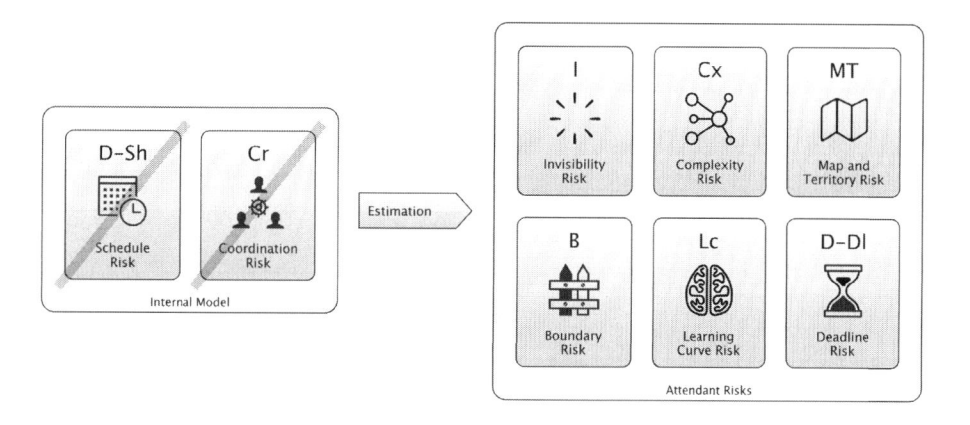

Figure 26.1: Estimates: Attendant Risks

- The developer and the client likely don't agree on exactly what X is, and any description of it is inadequate anyway (Invisibility Risk).
- The developer has a less-than-complete understanding of the environment he will be delivering X in (Complexity Risk and Map And Territory Risk).
- The developer has some vague ideas about how to do X, but he'll need to try out various approaches until he finds something that works (Boundary Risk and Learning Curve Risk).
- The developer has no idea what Hidden Risk will surface when he starts work on it.
- The developer has no idea what will happen if he takes too long and misses the date by a day/week/month/year (Schedule Risk).
- The developer now has a Deadline

... and so on. This is summarised in Figure 26.1. It's no wonder people hate estimating: the treatment is worse than the disease.

So what are we to do? It's a problem as old as software itself, and in deference to that, let's examine the estimating problem via some "Old Saws".

26.4 Old Saw No. 1: The "10X Developer"

"A 10X developer is an individual who is thought to be as productive as 10 others in his or her field. The 10X developer

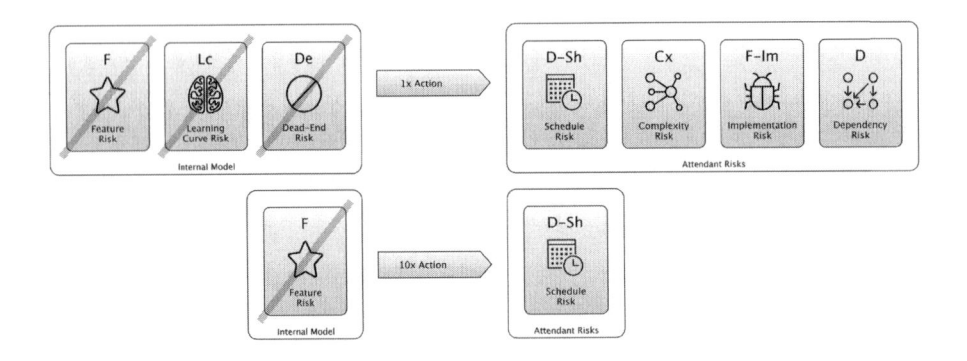

Figure 26.2: 1X Task vs 10X Task

would produce 10 times the outcomes of other colleagues, in a production, engineering or software design environment."

—10X Developer, *Techopedia*[3]

Let's try and pull this apart:

- How do we measure this "productivity"? In Risk-First terms, this is about taking action to change our current position on the Risk Landscape to a position of more favourable risk. A "10X Developer" then must be able to take actions that have much higher Payoff than a "1X Developer". That is, mitigating more existing risk, and generating less Attendant Risk.
- It stands to reason then, that someone taking action *faster* will be leaving us with less Schedule Risk.
- However, if they are *more expensive*, they may leave us with greater Funding Risk afterwards.
- But Schedule Risk isn't the only risk being transformed: the result might be bugs, expensive new dependencies or spaghetti-code complexity.
- The "10X" developer *must* also leave behind less of these kind of risks too.
- That means that the "10X Developer" isn't merely faster, but *taking different actions*. They are able to use their talent and experience to see actions with greater Payoff than the 1X Developer.

Does the "10X Developer" even exist? Crucially, it would seem that such a thing would be predicated on the existence of the "1X Developer", who gets

---

[3]https://www.techopedia.com/definition/31673/10X-developer

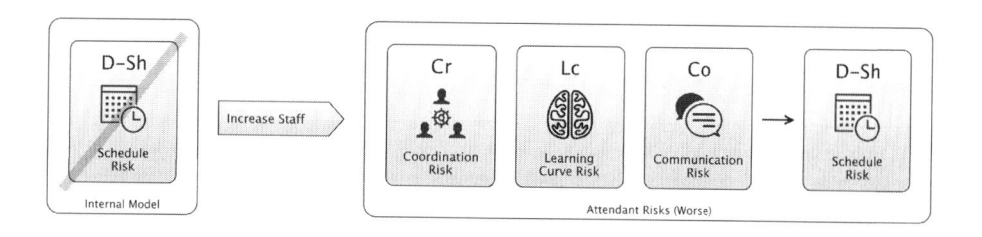

Figure 26.3: Brooks' Law, Risk-First Style

"1X" worth of work done each day. It's not clear that there is any such thing as an average developer who is mitigating risk at an average rate.

Even good developers have bad days, weeks or projects. Taking Action is like placing a bet. Sometimes you lose and the Payoff doesn't appear:

- The Open-Source software you're trying to apply to a problem doesn't solve it in the way you need.
- A crucial use-case of the problem turns out to change the shape of the solution entirely, leading to lots of rework.
- An assumption about how network security is configured turns out to be wrong, leading to a lengthy engagement with the infrastructure team.

The easiest way to be the "10X developer" is to have *done the job before*. If you're coding in a familiar language, with familiar libraries and tools, delivering a cookie-cutter solution to a problem in the same manner you've done several times before, then you will be a "10X Developer" compared to *you doing it the first time* because:

- There's no Learning Curve Risk, because you have already learnt everything.
- There's no Dead End Risk because you already know all the right choices to make and all the right paths to take on the Risk Landscape.

26.5 Old Saw No. 2: Quality, Speed, Cost: Pick Any Two

"The Project Management Triangle (called also the Triple Constraint, Iron Triangle and Project Triangle) is a model of the constraints of project management. While its origins are unclear, it has been used since at least the 1950s. It contends that:

1. The quality of work is constrained by the project's budget, deadlines and scope (features).

2. The project manager can trade between constraints.

3. Changes in one constraint necessitate changes in others to compensate or quality will suffer."

—Project Management Triangle, *Wikipedia*[4]

From a Risk-First perspective, we can now see that this is an over-simplification. If *quality* is a Feature Fit metric, *deadlines* is Schedule Risk and *budget* refers to Funding Risk then that leaves us with a lot of risks unaccounted for:

- I can deliver a project in very short order by building a bunch of screens that *do nothing* (accruing *stunning* levels of Implementation Risk as I go).

- Or, by assuming a lottery win, the project's budget is fine. (Although I would have *huge* Funding Risk because *what are the chances of winning the lottery?*)
- Brooks' Law (see Figure 26.3) contradicts the iron triangle by saying you can't trade budget for deadlines:

    "Brooks' law is an observation about software project management according to which 'adding human resources to a late software project makes it later'.
    —Brooks Law, *Wikipedia*[5]

So the conclusion is: **Focusing on the three risks of the iron triangle isn't enough.** You can game these risks by sacrificing others: we need to be looking at the project's risk *holistically*.

- There's no point in calling a project complete if the dependencies you are using are unreliable or undergoing rapid change
- There's no point in delivering the project on time if it's an Operational Risk nightmare, and requires constant round-the-clock support and will cost a fortune to *run*. (Working on a project that "hits its delivery date" but is nonetheless a broken mess once in production is too common a sight.)
- There's no point in delivering a project on-budget if the market has moved on and needs different features.

---

[4]https://en.wikipedia.org/wiki/Project_management_triangle
[5]https://en.wikipedia.org/wiki/Brooks_law

26.6 Old Saw No. 3: Parkinson's Law

> "Parkinson's law is the adage that 'work expands so as to fill the time available for its completion'."
> —Parkinson's Law, *Wikipedia*[6]

Let's leave aside the Devil Makes Work-style Agency Risk concerns this time. Instead, let's consider this from a Risk-First perspective. *Of course* work would expand to fill the time available: *Time available* is an *absence of Schedule Risk*. It's always going to be sensible to exchange free time to reduce more serious risks.

This is why projects will *always* take at least as long as is budgeted for them.

A Case Study

Let's look at a quick example of this in action, taken from Rapid Development by Steve McConnell[7]. At the point of this excerpt, Carl (the Project Manager) is discussing the schedule with Bill, the project sponsor:

> "I think it will take about 9 months, but that's just a rough estimate at this point," Carl said. "That's not going to work," Bill said. "I was hoping you'd say 3 or 4 months. We absolutely need to bring that system in within 6 months. Can you do it in 6?" (1)

Later in the story, the schedule has slipped twice and is about to slip again:

> ... at the 9-month mark, the team had completed detailed design, but coding still hadn't begun on some modules. It was clear that Carl couldn't make the 10-month schedule either. He announced the *third schedule slip* to 12 months. Bill's face turned red when Carl announced the slip, and the pressure from him became more intense. (2)

At point (2), Carl has tried to mitigate Feature Risk by increasing Schedule Risk, although he knows that Bill will trust him less for doing this, as shown in Figure 26.4. Let's continue...

---
[6]https://en.wikipedia.org/wiki/Parkinsons_law
[7]http://amzn.eu/d/eTWKOsK

Figure 26.4: Carl's Schedule Slip increases Trust and Belief Risks

Figure 26.5: Bill's Ultimatum

Carl began to feel that his job was on the line. Coding proceeded fairly well, but a few areas needed redesign and reimplementation. The team hadn't coordinated design details in those areas well, and some of their implementations conflicted. At the 11-month oversight-committee meeting, Carl announced the fourth schedule slip— to 13 months. Bill became livid. "Do you have any idea what you're doing?" he yelled. "You obviously don't have any idea! You obviously don't have any idea when the project is going to be done! I'll tell you when it's going to be done! It's going to be done by the 13-month mark, or you're going to be out of a job! I'm tired of being jerked around by you software guys! You and your team are going to work 60 hours a week until you deliver!" (3)

At point (3) in McConnell's Case Study, the schedule has slipped again and Bill has threatened Carl's job. Why did he do this? Because *he doesn't trust Carl's evaluation of the Schedule Risk*. By telling Carl that it's his job on the line he makes sure Carl appreciates the Schedule Risk.

However, forcing staff to do overtime is a dangerous ploy: it could disenfranchise the staff, or cause corners to be cut, as shown in Figure 26.5.

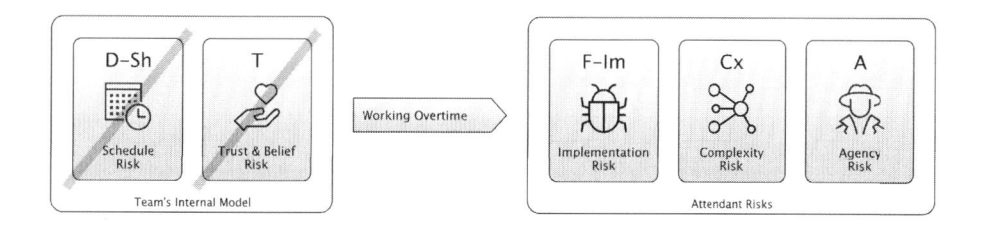

Figure 26.6: Team Response

> Carl felt his blood pressure rise, especially since Bill had backed him into an unrealistic schedule in the first place. But he knew that with four schedule slips under his belt, he had no credibility left. He felt that he had to knuckle under to the mandatory overtime or he would lose his job. Carl told his team about the meeting. They worked hard and managed to deliver the software in just over 13 months. Additional implementation uncovered additional design flaws, but with everyone working 60 hours a week, they delivered the product through sweat and sheer willpower. " (4)
>
> —McConnell, Steve, *Rapid Development*[8]

At point (4), we see that Bill's gamble worked (for him at least): the project was delivered by the team working overtime for two months. This was lucky - it seems unlikely that no-one quit and that the code didn't descend into a mess in that time.

Figure 26.6 shows the action taken, *working overtime*. Despite this being a fictional (or fictionalised) example, it rings true for many projects. What *should* have happened at point (1)? Both Carl and Bill estimated incorrectly... Or did they? Was this just Parkinson's Law in operation?

26.7 Agile Estimation

One alternative approach, much espoused in DevOps/Agile is to pick a short-enough period of time (say, two days or two weeks) and figure out what the most meaningful step towards achieving an objective would be in that time. By fixing the time period, we remove Schedule Risk from the equation, don't we?

---

[8] http://amzn.eu/d/eTWK0sK

Well, no. First, how to choose the time period? Schedule Risk tends to creep back in, in the form of something like Person-Hours[9] or Story Points[10]:

> "Story points rate the relative effort of work in a Fibonacci-like format: 0, 0.5, 1, 2, 3, 5, 8, 13, 20, 40, 100. It may sound counter-intuitive, but that abstraction is actually helpful because it pushes the team to make tougher decisions around the difficulty of work."
>
> —Story Points, *Atlassian*[11]

Second, the strategy of picking the two-day action with the greatest Payoff is *often good*. (After all, this is just Gradient Descent and that's a perfectly good way for training Machine Learning[12] systems.) However, just like following a river downhill from the top of a mountain will *often* get you to the sea, it probably won't take the shortest path and sometimes you'll get stuck at a lake.

The choice of using gradient descent means that you have given up on Goals: essentially, we have here the difference between "Walking towards a destination" and "Walking downhill". Or, if you like, a planned economy and a market economy. But, we don't live in *either*: everyone lives in some mixture of the two: our governments *have plans* for big things like roads and hospitals, and taxes. Other stuff, they leave to the whims of supply and demand. A project ends up being the same.

26.8 Risk-First Estimating

Let's figure out what we can take away from the above experiences:

- **From the "10X Developer" Saw**: the difference made by experience implies that a lot of the effort on a project comes from Learning Curve Risk and Dead End Risk.
- **From "Quality, Speed, Cost"**: we need to be considering *all* risks, not just some arbitrary milestones on a project plan. Project plans can always be gamed, and you can always leave risks unaccounted for in order to hit the goals.

---

[9] https://en.wikipedia.org/wiki/Man-hour
[10] https://www.atlassian.com/agile/project-management/estimation
[11] https://www.atlassian.com/agile/project-management/estimation
[12] https://en.wikipedia.org/wiki/Machine_learning

- **From "Parkinson's Law"**: giving people a *time budget*, you absolve them from Schedule Risk... at least until they realise they're going to overrun. This gives them one less dimension of risk to worry about, but means they end up taking all the time you give them, because they are optimising over the remaining risks.
- Finally, the lesson from **Agile Estimation** is that *just iterating* is sometimes not as efficient as *using your intuition and experience* to plan a more optimal path.

How can we synthesise this knowledge, along with what we've learned into something that makes more sense?

Tip #1: Estimating Should be About *Estimating Payoff*

For a given action / road-map / business strategy, what Attendant Risks are we going to have?

- What bets are we making about where the market will be?
- What Communication Risk will we face explaining our product to people?
- What Feature Fit risks are we likely to have when we get there?
- What Complexity Risks will we face building our software? How can we avoid it ending up as a Big Ball Of Mud?
- Where are we likely to face Boundary Risks and Dead End Risks?

Instead of the Agile Estimation being about picking out a story-point number based on some idealised amount of work that needs to be done, it should be about surfacing and weighing up risks. e.g:

- "Adding this new database is problematic because it's going to massively increase our Dependency Risk."
- "I don't think we should have component A interacting with component B because it'll introduce extra Communication Risk which we will always be tripping over."
- "I worry we might not understand what the sales team want and are facing Feature Implementation Risk. How about we try and get agreement on a specification?"

Essentially, this is what we are trying to capture with Risk-First Diagrams (Figure 26.7 being the template for this).

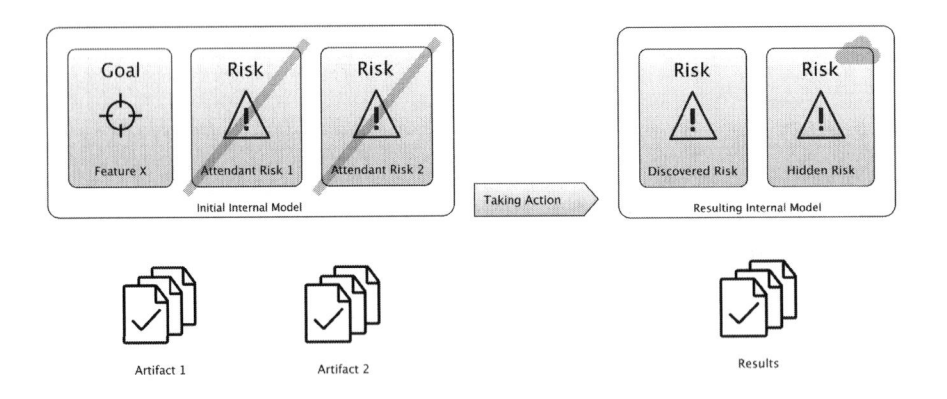

Figure 26.7: Risk-First Diagram Language

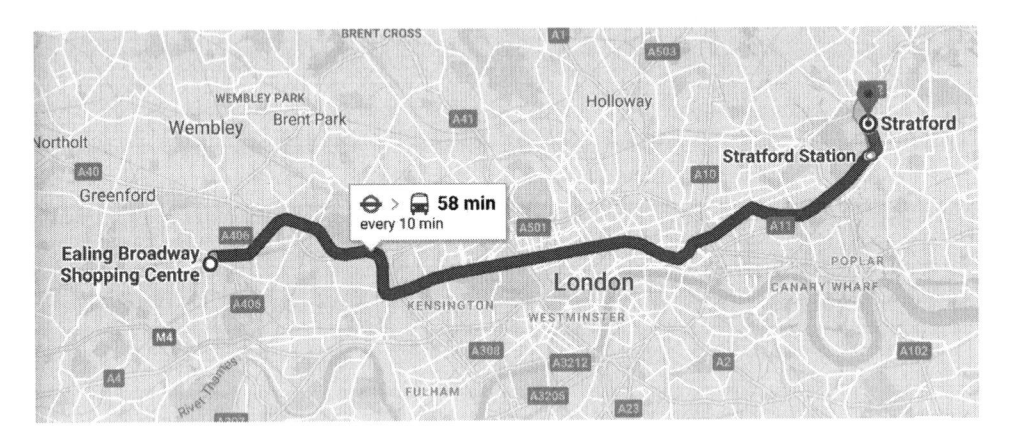

Figure 26.8: Journey via the Central Line

Tip #2: The Risk Landscape is Increasingly Complex: Utilise This

If you were travelling across London from Ealing (in the West) to Stratford (in the East) the *fastest* route might be to take the Central Line. You could do it via the A406 road, which would take a *bit* longer. It would *feel* like you're mainly going in completely the wrong direction doing that, but it's much faster than cutting straight through London and you don't pay the congestion charge.

In terms of risk, they all have different profiles. You're often delayed in the car, by some amount. The tube is *generally* reliable, but when it breaks down or is being repaired it might end up quicker to walk.

If you were doing this same journey on foot, it's a very direct route, but would

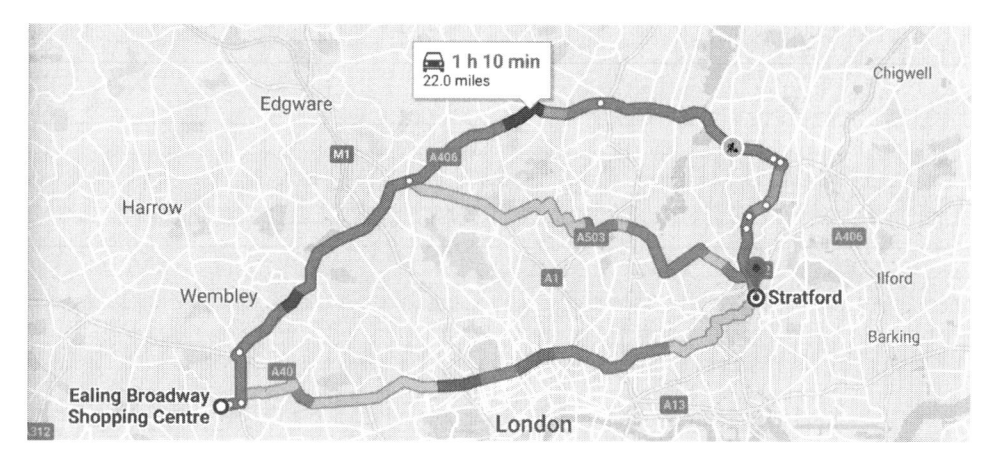

Figure 26.9: Journey by Car

Figure 26.10: Journey on Foot

take five times longer. However, if you were making this journey a hundred years ago that might be the only choice (horseback might be a bit faster).

In the software development past, *building it yourself* was the only way to get anything done. It was like London *before road and rail*. Nowadays, you are bombarded with choices. It's actually *worse than London* because it's not even a two-dimensional geographic space and there are multitudes of different routes and acceptable destinations. Journey planning on the software Risk Landscape is an optimisation problem *par excellence*.

Because the modern Risk Landscape is so complex:

- There can be orders of magnitude difference in *time*, with very little difference in destination.
- If it's Schedule Risk you're worried about, *Code Yourself* isn't a great solution (for the whole thing, anyway). "Take the tube" and at least

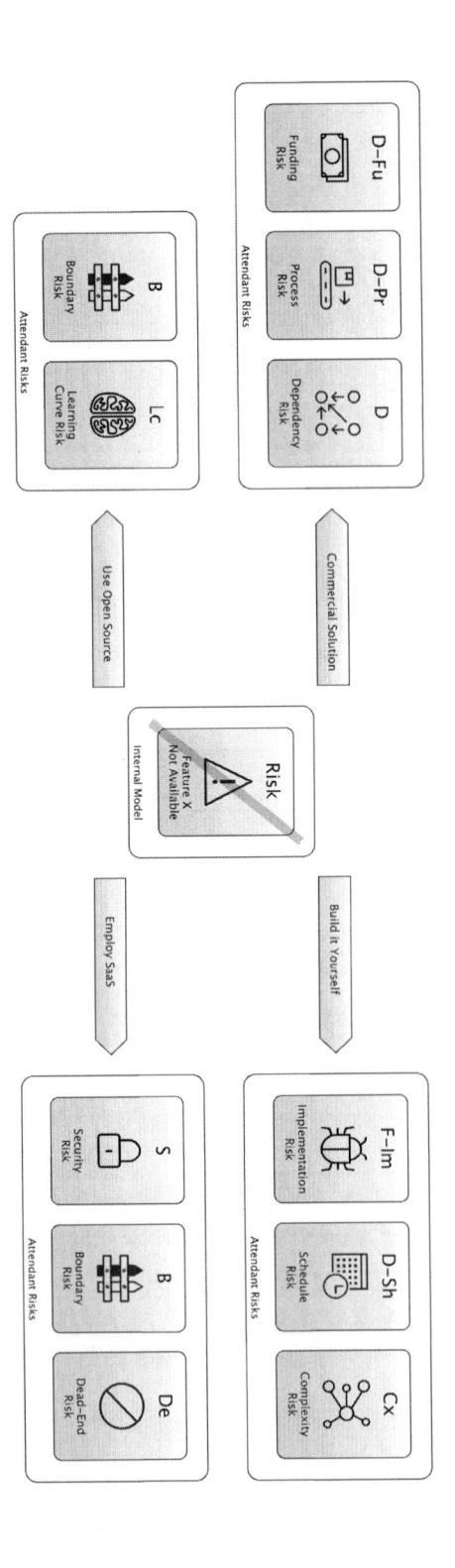

Figure 26.11: Possible Moves On The Risk Landscape

252

partly use something someone built already. There are probably multiple alternatives you can consider.
- If no one has built something similar already, then why is that? Have you formulated the problem properly?
- Going the wrong way is *so much easier*.
- Dead-Ends (like a broken Central Line) are much more likely to trip you up.
- You need to keep up with developments in your field. Read widely.

Tip #3: Meet Reality Early on the Biggest Risks

In getting from A to B on the Risk Landscape imagine that all the Attendant Risks are the stages of a journey. Some might be on foot, train, car and so on. In order for your course of action to work all the stages in the journey have to succeed.

Although you might have to make the steps of a journey in some order, you can still mitigate risk in a different order. For example, checking the trains are running, making sure your bike is working, booking tickets and taxis, and so on.

The *sensible* approach would be to test the steps *in order from weakest to strongest*. This means working out how to meet reality for each risk in turn, in order from biggest risk to smallest.

Often, a *strategy* will be broken up into multiple actions. *Which are the riskiest actions?* Figure this out, using the Risk-First vocabulary and the best experience you can bring to bear, then, perform the actions which Payoff the biggest risks first.

As we saw from the "10X Developer" Saw, Learning Curve Risk and Dead End Risk, are likely to be the biggest risks. How can we front-load this and tackle these earlier?

- *Having a vocabulary* (like the one Risk-First provides) allows us to *at least talk about these*. e.g. "I believe there is a Dead End Risk that we might not be able to get this software to run on Linux."
- Build mock-ups:
    - UI wireframes allow us to bottom out the Communication Risk of the interfaces we build.
    - Spike Solutions allow us to de-risk algorithms and approaches before making them part of the main development.
    - Test the market with these and meet reality early.

- Don't pick delivery dates far in the future. Collectively work out the biggest risks with your clients, and then arrange the next possible date to demonstrate the mitigation.
- Do actions *early* that are *simple* but are nevertheless show-stoppers. They are as much a source of Hidden Risk as more obviously tricky actions.

Tip #4: Talk Frankly About All The Risks

Let's get back to Bill and Carl. What went wrong between points (1) and (2)? Let's break it down:

- **Bill *wants* the system in 3-4 months.** It doesn't happen.
- **He says it "must be delivered in 6 months", but this doesn't happen either.** However, the world (and the project) doesn't end: *it carries on*. What does this mean about the truth of his statement? Was he deliberately lying about the end date, or just espousing his view on the Schedule Risk?
- **Carl's original estimate was 9 months.** Was he working to this all along? Did the initial brow-beating over deadlines at point (1) contribute to Agency Risk in a way that *didn't* happen at point (2)?
- **Why *did* Bill get so angry?** His understanding of the Schedule Risk was, if anything, *worse* than Carl's. It's not stated in the account, but it's likely the Trust Risk moved up the hierarchy: Did his superiors stop trusting him? Was his job at stake?
- **How could including this risk in the discussion have improved the planning process?** Maybe the conversation have started like this instead:

> "I think it will take about 9 months, but that's just a rough estimate at this point," Carl said. "That's not going to work," Bill said. "I was hoping you'd say 3 or 4 months. I need to show the board something by then or I'm worried they will lose confidence in me and this project".
>
> "OK," said Carl. "But I'm really concerned we have huge Feature Fit Risk. The task of understanding the requirements and doing the design is massive."
>
> "Well, in my head it's actually pretty simple," said Bill. "Maybe I don't have the full picture, or maybe your idea of what to build

Figure 26.12: Identifying The Action

is more complex than I think it needs to be. That's a massive risk right there and I think we should try and mitigate it right now before things progress. Maybe I'll need to go back to the board if it's worse than I think."

Tip #5: Picture Worrying Futures

The Bill/Carl problem is somewhat trivial (not to mention likely fictional). How about one from real life? On a project I was working on in November some years ago, we had two pieces of functionality we needed: "Bulk Uploads" and "Spock Integration". (It doesn't really matter what these are). The bulk uploads would be useful *now*. But, the Spock Integration wasn't due until January. In the Spock estimation meeting I wrote the following note:

> "Spock estimates were 4, 11 and 22 until we broke it down into tasks. Now, estimates are above 55 for the whole piece. And worryingly, we probably don't have all the tasks. We know we need bulk uploads in November. Spock is January. So, do bulk uploads?"

The team *wanted* to start Bulk Uploads work. After all, from these estimates it looked like Spock could easily be completed in January. However, the question should have been:

> "If it was February now, and we'd *got nothing done*, what would our biggest risk be?"

Missing Bulk Uploads wouldn't be a show-stopper, but missing Spock would be a huge regulatory problem. *Start work on the things you can't miss.*

26.9 In Summary...

Let's recap those again, in reverse order:

- **Tip #5: Picture Worrying Futures**. For some given future point in time, try considering which risks you *don't* want to be facing.
- **Tip #4: Talk Frankly About All The Risks**. Apply the Risk-First vocabulary to help.
- **Tip #3: Meet Reality Early on the Biggest Risks**.
- **Tip #2: The Risk Landscape is Increasingly Complex**: This means you have a wide variety of possible actions to take, so consider all the options.
- **Tip #1: Estimating Should be About *Estimating Payoff***. For your action, don't just get stuck on Schedule Risk. Consider the whole cast.

Glossary

Abstraction

The process of removing physical, spatial, or temporal details or attributes in the study of objects or systems in order to more closely attend to other details of interest.

Agent

Agency is the capacity of an actor to act in a given environment. We use the term *agent* to refer to any process, person, system or organisation with agency.

Feedback Loop

The process of testing an Internal Model, through taking action to Meet Reality. Typically, we talk about short or long feedback loops, depending on the intervals between Meeting Reality.

Goal In Mind

A picture of the future that an individual or team carries within their Internal Model; An imagined destination on the Risk Landscape.

Internal Model

The model of reality held by an individual, team, software system or other Agent. You can regard the concept of Internal Model as being what you *know* and what you *think* about a certain situation. An internal model *represents* reality: reality is made of matter, whereas the internal model is information.

Obviously, because we've all had different experiences, and our brains are wired up differently: everyone will have a different Internal Model of reality.

- Within an organisation, we might consider the Internal Model of a *team of people* to be the shared knowledge, values and working practices of that team.
- Within a software system, we might consider the Internal Model of a single server, and what knowledge it has of the world.
- A codebase is a team's Internal Model written down and encoded as software.

Meet Reality

Any moment where we test an Internal Model by exposing it's predictive power against reality. Note that "Reality" might be limited in some way, for example, a trial period or test users.

Payoff

Payoff refers to the *value* of the actions we take. When we decide on a course of action, we have in mind a risk we wish to manage. If the action is likely to have a big positive effect on the risk of a project, we say it has a promising payoff, whereas if the action fails to manage the risk, then it hasn't *paid off*.

Risk

A possibility of loss or cost. Anything that *can* go wrong on a project, or is *going* wrong, but resists exact realization. We talk about risk because we wish to recognise both the range of possibilities and the range of cost.

Usually broken down into:

Attendant Risk

A Risk you expect to face as the result of Taking Action.

Hidden Risk

Risks you aren't aware of when you consider Taking Action. i.e. an *unknown unknown*.

Mitigated Risk

Risks that, as a result of Taking Action have been minimized.

Upside Risk

The possibility of things going well, and leaving us with a benefit. We may take action to maximize the likelihood and return of upside risks.

Risk Landscape

A hypothetical landscape on which risks can be placed. Taking Action means making a move on the Risk Landscape to reposition a project so that it has a different profile of Attendant Risks.

Taking Action

Refers to any activity in the project. Actions are taken in order to manage some risk. At the same time, Taking Action usually means interacting with reality and updating the Internal Model.

Index

10X Developer, 241

Transmission Control Protocol (TCP), **90**

Abstraction, 105, 230, 232, 233, 257
Agency, 158, 179
Agile, 58, 247
Agile Estimation, **247**, 249
Agile Manifesto, viii
Amazon Web Services, 150, 176
Android, 176
Apple Watch, 129
ASCII, 174
Audience, 208
Audit, 46, 163, 223
Availability Heuristic, 216, 217

Backwards Compatibility, 94
Bandwagon Effect, 216
Beck, Kent, viii, 20, 59
Big Ball Of Mud, 116, 249
Big O, 49, 115
Bitcoin, **203**
Bounded Rationality, 145
Brooks' Law, 244
Buffers, 131
Business Analyst, 7, 8, 10

CAP Theorem, **199**, 200
Clojure, 93, 117
Code Coverage, xi, 213
Code Golf, 105

Compilation, 42, 138
Concurrency, 116
Connectivity, **106**, 108, 116, 148
Consensus, 192
Contention, 193, 201, 240
Continuous Integration, xi
Conway's Law, **143**, 144
Correlation, **70**, 71, 213
Crisis Management, 31
Crunch Time, 180
CV Building, **181**

Deadlock, 116, 193, 199
Decoding, 84
Delight, 79
Demand Management, 131
Design Patterns, vii
Devil Makes Work, **181**, 245
DevOps, 60, 225, 247
Diminishing Returns, **190**
Discount Factor, 36, 37
Discounting, 35
Division Of Labour, 124
Domain Name System, 89
Domain Name System (DNS), 89
Drupal, 168–170
Duke Nukem Forever, 130

ECMAScript, 138
Ecosystems, 169, 171
Eisenhower's Box, **34**
Employee Stock Options, 186

261

Encoding, 84, 138
Estimates, 239, 240
Evolution, 81, 158, 212

Factions, 192
Failure, 25, 61
Failure Mode and Effects Analysis (FEMA), 122
Fashion, 79
Feature Creep, 112
Fit, 55, 73, 81, 207
Fixed Price, 57, 186
Forecasting, 222
Forwards Compatibility, 94

Gantt Charts, 124
Git, 202
Goal In Mind, 3, 257
Graceful Degradation, 131
Gradient Descent, 67, 248

Hawthorne Effect, 184
Hickey, Rich, 124, 193
Hierarchies, **108**, 109, 124, 198, 206
Homeostasis, 223
Horizontal Scaling, 131
Huffington Post, 217
Hype Cycle, 209
Hypertext Transfer Protocol (HTTP), **90**

Inadequate Equilibria, 218
Interest Rates, 35
Internet Protocol (IP), **89**, 175
Interpretation, **96**, 97, 100, 205, 221
iPad, **129**

Key Performance Indicators, 135, 223
Kolmogorov Complexity, 103, 137
Korzybski, Alfred, 206

Lean Software Development, 60, 67

Learned Helplessness, **48**
Logistics, 132, 193
London, 230, 250, 251

Marketing Communications, **87**, 99
McClelland, David, 186
McConnell Steve, 34, 245
Meeting Reality, 5, 15, 18
Merging Data, 192
Message, 95
Metrics, 212
Modularisation, 108
MongoDB, **17**
Morale, **182**, 195
Motivation, 182, 186, 187
Mutability, 116

Net Present Value, 32, 35
Network Effect, 150, 169, 170
Networking, 117
Nice Problem to Have, A, **47**

Ostrich Effect, 216
OWASP, 223

Pair Programming, xi, 87, 187
Panic Invariance, **31**, 32
Parkinson's Law, 245
Periodic Table, vii, 230
PEST, 223
Pet Project, **181**, 182
Peter Principle, 171, 212
Pools, 131, 203
Precision, 39
Prince2, v, viii
Principal-Agent Problem, 183
Procrastination, 37, 128
Project Management, 60, 124, 132, 243, 244
Project Management Triangle, 243
Protocol, 88, 90, 94, 95, 116, 139

Queues, 131

Race Condition, 116, 193, 199, 200
RAG Status, xi
RAID logs, xi
Reception, 84
Redundancy, xiv, 24, 98, 122, 123
Regression, 75
Reliability Engineering, 122
Reservation Systems, 131
Resource Allocation, 193, 197, 201
Risk
    Agency, 158, 179
    Channel, **86**, 87
    Codebase, 103
    Communication, 83, 85, 100
    Complexity, 103, 147
    Conceptual Integrity, 75
    Credit, xii, 71
    Dead-End, 113
    Deadline, 133
    Dependency, 119, 124, 137, 233
    Exploiting, 49
    Feature, 73, 82, 233
    Feature Access, 76
    Feature Drift, 78
    Feature Fit, 73
    Funding, 125
    Implementation, 74, 95
    Internal Model, **95**
    Invisibility, 97, 123
    Key Person, xiii, 47, 127, 187, 197
    Liquidity, xii, 71
    Map And Territory, 205
    Market, 77
    Message, **96**
    Misinterpretation, **96**, 97, 100
    Operational, 219
    Opportunity, 129
    Process, 155
    Protocol, 91
    Protocol Implementation, **95**
    Protocol Incompatibility, **93**
    Protocol Versioning, **94**
    Red-Queen, **130**
    Regression, **75**, 81
    Reliability, **121**, 123, 125, 131, 219
    Scarcity, 125
    Schedule, 136
    Security, 112, 185
    Software Dependency, 137
    Staff, **127**, 159, 187, 219
    Trust and Belief, **98**, 99, 225, 226
    Upside, 32, 259
Risk Landscape, 15, 250, 259
Risk Matrix, **28**
Risk Register, **27**, 30, 49

Scale Invariance, **32**, 189, 199
Security, 117, 184
Shannon, Claude, 83, 84, 86, 95
Sign-Off, 158
Slack, 134
Slack, Nigel, 221
Software as a Service, 141
Software Libraries, 144, 145
Specification, 9
Spolsky, Joel, 114
Sprint, 31, 213
Standards, 174
Student Syndrome, 128
Sunk Costs, 31

Taleb, Nassim Nicholas, i, 53, 186
Technical Debt, 110
Testing Pyramid, 43
Transmission, 90
Tuckman, Bruce, 196
TVTropes, vi

Unit Testing, xi, 12, 16, 42, 49
Unknown Unknowns, 30
Urgency, 35

Veritasium, 109
Vroom and Yetton, 194, 197, 199, 203
Vulnerability Management, 224

Window Of Opportunity, 129
Windows, 52, 167, 175, 176

YAGNI, **18**, 19, 20

ZooKeeper, **201**, 202

Printed in Great Britain
by Amazon